The Chase Court

ABC-CLIO SUPREME COURT HANDBOOKS

The Burger Court, Tinsley E. Yarbrough
The Chase Court, Jonathan Lurie
The Fuller Court, James W. Ely, Jr.
The Hughes Court, Michael E. Parrish
The Stone Court, Peter G. Renstrom
The Taft Court, Peter G. Renstrom
The Taney Court, Timothy S. Huebner
The Vinson Court, Michal R. Belknap
The Waite Court, Donald Grier Stephenson, Jr.
The Warren Court, Melvin I. Urofsky
The White Court, Rebecca S. Shoemaker

Forthcoming:
The Jay/Ellsworth Court, Matthew P. Harrington
The Marshall Court, Robert L. Clinton
The Rehnquist Court, Thomas R. Hensley

Peter G. Renstrom, Series Editor

ABC-CLIO SUPREME COURT HANDBOOKS

The Chase Court

Justices, Rulings, and Legacy

Jonathan Lurie

ABC-CLIO

Santa Barbara, California • Denver, Colorado • Oxford, England

Library of Congress Cataloging-in-Publication Data

Lurie, Jonathan, 1939–
The Chase Court : justices, rulings, and legacy / Jonathan Lurie.
p. cm. — (ABC-CLIO Supreme Court handbooks)
Includes bibliographical references and index.
ISBN 1-57607-821-3 (hardback : alk. paper) — ISBN 1-57607-822-1 (e-book) 1. United States. Supreme Court—History—19th century. 2. Constitutional history—United States. 3. Chase, Salmon P. (Salmon Portland), 1808–1873. I. Chase, Salmon P. (Salmon Portland), 1808–1873. II. Title. III. Series.

KF8742.L87 2004
347.73'26'09—dc22

2004019644

08 07 06 05 04 10 9 8 7 6 5 4 3 2 1

This book is also available on the World Wide Web as an e-book. Visit abc-clio.com for details.

ABC-CLIO, Inc.
130 Cremona Drive, P.O. Box 1911
Santa Barbara, California 93116-1911

This book is printed on acid-free paper ∞.
Manufactured in the United States of America

For Mac,
my most favorite editor-in-chief for
more than thirty-six years,
and for our family:
David and Hikari,
Debbie and Jason,
Daniel and Katherine

Contents

Series Foreword, ix
Preface, xiii

PART ONE
Justices, Rulings, and Legacy, 1

1 ***The Chase Court and the Period,*** 3
References, 16

2 ***The Justices,*** 19
Salmon P. Chase, 20
James Wayne, 27
John Catron, 30
Samuel Nelson, 32
Robert C. Grier, 35
Nathan Clifford, 37
Noah H. Swayne, 39
Samuel F. Miller, 41
David Davis, 43
Stephen J. Field, 46
William Strong, 48
Joseph P. Bradley, 50
Ward Hunt, 52
References, 52

3 ***Major Decisions,*** 55
Military Commissions: *Ex Parte Milligan* (1866), 55
Test Oath Cases: Cummings v. Missouri (1867), 58

Ex Parte Garland (1867), 59
Congress and the Court: *Ex Parte McCardle* (1869), 62
Congressional Reconstruction and the Court:
Mississippi v. Johnson (1867), 66
Georgia v. Stanton (1868), 66
Texas v. White (1869), 67
Federalism—State and Federal: *Crandall v. Nevada* (1868), 68
Veazie Bank v. Fenno (1869), 70
Collector v. Day (1871), 71
Legal Tender Cases: Hepburn v. Griswold (1870), 73
Knox v. Lee and *Parker v. Davis* (1871), 77
State Police Power and the Fourteenth Amendment:
The Slaughterhouse Cases (1873), 79
Bradwell v. Illinois (1873), 84
References, 85

4 ***Legacy and Impact,*** 87
State Authority, 88
Due Process in Wartime, 95
Conclusion, 100
References, 101

PART TWO
Reference Materials, 103

Key People, Laws, and Events, 105

Appendix: Documents, 173

Chronology, 203

Table of Cases, 211

Glossary, 213

Annotated Bibliography, 225

Index, 231
About the Author, 247

Series Foreword

There is an extensive literature on the U.S. Supreme Court, but it contains discussion familiar largely to the academic community and the legal profession. The ABC-CLIO Supreme Court series is designed to have value to the academic and legal communities also, but each volume is intended as well for the general reader who does not possess an extensive background on the Court or American constitutional law. The series is intended to effectively represent each of fourteen periods in the history of the Supreme Court with each of these fourteen eras defined by the chief justice, beginning with John Marshall in 1803. Each Court confronted constitutional and statutory questions that were of major importance to and influenced by the historical period. The Court's decisions were also influenced by the values of each of the individual justices sitting at the time. The issues, the historical period, the justices, and the Courts' decisions in the most significant cases will be examined in the volumes of this series.

ABC-CLIO's Supreme Court series provides scholarly examinations of the Court as it functioned in different historical periods and with different justices. Each volume contains information necessary to understand each particular Court and an interpretative analysis by the author of each Court's record and legacy. In addition to representing the major decisions of each Court, institutional linkages are examined as well—the political connections among the Court, Congress, and the executive branch. These relationships are important for several reasons. Although the Supreme Court retains some institutional autonomy, all the Court's justices are selected by a process that involves the other two branches. Many of the significant decisions of the Court involve the review of actions of Congress or the president. In addition, the Court frequently depends on the other two branches to secure compliance with its rulings.

The authors for the volumes in this series were selected with great care. Each author has worked extensively with the Court, the period, and the personalities about which he or she has written. ABC-CLIO wanted each of the volumes to examine several common themes, and each author agreed to work within certain guidelines. Each author was free, however, to develop the content of each volume, and many of the volumes advance new or distinctive conclusions about the Court under examination.

Each volume contains four substantive chapters. The first chapter introduces the Court and the historical period in which it served. The second chapter examines each of the justices who sat on the particular Court. The third chapter represents the most significant decisions rendered by the particular Court. Among other things, the impact of the historical period and the value orientations of the individual justices are developed. A fourth and final chapter addresses the impact of each particular Court on American constitutional law—its doctrinal legacy.

Each volume contains several features designed to make it more valuable to those whose previous exposure to the Supreme Court and American constitutional law is limited. Each volume has a reference section that contains brief entries on some of the people, statutes, events, and concepts introduced in the four substantive chapters. Entries in this section are arranged alphabetically. Each volume also contains a glossary of selected legal terms used in the text. Following each of the four chapters, a list of sources used in the chapter and suggestions for further reading appears. Each volume also has a comprehensive annotated bibliography. A listing of Internet sources is presented at the end of the bibliography. Finally, there is a comprehensive subject index and a list of cases (with citation numbers) discussed in each volume. ABC-CLIO is delighted with the quality of scholarship represented in each volume and is proud to offer this series to the reading public.

Permit me to conclude with a personal note. This project has been an extraordinarily rewarding undertaking for me as series editor. Misgivings about serving in this capacity were plentiful at the outset of the project. After tending to some administrative business pertaining to the series, securing authors for each volume was the first major task. I developed a list of possible authors after reviewing previous work and obtaining valuable counsel from several recognized experts in American constitutional history. In virtually every instance, the first person on my list agreed to participate in the project. The high quality of the series was assured and enhanced as each author signed on. I could not have been more pleased. My interactions with each author have been most pleasant, and the excellence of their work will be immediately apparent to the reader. I sincerely thank each author.

Finally, a word about ABC-CLIO and its staff. ABC-CLIO was enthusiastic about the project from the beginning and has done everything necessary to make this series successful. I am very appreciative of the level of support I have received from ABC-CLIO. Alicia Merritt, senior acquisitions editor, deserves special recognition. She has held my hand throughout the project. She has facilitated making this project a reality in every conceivable way. She has encouraged me from the beginning, provided invaluable counsel, and given me latitude to operate as I wished while keeping me on track at the same time. This project would not have gotten off the ground without Alicia, and I cannot thank her enough.

Peter G. Renstrom
Series Editor

Preface

Change and continuity form the outer boundaries of U.S. constitutional history. We like to believe that throughout its course of more than two centuries, amid crisis, war, depression, political upheaval, and terrorism, the U.S. Supreme Court has continually functioned well. To many, it is a symbol of stability, permanence, and continuity; a sort of anchor in the sometimes turbulent seas of change. Wars begin and end, technology and economic growth transform our land, the worst depression in our history lays a heavy hand on U.S. citizens, political crises from time to time absorb our energies. And through it all, this tribunal goes about its business: hearing and deciding cases, interpreting a 200-plus-year-old document in the light of modern needs.

But, of course, this function is not new. Through constitutional change—and there has been so much of it, either because of amendment or judicial interpretation—the High Court continually seeks to reconcile our fundamental law with the new, the unexpected, the unpredictable. With what success or failure the Court has done this remains very much a matter of debate. Further, the Court's efforts at such reconciliation reflect more than its view of constitutional law. The justices are creatures of their time. Their contribution is based on their own sense of political values and convictions. This combination of personal and political predilection in the context of a specific legal controversy helps explain why U.S. constitutional history can be described as an intriguing synthesis of principle and expediency.

This generalization seems especially valid when one examines the crisis facing the United States in 1860, when Abraham Lincoln was elected and some Southern states tried to secede. Whether they actually did secede—as they claimed—or merely attempted to do so—as Lincoln insisted to his dying day—the result was the bloodiest war ever fought in U.S. history and on American soil. As the war ran its course, the South was defeated in battle, though not in its undying insistence on the righteousness of its cause. It anticipated some sort of political reunion, if not reconciliation, but the conflict had raised new questions about the nature of union and the extent of executive authority and of federal power. Inevitably the Supreme Court would confront these questions, much as it had been doing since the days of Chief Justice John Marshall in 1803.

But in the 1860s, the context was very different. Determined to save the Union, what he described as "the last, best hope of Earth," President Lincoln had suspended the writ of habeas corpus, imposed a blockade on Southern ports, and in 1862 issued the Emancipation Proclamation. No other president had taken such actions before. Nor was this all. During the era of the Civil War, the army employed military commissions to try civilians who supposedly had run afoul of its operations. The Supreme Court had to consider the constitutionality of a number of these actions. Yet between 1861 and 1864, the Court had also changed. By the time of his death, Lincoln had named five new justices. As will be seen, they varied widely in background and experience, yet they were all committed to Lincoln's position on the permanency of the Union.

Finally, as the war ended, issues of peace and punishment as well as questions relating to the ongoing economic growth and expansion of the country—a course that the war had possibly delayed but not diminished—confronted the High Court. This is the era in which the Chase Court operated. The term describes the period when Salmon Chase served as chief justice, from 1864 until his death in 1873. He took his center seat on the eve of Union military victory. He died as Reconstruction was winding down, and his tenure as chief reflected the legacies of war and the complex logistics of its aftermath. It remains a fascinating story, as I hope these chapters will illustrate.

I want to acknowledge with much gratitude the consistent support offered by Peter Renstrom, who almost convinced me that this volume would require only a few months of work, as well as by Alicia Merritt and Melanie Stafford of ABC-CLIO. I only hope that their patience has been worth the wait. Heartfelt thanks also go to Rutgers Law School Librarian Carol Roehrenbeck for invaluable aid in obtaining many of the case decisions discussed in this volume.

Jonathan Lurie

PART ONE

Justices, Rulings, and Legacy

1

The Chase Court and the Period

In one respect, Salmon Chase's appointment as chief justice of the Supreme Court on December 6, 1864, was not unusual. He had been a member of his president's cabinet, as had been true of his two immediate predecessors, John Marshall and Roger Taney. But when Chase took his seat, the United States, about to be successfully reunited by military might, was in the midst of tumultuous change. The new chief faced challenges unlike any confronted by his predecessors.

Marshall's and Taney's tenure each spanned more than a generation. Marshall served from 1810 to 1835. His Court played an important role in transforming the nature of federalism as well as the role of the Supreme Court. Taney served from 1836 to 1864. His Court harmonized economic growth with an expanding Union. The Marshall Court witnessed the waning of the Federalists (his own party), the rise of the Jeffersonian Democrats, and the triumph of Jacksonian politics. The Taney Court witnessed the expansion of state power, refined some important distinctions between state and federal jurisdictions, and unfortunately stumbled over the issue of slavery. The Chase Court participated in, witnessed, and reshaped the reemerging federalism of the post–Civil War era.

The opportunity to hold judicial office for anything approaching the terms of his predecessors was not given to Chase. He only served eight years, less than one-quarter of the Marshall era, and barely one-third of Taney's. For these two jurists, who together held office for more than sixty years, change was an evolving process that had occurred over a period of many years. But for Americans of Salmon Chase's generation, the Civil War was its defining event. And like most Americans, the members of his Court had observed the transformation four years of war had wrought. If asked, the justices might not have been able to explain how this had happened and to what extent the conflict had specifically affected them. But the bloodiest war in U.S. history had featured the worst carnage ever recorded on this continent, a conflict that ended with more than 620,000 dead and 4 million human beings set free. As Philip Paludan wrote, "vast fields, busy cities, quiet villages destroyed, new economic paths charted with unknown costs and consequences ahead"—all these had reshaped the legal environment in which they operated (Paludan 1988, 304). Though the justices might not explicitly refer to this transformation in their opinions, some of their writing reflects it; and we cannot understand the key decisions of the Chase Court without a sense of the altered context in which the Court operated from 1863 to 1873.

Although historians have long argued that slavery was a major cause of the war, other contributing factors should be considered. From 1800 to 1860, industrial, economic, and social development varied widely within the United States. By 1861, these differences between the free states (North and West) and the slave states (South) were marked. A few statistics well illustrate this fact.

In 1860, the urbanized population—those living in towns of 2,500 or more—was 26 percent in the free states and 10 percent in the slave states. The value of farmland per acre in the free states was $25.67, in the slave states $10.40. The percentage of capital invested in manufacturing, based on U.S. total per capita in 1860, tells a similar story: 84 percent in the free states, or $43.73 per capita, compared with 16 percent in the slave states, or $13.25 per capita. The percentage of literacy in the total population contrasted with the free population was 94 percent in the free states, and 94 percent of the free population, compared with 58 percent in the slave states, which represented 83 percent of the free population in the South. In the North, 72 percent of the free population was enrolled in school; in the South, only 35 percent.

Perceptive Southern observers had long realized the implications of these statistics. In 1851, with some exaggeration but much accuracy, a Southerner reflected that

> we purchase all our luxuries and necessities from the North. . . . Our slaves are clothed with Northern manufactured goods, have Northern hats and shoes, work with Northern hoes, ploughs. . . . The slaveholder dresses in Northern goods, rides [on] a Northern saddle, sports his Northern carriage, reads Northern books. In Northern vessels his products are carried to market, his cotton is ginned with Northern gins, his sugar is crushed and preserved by Northern machinery; his rivers are navigated by Northern steam boats. His son is educated at a Northern college . . . his schools are furnished with Northern teachers, and he is furnished with Northern inventions. (McPherson 2001, 537)

Although this is a study of justices and decisions, brief attention must focus on the industrial and economic transformations just cited above. Between 1861 and 1865, for example, the Northern states provided more than enough food to feed the Union Army, which by 1865 had "consumed more food per man than any previous army in history" (McPherson 2001, 400). Innovations in grain harvesting had revolutionized grain collection since the 1850s, as had improvements in manufacturing. The standardization of uniform sizes, new methods of boot production, as well as new techniques in food preservation were also significant. In railroad growth, the War Department created the United States Military Railroads (USMRR), which were especially important as the Union armies penetrated deeper into the South. By 1865, with its 2,105 miles of track, more than 400 engines, and 6, 300 cars, the USMRR operated "the largest railroad in the world at that time." In short, the four years of war contributed to a powerful "acceleration of prewar modernizing trends" (McPherson 2001, 400–402).

These trends were successful for yet another reason. Secession meant that the Deep South was no longer represented in Congress, and its withdrawal from Congress had major implications. The absence of a state-oriented ideology that had consistently opposed internal improvements and massive federal economic involvement was extremely significant. It paved the way in 1862 for both the Homestead Act, which gave 160 acres of the public domain to a settler who lived on it for five years, and the Morrill Land Grant Act, which enabled each state to set aside a public college for "agricultural and mechanical arts." In its long-term results, the Morrill Act represented the "most important instance of federal aid to education in American History" (McPherson 2001, 405). Further, by1863, Congress had enacted legislation to finance the war, to establish a sort of national banking system, to increase the tariff (something that had been anathema to the Deep South), and to provide federal support for a transcontinental railroad. Behind all these statutes lay a common policy commitment: to insure sustained economic growth to an extent not yet seen in U.S. history. Such was the environment in which the Chase Court came into existence in December, 1864.

Because politics has always been a factor in selecting members of the High Court, one must also be aware of the changing political perimeters as they affected the tribunal. On the eve of the Civil War, as the country awaited word of the presidential winner, the Court, like the Congress and, with few exceptions, the presidents, had reflected Democratic dominance. Indeed, those opposed to secession frequently pointed out that with Congress and the Court still heavily Democratic in political strength, even a new Republican president's potential for "abuse" might be contained. But these views were rejected in favor of direct action, and shortly after Lincoln's election, a number of Southern states seceded. More would join them by the spring of 1861. Although virtually all Southern congressmen followed their states into secession, only one member of the High Court did so, John Campbell of Alabama. Appointed in 1853 by President Franklin Pierce, he left Washington barely two weeks after Southern troops had fired on Fort Sumter. On paper, at least the Court remained Democratic as the war began. (See the next chapter for biographical material on the members of the Chase Court.)

Between 1857 and 1863, the Supreme Court kept a relatively low profile, possibly because of the strong public reactions to the 1857 High Court decision in *Dred Scott.* In this decision, by a vote of 7–2, the Court had denied congressional authority to regulate slavery in the territories, held the famous compromise of 1850 to be unconstitutional, and hinted that efforts to ban slavery anywhere might be of dubious legal validity (Finkelman 1997, 47–49). During the early years of the war, the justices avoided dramatic judicial activism, especially if it involved confrontation between the Court and the legislative or executive branches of the federal government. Moreover, between 1862 and 1864, five new justices took their seats, reflecting the fact that Abraham Lincoln had an unusual opportunity to create a new Court majority committed to the Union by the end of 1864. One vacancy existed before Lincoln took the oath of office, simply because Republicans in the Senate, possibly with Lincoln's tacit approval, blocked Buchanan's nomination of a replacement for Justice Peter Daniel, who had died even before Lincoln was nominated.

One month after his inauguration in March 1861, the new chief executive had two more vacancies to fill. Justice John McClean died on April 4, and Justice John Campbell resigned to follow his state of Alabama into secession. Coping with the Fort Sumter crisis occupied the president, and he did not make his first High Court appointment until January 1862. Before year's end, he had filled the other two vacancies. In1863, Congress expanded the size of the Court to ten justices, giving Lincoln his fourth appointment. When the elderly Roger Taney finally passed away in October 1864, after some reflection and delay, Lincoln moved to name his former treasury secretary, Salmon Chase, as chief justice. The Unionist president had constructed a new judicial bloc. As will be seen, his five appointees had very different judicial philosophies. But on one point they were unanimous; survival of the federal Union had to be the first goal of war.

Although the Court as a whole tried, for the most part successfully, to avoid confrontation, the same cannot be said for its chief justice, Roger Taney. Aged and ailing, sitting as a Maryland circuit justice in 1861, Taney moved to block the new Lincoln administration's initial suspension of the writ of habeas corpus, in the case of *Ex parte Merryman.* Well aware of its importance as a conduit for Northern troops passing through the state to defend Washington, Lincoln suspended the writ in April 1861 as part of his effort to insure that Maryland did not secede. A pro-Confederate partisan from Maryland (he had been caught burning railroad bridges and seeking recruits for the Confederacy), John Merryman was arrested and imprisoned by federal troops (Paludan 1988, 28). He obtained a writ from the Southern-sympathizing chief justice, but the military authorities politely ignored it. Angry as well as frustrated, Taney ordered the arrest of the commander, only to be ignored once again. Writing from the security of his chambers in Washington, the chief justice denounced Merryman's arrest and confinement as unconstitutional and filed his opinion, acknowledging in its conclusion that there was nothing else he could do.

Taney denied that Lincoln had any authority to suspend the writ in the first place. He argued, correctly, that the constitutional provision banning its suspension was located in that section of the Constitution dealing with legislative authority; indicating, at least to him, that only Congress could take such a step. A few months later, in his

July 4 message to Congress, Lincoln responded, also correctly, that the document did not specify by whom the writ might be suspended but that this step could be taken only "when in cases of rebellion or invasion the public safety may require it." With armed conflict raging, with a number of states in open rebellion against federal authority, here, Lincoln insisted, was such a case. "Are all the laws *but one* to go unexecuted," he asked, "and the Government itself go to pieces, lest that one be violated?" The beleaguered president had no doubt as to the answer, and in due course Congress ratified Lincoln's actions while the Confederate press denounced them. Before the war was over, however, the Confederacy would also find it necessary to suspend the writ, recognizing that constitutional survival might be more important than apparent constitutional consistency.

Three decisions handed down during the early years of the war illustrate the pre–Chase Court's effort to avoid confrontation with Lincoln's administration yet retain its independence as a coequal part of the federal government. The first case concerned the military, the second dealt with matters on the high seas, and the third reflected the fact that state economic activities continued even as the war ran its course.

In 1863, a Democratic malcontent, Clement Vallandigham, while running for the Ohio Democratic gubernatorial nomination, ran afoul of an order from the Union commander in Ohio requiring citizens in areas under his jurisdiction not to offer public support for the Confederacy. Vallandigham spoke at a political rally and called the war "wicked, cruel and unnecessary," a needless war being fought for the "freedom of the blacks and enslavement of the whites," with the goal of "crushing out liberty and to erect a despotism." That was enough for the commander, General Ambrose Burnside, who ordered Vallandigham's arrest and trial by a military commission. Other Northern Democrats denounced this action, later leading Lincoln to ask, "Must I shoot a simple minded soldier boy who deserts, while I must not touch a hair of a wily agitator who induces him to desert?" (Lurie 1992, 32–33).

Promptly confined after his conviction by the military commission, upon Lincoln's orders, Vallandigham was released behind Confederate lines. This did not prevent him later from seeking relief in the Ohio federal circuit court; a prospect that so disturbed Lincoln that he seriously considered another suspension of the writ of habeas corpus. Former Ohio governor and current Treasury Secretary Salmon Chase predicted to his chief, however, that Vallandigham would not prevail, as indeed turned out to be the case. Next Vallandigham appealed to the Supreme Court, only to be rejected once again.

Speaking for a unanimous Court, Justice James Wayne concluded that a military commission was not in fact a court. Thus the justices had no jurisdiction over it, even though Wayne admitted that just like a court, the commission exercised a "discretion to examine, to decide and sentence." But it exercised a special military authority, one that supposedly was not reviewable by civilian tribunals. It might be that Wayne's opinion was more an exercise in judicial avoidance than in sound jurisprudence. On the other hand, one can understand why in 1864 the Supreme Court would choose not to confront the United States Army, now the largest thus far in U.S. history, over a notorious Ohio malcontent—particularly because Lincoln had already resolved his case. But Wayne had merely avoided, through an expedient decision based on jurisdiction, the much more difficult question of a military commission's authority to try a civilian accused of a nonmilitary offense. Although Chase did not know it, this question would arise again during his tenure as chief justice, and his Court would come up with what appeared to be very different results (Lurie 1992, 34–35).

Even though early in April 1861, the Union Navy had far from sufficient ships to undertake a blockade of the Southern coast, this fact did not prevent Lincoln from ordering that such action be taken. There were two very serious implications for such a move. First, according to international law, in order to be recognized as legitimate, a blockade had to be effective. Such was surely not the case with the Union Navy until 1863–1864. Therefore, was the blockade unlawful, and if so, was the ever-increasing seizure of ships heading for Southern ports illegal?

Second, under traditional canons of international law, a formal declaration of war permitted establishing a blockade, one that neutral powers were supposed to recognize and accept. But from the day shots were fired over Sumter to the day he died, Lincoln consistently declined, as a matter of international law, to accept the claim that the South had seceded. He never wavered from his insistence that one of the basic purposes of the war, indeed until late in 1862 *the* sine qua non of the conflict, was to prevent the South from seceding. Lincoln led the bloodiest war in U.S. history without a formal declaration of war from Congress. But as the casualties increased, and by 1865 they would reach more than a half-million dead, how could an undeclared war in name be anything but a real war in fact? These were the questions at issue in the *Prize Cases*—an 1863 decision that represented the most significant potential for a clash between the judiciary and the executive thus far—as the war dragged on (Morris 2001, 243–244).

Both sides in the litigation were nervous about its possible outcome but for different reasons. Early in 1863, the stakes were high in these four cases that focused on the legality of the Union naval forces intercepting ships, some from neutral powers, loaded with cargoes entering and exiting Southern ports. Not yet convincingly successful on the battlefield, the Union strategists badly needed the blockade, which grew more effective as the months passed. The South awaited the decision with even more trepidation. If the blockade withstood High Court scrutiny, it could ultimately strangle the Confederacy; a fact well understood as early as 1862. One observer noted that "we cannot eat cotton, nor dine off tobacco and sugar" (Morris 2001, 244). Indeed, the Deep South had never been economically self-sufficient; thus an internationally recognized blockade was worrisome, even if at first it was only effective on paper.

Two attorneys, Richard Henry Dana and William Evarts, represented the United States. More familiar perhaps to the public as the author of *Two Years Before the Mast*, a popular account of the author's experience as a common seaman, published in 1840, Dana had become a recognized legal expert on maritime law. His cocounsel, William Evarts, already a well-known appellate lawyer from New York, would later defend Lincoln's successor, Andrew Johnson, in his congressional impeachment trial. A Washington, D.C., attorney specializing in international cases, James M. Carlisle, represented the ship owners. Both sides squared off before the Supreme Court in February 1863, and their respective counsel made compelling arguments.

Insisting that the blockade was unlawful, Carlisle noted that under the Constitution *only* Congress could declare war, and Congress had not done so. Indeed, it had not even been *requested* to do so. What new and implied constitutional powers did Abraham Lincoln possess, and since when were they limited only by "necessity"? Nowhere did the Constitution empower the chief executive to act as a sovereign power. After all, the president was empowered to "faithfully execute" the law, but not to alter it. Only Congress could do that. In truth, Carlisle insisted, "there was no war in [any] legal sense," and thus "the federal government could not claim belligerent rights," either against the Confederate states or neutral powers (Morris 2001, 244).

Evarts and Dana focused less on constitutional rhetoric and more on the realities of armed conflict. Surely a sovereign could exercise inherent powers to put down a rebellion. Lincoln had simply sought to do this, and by endorsing his actions of July 1861 and thereafter, Congress had acquiesced. Thus both legislature and executive *had* acted, according to Dana. They had resolved a political question, and their action ought to be conclusive (Morris 2001, 244). If so, what was left for the Court to decide?

Speaking for a five-member majority that included one Southern slave-owning Democrat, Justice Robert Grier sustained the Union position. As with Evarts and Dana, he minimized legal technicalities. A civil war might be called a rebellion, but "its actual existence is a fact in our domestic history which the court is bound to notice and know." The claim that in fact there was no existing legal and hence legitimate war in progress was irrelevant. Indeed, all knew that the current conflict was "the worst civil war in history." There was no legal justification to "paralyze" the government "by subtle definitions and ingenious sophisms." Lincoln's response to the war was appropriate and lawful (Finkelman 1992, 681; Morris 2001, 245).

The four remaining Democratic judges, including Roger Taney, dissented. A native New Yorker, Samuel Nelson, explained why. He accepted Carlisle's contentions, and conceded that Congress had authorized Lincoln to seek to block trade with the South. But this had taken place after Lincoln's illegal proclamation of a blockade. Congress could not make presidential actions that were unlawful when they were taken, legitimate by later resolution (Morris 2001, 245).

The majority studiously avoided the issue of secession, focusing instead on its existence as the basis for an actual war, rather than its legality. Such action, as was also seen in the *Vallandigham* case, only postponed the inevitable. Sooner or later, the Court would have to confront difficult issues arising from secession and its consequences. On the other hand, the justices may have believed that ultimately, once the Confederacy was soundly defeated, there would be time enough to take them up. Such turned out to be the case, and the resulting decisions formed the great bulk of significant jurisprudence for the Chase Court, between 1865 and 1873.

Early in 1864, the Court handed down a decision in the case *of Gelpcke v. Dubuque,* a holding that reflected a sometimes neglected fact. For much of the United States, especially in the Northeast and Midwest, industrial and economic expansion continued unabated during the Civil War. This case resulted from the earlier frenetic efforts of states to encourage railroad construction—often through the sale of municipal bonds used to finance them. The results were ultimately failures, causing in turn temporarily popular revulsion against railroading and its financing. Not infrequently, "local government and state courts" repudiated the municipal bonding that had been undertaken with such enthusiasm (Gillette 1969, 995–996).

In Dubuque, railroad promoters had sold bonds in amounts far beyond the debt limit specified by Iowa law. Although one state supreme court decision had upheld the sale, a later "reform-minded" high court reversed itself and found both the law and the bonds invalid. The bondholders appealed to the United States Supreme Court, where they found a sympathetic voice in Justice Noah Swayne, a former railroad lawyer and Lincoln's first appointment to the Court. He dismissed the latest Iowa reversal, insisting that federal judges could not be bound by "state court oscillations." Moreover, he said, "We shall never immolate truth, justice and the law, because a State tribunal has erected the altar and decreed the sacrifice." In dissent, Samuel Miller—Lincoln's second appointment and a resident of Iowa—argued that state judges had to have final authority to construe their constitution and statutes (Hyman 1992, 327). The clash between the rights of property (bondholders) and burdens on the community as a whole, at issue in this case, would be replayed in different legal forums for the next eighty years or so (Wiecek 1998).

These three cases reflected the fact that the High Court had yet to deal with the actual results of the Civil War, once hostilities had ended. When Chase took his seat as chief justice in December 1864, although the future appeared increasing bleak for the Confederacy, in fact several more months of military conflict lay ahead before Lee surrendered to Grant on April 9, 1865. Five days later, President Lincoln was assassinated. While the North mourned, the Chase Court prepared to confront serious issues. For the newly appointed chief justice, the political instincts honed from two terms as Ohio's governor, plus election to two terms as U.S. senator, had given him sound experience in "the art of governing." He would surely need it as chief justice.

The Chase Court in 1865: (left to right) John Catron, David Davis, Noah H. Swayne, Robert C. Grier, James Wayne, Salmon P. Chase, Samuel Nelson, Nathan Clifford, Samuel F. Miller, Stephen J. Field (Mathew Brady, Handy Studios, Collection of the Supreme Court of the United States).

Part of the great challenge facing Chase and his Court was the sense of national uncertainty in the wake of Lincoln's sudden murder. A mood of vengeance for the assassination swept the North. "Beware the people weeping," wrote Herman Melville, "when they bare the iron hand." But in fact, such desire for vengeance was more transitory than lasting. Northern sentiment was ambivalent and uncertain; especially toward the ex-slave. A variety of motivation and sentiments: revenge, restoration, reconciliation, racism, and restitution characterized Northern Reconstruction. As will be seen, they represented potentially explosive minefields through which emerging national policy, both political and judicial, would have to navigate.

Although we can never know how Lincoln would have handled this very difficult challenge, he did leave some hints of his intentions. A shrewd political tactician as well as an urbane human being capable of impressive social and political adaptation, Lincoln had apparently not revealed any detailed plans for reconstructing the South. He lived long enough, however, to see a number of Southern states, including Louisiana and Tennessee, fall under virtually undisputed Union control. His policies indicated a disinclination toward any actions that smacked of revenge or brutality. His initial proposal for Reconstruction, for example, was notable for its simplicity: When 10 percent of the voters who had voted in the 1860 election had taken an oath to support the federal authority and to abolish slavery, the state could be readmitted to the Union. Apparently, Lincoln envisaged no treason trials, no war crimes trials for defeated Confederate commanders, no major confiscation of Confederate property, and only a tiny fraction "of the voting population to begin the process" (McPherson 2001, 426). Moreover, his plan made no mention of congressional involvement.

Lincoln realized, however, that four years of war had changed the traditional dynamic between Congress and the president. Although not yet a majority of the Republican Party, by July 1864 the Radical Republicans were able to gain almost unanimous party support for a bill sponsored by Senator Benjamin Wade and Congressman Henry Davis. It revealed the growing gap between Lincoln's moderate Reconstruction policy and a more militant position held by an increasingly large segment of his own party. Lincoln required only 10 percent to start his Reconstruction process; the Wade-Davis bill required 50. Further, it "enacted specific legal safeguards of the freedman's liberty, which were to be enforced by federal courts" (McPherson 2001, 439).

Passage of the bill in the final hours of the congressional session gave Lincoln an opportunity to reject the bill without the necessity for a presidential veto. His action gave rise to the popular term "pocket veto." Wade and Davis denounced Lincoln's ploy, noting that "a more studied outrage on the legislative authority of the people has never been perpetrated," and that if Lincoln wished for support from Republican members of Congress, he would do well to "obey and execute, not to make the laws—to suppress by arms armed rebellion, [and] leave political organization to Congress" (McPherson 2001, 440). Even though Lincoln's plan left little to Congress besides approval once implemented, he was too adept a politician not to realize that in the war's aftermath congressional and presidential prerogatives concerning Reconstruction would have to be reconciled. He had no opportunity, however, to undertake such a move. The tragedy of his sudden assassination was matched by another—the total inability of his successor to grasp this fundamental fact of political reality.

One suspects that, as frequently has been the case in U.S. history, issues of expediency not foresight had guided Lincoln's acceptance of Andrew Johnson as his running mate in 1864. Racist in outlook, strongly in favor of states' rights and a limited federal presence, Johnson came from a background of poverty similar to that of Lincoln. As a Tennessee politician, he railed against the dominant slave-owning planter aristocracy, not just because he disapproved of slavery as much as he resented his inability to become a part of this social and cultural elite. As a U.S. senator, his opposition to secession, his identification as a Democrat Southern loyalist, and his refusal to follow Tennessee into secession all appealed to Lincoln's reelection operatives. Johnson was selected as Lincoln's running mate, and for the 1864 campaign the Republican Party became the National Union Party, "in an attempt to attract [both] War Democrats and loyal Southerners to the party's banner" (McPherson 2001, 441).

Suddenly thrust into high office early in the morning of April 15, Johnson remained susceptible to flattery, especially from wealthy Southerners, even as he denounced Lincoln's murder, warning that treason must be made odious. Moreover, instead of consulting Congress, Johnson ignored the legislative branch, which had adjourned even before Lincoln's death. He declined to call Congress into special session. Thus from April through December 1865, Johnson fashioned his own form of Reconstruction temporarily free from congressional involvement. Self-righteous as well as racist, he built upon Lincoln's mild 10 percent plan, but made some changes. He made wholesale use of the presidential pardon, facilitated the return of all adult (and white) males to the franchise, conditional only upon an oath of future allegiance, and minimized the changes necessary for "restoration" to the Union. By the time Congress convened in December, all the Southern states had elected their congressional representatives, often the same individuals who had served in the Confederacy. Assuming that the Republican leadership would simply approve admission of these Southern delegates, Johnson considered Reconstruction essentially ended. It was the first of many miscalculations that would end with his impeachment.

Presented with what Johnson assumed to be a fait accompli, his version of presidential Reconstruction, Congress reflected a very different perception. The Republicans certainly disagreed among themselves about how much federal involvement and/or obligations were due the former slaves; but they were virtually unanimous—especially in the year after Lincoln's death—that the results of four years of bloodshed meant more than just a restoration of white rule in the South as it had been in 1861, minus slavery. At the same time, they were anxious to avoid, if at all possible, major confrontation with Andrew Johnson. Their initial legislation in 1866 reflected these dual concerns.

Under the leadership of Illinois Senator Lyman Trumbull, Congress approved an extension of the Freedman's Bureau, but with important limitations, even as the bill appeared to expand its jurisdiction. It limited freedmen occupation of land opened up for black settlement by General Sherman, and it accepted Johnson's order "restoring confiscated lands to pardoned rebels" (Perman 2003, 53). Trumbull also introduced a new "civil rights" bill. This measure declared all persons of African descent born in the United States to be U.S. citizens; he further declared that "there shall be no discrimination in civil rights or immunities among the inhabitants of any state . . . on account of race, color or previous condition of slavery." He assured his fellow senators that his bill had "nothing to do with political rights or status of parties. It is confined exclusively to their civil rights, such rights as should appertain to every free man" (Lurie 1983, 8).

Trumbull's bill passed the Senate by a vote of 33–12, but the House debates reflected the ambivalent attitude toward race that bedeviled Republicans and Reconstruction. The bill's sponsor insisted that civil rights meant "simply the absolute rights of individuals, such as the right of personal security, the right of personal liberty, and the right to acquire and enjoy property." But he emphasized that the right to vote or to attend an integrated school, "or that all citizens shall sit on the juries. . . . These are not civil rights." Indeed, Republicans forced the bill's recommitment, and when it was brought back to the floor, all the references to civil rights had been deleted. As amended, it easily passed the House, and the Senate concurred in the changes. But not Johnson. He vetoed both the extension of the Freedman's Bureau and the civil rights bill.

The latter measure "if acquiesced in, must sap and destroy our federative system of limited powers," Johnson said. Further, it "invaded the judicial power of the state." The vehemence of Johnson's veto gave the congressional leadership pause. It came at a time when the Republicans were seeking to transform themselves from a sectional party into a national coalition. Although they easily succeeded in overriding the civil rights veto, they knew that future congressional statutes might be held hostage by an unfriendly Supreme Court—whose members could well be screened by the "southern oriented" chief executive. Moreover by mid-1866 it was clear that Johnson intended to form what he hoped would be a viable alternative to the Republican Party: a national Union party. Finally, two bloody race riots during June and July 1866, one in Memphis and the other in New Orleans, had made it very clear that the South, even if it had lost the war, was far from losing the peace.

This was the context in which Congress enacted the Fourteenth Amendment. It was intended to place the very limited objectives of the civil rights bill beyond both executive and judicial interference. But, again reflecting Republican ambivalence, the all-important first section made no mention of civil rights, civil liberties, or racial equality. On the other hand, its language was broad and replete with phrases such as due "process" or "equal protection"—phrases that invited future interpretation. As the House prepared to send the new amendment to the states for ratification, Congressman Thaddeus Stevens candidly confessed that "it falls far short of my wishes." But it was all he could hope for in June 1866, and, he said, "I will take all I can get in the cause of humanity and leave it to be perfected by better men in better times" (Perman 2003, 56).

Apparently Stevens did not have Andrew Johnson in mind, if only because Johnson urged all Southern states to reject the new amendment, which they did, leading to a rupture between the executive and Congress on a level that neither branch had yet experienced in U.S. history. It resulted in passage of several Reconstruction measures, as well as impeachment of the president and efforts to remove him from office—an attempt that failed by only one vote. Further, the antagonism between Johnson and some Republicans was exacerbated by inner doubts within the Republican ranks about the suffrage. This can be seen in the peculiar wording of the Fifteenth Amendment.

Although Republicans were sympathetic to ex-slaves receiving the franchise in the South, all the more if they voted Republican, it was a very different story closer to home. Most Northern states refused to allow blacks the vote, and the issue frequently cost the Republicans support. By 1868, the party disregarded any notion of black suffrage in the North, even as they endorsed its imposition on the reconstructed Southern states. Indeed, by 1869 the Republicans determined to "nationalize black voting rights" throughout the country "by constitutional amendment." But the wording they employed reflected their fear of Northern white voter backlash.

The Fifteenth Amendment said nothing about granting the right to vote but only forbade its denial because of race. Other grounds, which would be dredged up later, including a property restriction or a literacy test, would be sustained by the Supreme Court (Perman 2003, 125). Thus, by their deeds but not their words the Republicans were forced to admit that native Northern opposition to equal rights had undercut their central promise of black suffrage—a commitment vital to the party gaining a national political presence. All these developments formed the background for the Chase Court, which effectively functioned from 1865 to 1873. The justices watched, read, and listened as Reconstruction unfolded; and we should not be surprised to see the ambivalence of the latter included in some rulings of the former.

In summary then, Chase faced a number of challenges as the war ended:

- He had to deal with self-confident if not egotistical colleagues while he sought a harmonious judicial environment, even as he accepted, and occasionally contributed to, doctrinal divergence.
- He had to mediate and work within an increasingly tense relationship between Congress and President Andrew Johnson, while at the same time charting a judicial path independent of both.
- His Court had to determine the changed boundaries of state and federal relationships in the wake of the war.
- He had to confront the difficult questions concerning constitutional rights of all citizens—not only the newly emancipated former slaves.

Above all, the Chase Court had to resolve and redefine constitutional issues posed by the new postwar industrial economy—and this in a shifting context of Reconstruction, race, republicanism, and the lingering resentments previously noted (Bodenhamer 1994, 102).

The Chase Court also had another unarticulated objective: to regain the power that the Supreme Court had held during the first half of the nineteenth century. Chase could only have been well aware of the denunciation the Supreme Court had received in 1857 after the *Dred Scott* decision. Indeed, he had contributed to it in his capacity

The Chase Court in 1867: (left to right) Stephen J. Field, Samuel F. Miller, Nathan Clifford, Samuel Nelson, Salmon P. Chase, Robert C. Grier, Noah H. Swayne, David Davis (Mathew Brady, Handy Studios, Collection of the Supreme Court of the United States).

as Ohio's governor. A measure of the success with which he reached this objective, even as he navigated all the issues just noted, can be seen in the exercise of judicial review. Before Chase became chief justice, thus far in its entire history the High Court had declared only two federal statutes unconstitutional, one in 1804, the other in 1857. Between 1865 and 1873, this number increased to twelve. In a four-year period, 1869–1873, the Court declared seven congressional acts unconstitutional. Who were the justices—those already on the Court, and those yet to be appointed—as Chase took his oath of office on December 13, 1864? What made it possible for them to exercise such enhanced judicial authority?

References

Bodenhamer, David J. 1994. "Salmon Chase." In Melvin I. Urofsky, ed., *The Supreme Court Justices: A Biographical Dictionary.* New York: Garland.

Finkelman, Paul. 1992. "The Prize Cases." In Kermit Hall, ed., *The Oxford Companion to the Supreme Court of the United States.* New York: Oxford University Press.

———. 1997. *Dred Scott. v. Sandford.* Boston: Bedford Books.

Friedman, Leon, and Fred Israel, eds. 1969. *The Justices of the United States Supreme Court, 1789–1969: Their Lives and Opinions.* 2 vols. New York: Chelsea House Publishers.

Gillette, William. 1969. "Noah Swayne." In Leon Friedman and Fred Israel, eds., *The Justices of the United States Supreme Court, 1789–1969: Their Lives and Opinions.* 2 vols. New York: Chelsea House Publishers.

Hyman, Harold M. 1992. "*Gelpcke v. Dubuque.*" In Kermit Hall, ed., *The Oxford Companion to the Supreme Court of the United States.* New York: Oxford University Press.

Lurie, Jonathan. 1983. *Law and the Nation: 1865–1912.* New York: Alfred A. Knopf.

———. 1992. *Arming Military Justice: Origins of the U.S. Court of Military Appeals, 1775–1950.* Princeton: Princeton University Press.

McPherson, James. 2001. *Ordeal by Fire.* 3rd ed. New York: McGraw-Hill.

Morris, Thomas. 2001. "Texas v. White." In John W. Johnson, ed., *Historic U.S. Court Cases.* 2nd ed. New York: Routledge.

Perman, Michael. 2003. *Emancipation and Reconstruction.* 2nd ed. Wheeling, IL: Harlan Davidson.

Paludan, Philip Shaw. 1988. *A People's Contest: The Union and Civil War 1861–1865.* New York: Harper and Row.

———. 1994. *The Presidency of Abraham Lincoln.* Lawrence: University Press of Kansas.

Wiecek, William. 1998. *The Lost World of Classical Legal Thought: Law and Ideology in America, 1886–1937.* New York: Oxford University Press.

2

The Justices

Members of the Chase Court shared several traits commonly found among Supreme Court justices during the nineteenth century: all were male, white, Protestant (with very few exceptions), and had been active in politics. They were exceptional, however, in the extent to which their political activity continued after appointment to the High Court. The chief justice, whose presidential ambitions were as considerable as his legal acumen, had sought the presidency in 1860 and 1864. He even solicited Democratic interest in his availability for 1868. Four years later, and in very precarious health, Chase allowed his name to be floated for yet another presidential candidacy. In 1872, Chase's colleague, David Davis, accepted the presidential nomination of the National Labor Union Reform Party, although he prudently declined to resign from the Court in advance of his most improbable election. As late as 1884, Stephen Field hoped for favorable consideration as the Democratic presidential nominee, and Samuel Miller had flirted with a possible run in 1880 and 1884. Though the line between political activism and life on the bench was sometimes blurred, judicial propriety was not the same in the nineteenth century as it is today. Stephen Field would not, for example, have thought it inappropriate to sit on cases in which his older brother David served as attorney. Indeed, he sometimes did.

Twelve justices served along with Chase during his tenure as chief justice of the U.S. Supreme Court. The oldest, John Catron, had been born in 1786, before the new Constitution had been drafted, let alone ratified. The youngest, Samuel Miller and Stephen Field, both born in 1816, were also two of the most distinguished jurists on the Chase Court. The great majority of its members were born within the first two decades of the nineteenth century. Its last surviving jurist died in 1899. For about six months after Chase began his tenure, there were ten justices on the High Court. Five of them had been appointed prior to 1861, and five would be selected by Lincoln. Less than one month into his term, Lincoln already had three High Court vacancies to fill. Justice Daniel had died in 1860, prior to Lincoln's election, and the Republicans in the Senate determined to deny confirmation of President Buchanan's nominee—thus leaving the newly elected Lincoln with a choice appointment. Justice Campbell had resigned his seat to follow his state of Alabama into secession, and Justice McLean died on April 4,

1861. Occupied with Fort Sumter and its aftermath, Lincoln did not get around to these nominations until 1862. By December 1864 he had named five justices.

Among his judicial brethren the chief justice ranks first among equals, so it is appropriate to begin with Salmon Chase, followed by the other justices in order of appointment. Actually, three-quarters of the Chase Court had already been appointed by the time Chase received his nomination. Abraham Lincoln's final choice for the High Court came only a few months before his assassination. It also represented one of his most unusual selections.

Salmon P. Chase

Salmon P. Chase was born in New Hampshire in 1808. Before he reached the age of twenty-one, he had graduated Phi Beta Kappa from Dartmouth. Apprenticed for a time to Attorney General William Wirt, by the mid-1840s, Chase had established a successful practice in Ohio, where he also became "involved in various reform causes, especially temperance" and abolition (Urofsky 1994, 101). But he suffered much personal tragedy in these early years. He lost three successive wives as well as a number of siblings due to illness and spent the remaining years of his life as a widower. Always a moralist, Chase emerged from these terrible events with a grim determination to find meaning in his life and work.

Ernest and eloquent, he also found himself drawn to a political career, in part because it was a path open to young attorneys with limited family connections. Although he prospered as a lawyer, Chase realized that many of his clients, who were bankers and businessmen, did not share his interest in antislavery agitation. For a time, he managed to separate his moral causes from those of his clients. Indeed, the wealth he attained from his practice made it possible for Chase to undertake an early form of pro bono work. He represented, usually without fee, a number of escaped slaves seeking freedom in Ohio. But Chase's inability to control his personal political ambitions rendered his rigorous personal morality somewhat suspect. Many times, it appeared that ambition rather than morality guided his course of action.

In 1849, he was elected to the Senate from Ohio, and upon completion of his term, served as Ohio's governor from 1855 to 1859. A year later, he was again elected to the U.S. Senate. But Chase was destined to serve less than a week as a third-term senator. In his four years as Ohio's governor, Chase had gained valuable experience solving Ohio's fiscal problems. Further, as his interests in abolition expanded, he had become a very effective communicator, maintaining a vast correspondence with reform elements all over the country. By 1860, no longer content with confining slavery within its traditional geographic limitations, Chase leaned toward a call for its outright abolition. In this regard he was ahead of Abraham Lincoln, who thus far in his

Salmon P. Chase (Harris and Ewing, Collection of the Supreme Court of the United States)

career had emphasized the need for the containment of slavery rather than its immediate elimination. But both Chase and his longtime acquaintance from Illinois shared a moral revulsion for human bondage.

By 1860, the Democratic Party had disintegrated as a national institution, largely over the issue of slavery. Ultimately the nominating convention split, producing two candidates—Douglas from the North and Breckenridge from the South—each claiming to be the legitimate party nominee. Thus the future for the new Republican Party looked promising. Along with its catchy motto of "free soil, free labor and free men," the party platform unequivocally affirmed the right of the Southern states to maintain slavery. Its expansion into the territories, however, was quite a different matter. Along with New York's Senator William Seward, Chase was one of the two early favorites to win the Republican presidential nomination. But both senators were considered too outspoken in their calls for abolition. As a regional party seeking to build a national coalition, the Republicans believed it necessary to focus on what would unify them: opposition to the expansion of slavery, a commitment for easy access to new western lands, a protective tariff, and an intercontinental railroad. These were the issues that apparently appealed to voters in the East and Midwest.

It becomes understandable then, why the convention turned to Abraham Lincoln, who was considered more moderate on the issue of abolition. Political realities, however, required that both Chase and Seward should be named to Lincoln's cabinet, as indeed they were. Seward served as Lincoln's only secretary of state, while Chase ran the Treasury Department. Both men considered themselves superior to Lincoln not only in intellect and ability, but in education as well. Both men believed themselves better suited and qualified for the presidency than the incumbent; and both—especially in the early months of the new administration—sought to undercut Lincoln's authority to their own advantage. There the similarities ended. Seward became a devoted and trustworthy subordinate to Lincoln. The same, unfortunately, could not be said for Chase.

Embodying an intriguing mixture of egotism and strict personal morality, Chase could find no remedy to bring down his ever-present presidential fever. Although he administered the Treasury with skill, and successfully financed the vast expenses of the war, he connived against Lincoln on several occasions, seeking to bolster his own political fortunes at the expense of his president. Whenever Lincoln called him on it, Chase threatened to resign, knowing that Lincoln valued his abilities. By mid-1864, however, after a successful campaign for renomination and increasingly favorable news on the military front, Lincoln's party was unified behind him, and he no longer needed to put up with Chase's tactics. When Chase tendered his resignation over a minor question of patronage concerning his department, Lincoln quickly accepted it. Chase's colleague, Justice Samuel Miller, recalled that Chase's considerable strengths were "warped, perverted and shrivelled by the selfishness generated by ambition."

But Chase had been indispensable to the war effort. More than any other member of Lincoln's cabinet, he realized the need for fiscal solvency as well as military supremacy if the Union was to survive. His appointment of thousands of Treasury agents, many of whom were black and/or female, was an important step toward the nationwide implementation of one of his major goals: broadening opportunities for segments of society usually neglected in mid-nineteenth-century urban America. Although these changes were less visible than emancipation and abolition, such changes were viewed by Chase as part of what the war was all about. Here his vast network of reform-minded correspondents was invaluable. Also, the political effects of such widespread use of patronage should not be underestimated.

A staunch fiscal conservative, he found the issuance of paper money contrary to his moral values. Yet secession was even more offensive. If the Union could be fragmented whenever a state objected to a federal policy or practice, how could the United States survive? Secession could not be an acceptable alternative to union. Thus Chase administered the distribution of greenbacks and encouraged massive sale of federal war bonds as necessary tools for a much greater goal. Ultimately he succeeded, and all one needs to do is compare Northern war financial management with that of the Confederacy to sense how effective—for the most part—his efforts were.

Alone among Lincoln's cabinet, Chase openly called for the abolition of slavery as early as 1862 and privately criticized the president for being so dilatory on the subject. Ambitious to succeed Lincoln in 1864 (after all, no president had been reelected since Andrew Jackson in 1832), Chase failed to understand and appreciate Lincoln's burdens: Lincoln had to run a war, seek to unify a diverse party, and deal with members of a Congress responsible to a "majority of their constituents" (Hyman 1997, 69). Slowly but surely, however, Lincoln came around to Chase's perspective, and by the time Chase had forced himself out of the cabinet in 1864, the president had come to embrace both union and abolition as the inseparable goals of war. "I do not claim," Lincoln wrote, "to have controlled events, but confess plainly that events have controlled me" (Lurie 1983, 5).

After his reelection, Lincoln began to focus increasingly on the issues of Reconstruction. When the ailing and aged Chief Justice Roger Taney died, Lincoln hesitated, considered his various options—and ultimately appointed Chase. It was a shrewd decision, for in one stroke Lincoln raised to the High Court an able lawyer, a staunch supporter of the Union, and a perennial political nuisance, albeit one with strong supporters in Lincoln's party. Chase was nominated and confirmed within a few hours by voice vote of the Senate on December 6, 1864. Although he had no prior judicial experience, Chase brought a well-honed sense of political awareness to the bench. His role on the Court and the major cases decided during his nine-year tenure will be discussed in the following chapter.

By 1872, Chase had already suffered a series of strokes, and while he recovered to the extent that he could participate in the hearing and adjudication of cases, his speech remained slightly slurred, he could write only with difficulty, and his leadership of the Court—not easy under any conditions with the likes of Justices Miller, Field, and Bradley as colleagues—became virtually nonexistent. He died in May 1873, within a few weeks after the *Slaughterhouse* and *Bradwell* decisions were announced. These cases represented two of the major judicial landmarks of the Chase Court.

No one doubted the legal or administrative abilities of Chase as *primus inter pares*, but the new "occupational" challenges Chase faced were different from what he had confronted as secretary of the treasury. He had to deal with a number of justices who believed that they were every bit as qualified as Chase—if not more so—to sit in the center seat on the High Court bench. Moreover, his aloof personality did not lend itself to the easy camaraderie ascribed to Marshall or the kindliness with which Roger Taney had been reputed to treat his fellow justices. He does not appear to have been a good "persuader." Nor did he seem to appreciate the difference between rendering judgement and the political administration of a cabinet department. Again unlike Marshall and Taney, not content with what he had attained, Chase continued to yearn for the presidency.

Like most Republicans, Chase had little concern with the personal lives of African Americans once they had been freed from slavery. But, apparently more than any of his cabinet colleagues, he realized that freedom by itself was not enough. How could the ex-slaves be integrated into the economic mainstream of the country? How could they insure receiving a fair price for their labor, or that they would not in effect be enslaved again under new types of Southern statutes such as the "Black Codes"? Upon taking over as chief justice early in 1865, Chase watched with dismay as the "defeated" Confederacy enacted such laws, encouraged by Lincoln's successor—a staunch Jacksonian Democrat and virulent racist, though strongly opposed to secession.

Increasingly ambivalent about the appropriate role of the federal government in responding to the resurgence of Southern recalcitrance, and ever mindful of his need to present himself as a suitable subject for a Democratic presidential nomination in 1868, Chase found himself pulled in different directions, as Reconstruction ran its course. Unnecessarily distracted from his judicial duties by the need to preside over the Johnson impeachment trial, his insistence that it be first and foremost a judicial rather than a political procedure may well have contributed to Johnson's ultimate acquittal. Further, Chase's effort to stand above the bitter conflict between the congressional Republicans and the White House was probably intended to persuade the Democrats of his presidential suitability. His efforts to reconcile his presidential ambitions with his long-term moral commitments concerning currency, slavery and its aftermath, and his growing doubts about the correct course for Reconstruction represented a difficult if not insuperable challenge.

By the time he joined Lincoln's cabinet, Chase had defined a trilogy of deadly evils: secession, slavery, and repudiation of debts legally incurred. The third of these "sins" also included issuance of paper money as legal tender. All three violated his sense of personal morality and figured in his post–Civil War jurisprudence. Moreover, taken together, they revealed their seeming incompatibility with each other, in what Harold Hyman describes as Chase's "triplex world." This environment included his devout Protestantism, his legal insights, and his presidential ambitions (Hyman 1997, 110).

The complexity of these positions can be seen by his stand in the *Legal Tender Cases*, *Test Oath Cases*, *Texas v. White*, and *In re Turner*. Chase's position as a strong opponent of paper money was well known. But to save the Union and destroy secession, abolishing slavery at the same time, Chase willingly quashed his qualms and resorted to issuing "greenbacks." Further, he had authorized borrowing millions of dollars through the sale of government bonds—hawked, it might be noted, by Jay Cooke, an agent later known as one of the most notorious market manipulators flourishing during the Gilded Age. Perhaps Chase saw greenbacks as an emergency measure, mandated by expediency. But once the war was over and he was ensconced in the center seat on the High Court, Chase dusted off his objections to paper money. In 1869 he spoke for a bare majority of four justices, holding its issuance unconstitutional.

But both the timing and the context in which Chase handed down the decision can be criticized. In the first place, there was not a full Court to hear this very important constitutional controversy. The conflict between Johnson and the Republicans in Congress had resulted not only in Johnson's impeachment—something with which Chase was all too familiar—but also a refusal to confirm any appointment to the High Court that Johnson might be able to make. Death, congressional decisions, and resignation had left the Court at seven instead of nine justices. Chase could have waited until the Court was at full strength; all the more as this case in particular was of critical concern for future U.S. economic development. As will be seen, President Grant moved very quickly to fill the two open seats but met with some unexpected difficulties.

Further, Chase did not give sufficient attention to the impact of his unfavorable decision concerning greenbacks on the country as a whole. The great majority of indebtedness incurred after 1862 was based upon the Legal Tender Act. It was one thing to hold that similar future commercial debts would be illegal after the Court's finding, but to void all of them on a retroactive basis was quite another, as one of Chase's newer colleagues would point out. Ultimately, emphasis on practicality rather than strict constitutional principal won out in spite of Chase's dogged insistence to the contrary.

The problem of loyalty oaths became more pronounced as the war had expanded both in length and intensity. For their supporters, requiring a loyalty oath seemed a reasonable policy during Reconstruction—unless, of course, the individual concerned had been disloyal. For a public figure with political aspirations, such as Chase, they represented a serious challenge. He had built much of his career insisting that blacks should not be excluded from the usual occupations open to whites without question. But the *Test Oath Cases* involved whites, not blacks. Moreover, they had political significance. If the Supreme Court held the oaths invalid, such a decision might slow—if not derail—Reconstruction, as well as aiding its opponents. Democrats in particular opposed the oaths, and it is no coincidence that the four Democratic justices who held the oaths unconstitutional were joined by Stephen Field, the only Lincoln appointment from that party. Indeed, Field delivered the opinion of the Court. All of the Republicans Lincoln had selected, dissented. For Chase, the *Test Oath Cases* were one example where his sense of moral outrage over the damage wrought by those who had seceded justified his insistence that such restrictive statutes were appropriate.

On the other hand, Chase was not about to get into a battle with Congress over Reconstruction in general, even as that body recovered from the impeachment imbroglio. The case of *Texas v. White* involved a question of state authority exercised by a state that had seceded. In his opinion for the Court, Chase held that secession had been illegal and unsuccessful. Thus Texas had never formally left the Union despite its attempts to do so. The Constitution, he wrote, "looks to an indestructible Union composed of indestructible states." Moreover, the direction of Reconstruction was a matter for the legislative branch, not the Court. In other words, congressional measures enacted by Republicans were presumed to be valid.

Perhaps the best example of a decision that clearly reflected Chase's values is the little-known case of *In re Turner.* Technically it was not heard by his Court, as it arose while Chase was riding circuit by himself. But the litigation should be discussed, as it formed a key part of his jurisprudence. Although Maryland had not seceded, it remained a slave state throughout most of the war. Literally next door to Washington, this border state could not remain immune to the pressures for abolition that had led to passage of the Thirteenth Amendment. It did not ratify the new enactment until 1865.

But while formal slavery was abolished, this Southern-oriented state was not about to elevate the former slaves to anything approaching equality with the white majority. In addition to ratification, Maryland enacted a new statute. Under its provisions many of the younger ex-slaves were promptly apprenticed to their former masters, usually without their consent. Such was the case of Elizabeth Turner, who until 1865 had been a slave in Maryland. Toward the end of the war, Turner's mother had her daughter apprenticed to her former master. This man may also have been Turner's father, although the evidence remains unclear (Hyman 1997, 125).

What is certain, however, is that Turner, as a minor, had been virtually re-enslaved as an apprentice under this new state statute, which discriminated against blacks. It permitted outrageous distinctions between white and black apprentices by the individual to whom the apprentices had been bound. He was, for example, supposed to teach such basic skills as "reading, writing and arithmetic," but only to whites, not blacks. Again, in contrast to white apprentices, black apprentices could be "reassigned" to "third parties unspecified in the original contract" without permission of their parents. In short, the law bound Turner "to a legal status inferior to that of a free" white worker—to what Chase labeled as involuntary servitude.

The chief justice heard the *Turner* case while on circuit duty. Somehow, Turner had obtained the pro bono services of a white attorney working for the Freedman's Bureau in Maryland. Henry Stockbridge asked Chase to issue a writ of habeas corpus freeing Turner from an indenture she had never sought. No attorney came forward, however, either to represent the master or to refute Stockbridge's insistence that Maryland law was in fact involuntary servitude under a different name. And indeed there were a number of arguments that could have been raised against his position. Chase may well have assumed that his decision would be appealed to the full Court so that the issues lurking in it could receive a full exploration from his colleagues.

With no opposing counsel either to argue or to raise an appeal, Chase ruled on Turner's behalf. The Thirteenth Amendment had banned involuntary servitude except as punishment for crimes, which clearly did not apply to Turner. Not only did her treatment violate the new amendment, but the obvious discrimination practiced under the Maryland statute violated the federal Civil Rights Act of 1866. All persons were entitled to equal rights and benefits of citizenship (Hyman 1997, 129)—such was the view of Chief Justice Chase. But since the case never reached the High Court, it is uncertain whether his holding reflected the view of his brethren.

The aura of Jacksonian politics still hung over the Court that Chase joined in December 1864. Indeed, until Lincoln's appointments began to change the Court's philosophy, Southern justices, sometimes associated with Northern "doughface" colleagues, had dominated it. (The term usually referred to a Northern lawyer, politician, or public official who was able to stretch his views much like a piece of dough into a position favorable to Southern interests.) Jackson had placed six justices on the Court between 1829 and 1837. Upon his arrival, Chase found two of Jackson's appointees still in service, and he himself had replaced another Jackson supporter, Roger Taney. The five justices associated with the pro-Southern viewpoint were John Catron, James Wayne, Samuel Nelson, Robert Grier, and Nathan Clifford. Wayne and Catron will be considered together. Both owed their nominations to Jackson, both were Southerners, in their jurisprudence both struggled over the issues of federal as opposed to state authority, and ultimately both chose to remain Unionists—a choice they made with great personal travail.

James Wayne

James Wayne was the senior justice as Chase took his seat. Born in Georgia in 1790, he graduated from what is now Princeton University before he was twenty. He immediately turned to the study of law, first in Connecticut, then, after his father's death in 1810, back in Georgia. After the War of 1812, in which he served but saw no military action, Wayne moved into a lifelong career synthesis of law and politics. On the local level, he was a member of the Georgia legislature and one of the youngest members of the Savannah board of aldermen. In 1817, while still in his twenties, he was elected mayor of Savannah, and by 1828, he had been elected to Congress as one of the earliest and staunchest Jacksonian Democrats.

James Wayne (Unknown, Collection of the Supreme Court of the United States)

As a first-term congressman, Wayne had to face a challenge to a duel from a disgruntled Savannah doctor, one William Daniell. Apparently the issue involved federal investigation concerning clearance of some obstructions to shipping in the Savannah River. Although an opponent of dueling, as a young congressman from Georgia Wayne found it impolitic to reject it. But as the challenged party, he insisted on the broad sword and rifle as his weapons of choice. This choice may have decreased Daniell's interest in pursuing the matter. At any rate, the dispute was ultimately settled without a duel (Cushman 1993, 113).

Reelected three more times, Wayne remained a staunch supporter of Andrew Jackson. Sensitive to his section's concerns with the protective tariff, he nevertheless parted company with partisans of the neighboring state of South Carolina as it moved toward the doctrine of nullification in 1832. This doctrine argued that the federal Union remained a compact between sovereign states, who had retained their sovereignty. Hence in voluntarily joining the Union, the states had retained the right to nullify a federal statute if it endangered a state's well-being or represented improper exercise of illegitimate federal authority. Wayne opposed both the tariff and nullification, and—alone among the Georgia congressional delegation—voted to support Jackson's notorious Force Bill. This law had been enacted at Jackson's behest as the climax of the nullification battle with John Calhoun. When Supreme Court Justice William Johnson from South Carolina died in 1834, Jackson—who may have been in no mood to offer patronage to South Carolina—instead selected another Southerner, James Wayne, as his replacement. Thirty years later, Wayne was still on the bench to greet Chief Justice Salmon Chase.

As a Southern, slave-owning jurist, Wayne reflected an intriguing mixture of juridical values. He maintained, for example, an almost doctrinaire insistence on national power to regulate commerce. Thus he dissented from the Taney Court's efforts to reconcile this power with legitimate state interests, as seen in the *Cooley* case (1851). On the other hand, Wayne was equally consistent in his support of slavery. Alone among his brethren, in the *Dred Scott* case (1857), Wayne came out in total and explicit endorsement of Taney's opinion for the Court. Yet support for the notion that Congress was powerless to ban slavery in the territories was far from the position that secession was appropriate and legitimate. Here Wayne drew the line.

When Georgia seceded, he refused to resign from the Court, remained in Washington, and supported the Union position on the major constitutional issues in cases between 1862 and 1865. Meanwhile, Wayne watched his son Henry resign his commission in the United States Army and rise to the rank of general as a Confederate officer. He saw his property confiscated by his own state, his citizenship revoked by a Georgia court, and himself described an "enemy alien" (Cushman 1993, 115). Like Lincoln, Wayne endorsed policies considered necessary to put down a rebellion. Thus he had broken ranks with his fellow Southern jurists Taney and Catron when he voted to uphold federal authority in the *Prize Cases* (see Chapter 1). Also like Lincoln, Wayne opposed harsh, punitive measures against the Confederacy. He refused, for example, to hold court in those Southern states under military reconstruction. And one of his final decisions was to join Lincoln Court appointee Justice Stephen Field in striking down test oaths. However, Wayne did not figure heavily in Chase Court jurisprudence, since he died in Washington during an epidemic of yellow fever in 1867.

John Catron

Born in Pennsylvania sometime in 1786, John Catron's family soon moved first to Virginia and then to Kentucky. After his marriage, Catron relocated again, this time to Tennessee. He became acquainted with Andrew Jackson, under whom he served during the War of 1812. It remains unclear how he obtained his legal training, but by 1815 he had been admitted to the Tennessee Bar. Nine years later, Catron won appointment to the highest state court, and in 1831, he became chief justice.

Early in his career, Catron was identified as a Jacksonian Democrat. In 1829, for example, he published a number of pieces denouncing the Bank of the United States, three years before Jackson's famous veto in 1832 of the congressional rechartering of that controversial institution. Like James Wayne, Catron played an important role in insuring that Tennessee supported President Jackson during the nullification crisis. A new state statute eliminated Catron's post of chief justice, but his respite from judicial functions was to be very brief. Two years later, Catron managed Martin Van Buren's successful presidential campaign in Tennessee. What role this action played in his future is uncertain, but on his very last day in office, March 3, 1837, Andrew Jackson nominated Catron to the High Court. And, like James Wayne, he was still in harness in December 1864 to greet Salmon Chase.

Although Wayne and Catron had many similarities as Southern Jacksonian justices, Catron differed from his Georgia colleague in a few interesting instances. A devoted slave owner, he was much less doctrinaire in its defense than Wayne. In the *Dred Scott* case, for example, Catron felt it unnecessary to go beyond the authority of the Missouri courts concerning the status of Scott. Although he agreed with Taney and Wayne that the Missouri Compromise was unconstitutional, Catron insisted that as a general principle, federal authority in the territories was both necessary and legitimate. Finally, he did not feel it necessary, unlike Taney, to explore the issue of whether or not "a free Negro was barred from citizenship" (Gatell 1969, 746–747).

Compared to Wayne, Catron demonstrated a more flexible viewpoint concerning regulation of commerce, an issue of major importance for the Taney Court. He tried to find a fair balance between state and federal jurisdiction. In cases involving importation of liquor into a state, either from abroad or from another state, Catron

John Catron (Handy Studios, Collection of the Supreme Court of the United States)

found regulation of such commerce within state authority. On the other hand, when a state sought to regulate entrance of immigrants through a tax, such action was unconstitutional as it impinged on federal jurisdiction. He also concurred in the *Cooley* case, which held that where uniform commercial regulation was a necessity, such regulation was strictly federal in character. In other instances, state commercial authority remained legitimate (Gatell 1969, 744).

Shortly after Lincoln took office, Catron returned to ride his circuit, which included the states of Tennessee, Kentucky, and Missouri. Although there was strong sympathy for the Confederate cause in all three, only Catron's home state of Tennessee ultimately seceded. He managed to hold court in St. Louis, even as he refused to release a number of secession activists, whom he denounced as rebels. Upon his return to Tennessee, the aged justice was given a choice by Confederate agents: either resign his seat on the High Court or leave the state. Catron left Tennessee, leaving behind much property, which was promptly confiscated. But if Catron denounced secession, like a good Jacksonian he also objected to what he considered over zealousness in Lincoln's conduct of the war. In yet another example of the difference between Wayne and Catron, Catron dissented in the *Prize Cases*, arguing that in fact Lincoln had proclaimed a blockade without congressional approval. He lived to see the end of secession, but his life ended at about the same time, May 1865 (Gatell 1969, 747–748).

Three other holdovers from the prewar Supreme Court were on hand to greet Chase. Although not appointed to the High Court by Jackson, and not from the South, Justices Samuel Nelson, Robert Grier, and Nathan Clifford may be considered prime examples of Northern justices who were willing to recognize slavery as an integral part of the federal Union. All would outlive their new chief, as the Chase Court grappled with Reconstruction. Their different perspectives on the war are of some interest when contrasted with Lincoln's five appointees.

Samuel Nelson

Like several of his colleagues, Nelson appears to have been a precocious young man. Born in New York in 1792, Nelson was already a sophomore at Middlebury College by his fifteenth birthday. After graduation, he chose a career in law in New York. It included serving as a delegate to the New York Constitutional Convention of 1821, when he was not yet thirty. Two years later, he began his judicial tenure, first as judge on the New York Sixth Circuit Court, followed by appointment to the New York Supreme Court in 1831. He became chief justice in 1837. Nelson was known as a competent, capable jurist, but not highly visible—characteristics that also reflected his work on the High Court.

Samuel Nelson (Mathew Brady, Handy Studios, Collecton of the Supreme Court of the United States)

Nelson was John Tyler's sixth or seventh choice as a replacement for Justice Smith Thompson, also from New York, who had died late in 1843. Tyler's machinations have been described as "one of those recurrent instances of appointment politics that do little to enhance the prestige of the Court" (Gatell 1969, 822). Nevertheless, on March 5, 1845, Nelson began what would ultimately be a twenty-seven-year term on the U.S. Supreme Court. He silently concurred in the *Passenger* and *License Cases*, as well as the *Cooley* case. But it was in the *Dred Scott* decision of 1857, that Nelson best revealed his traits of judicial conservatism and self-restraint.

Possibly reflecting Chief Justice Taney's preference that a nonsoutherner write the opinion for the Court, at his request Nelson had prepared such a draft. It avoided any question of congressional authority over slavery in the territories, as well as any resolution of the constitutionality of the Missouri Compromise. These were exceedingly controversial issues, but their resolution was not necessary in order for the Court to decide this case. Instead, Nelson merely sustained the decision of the Missouri Supreme Court, which had declined to grant Scott relief on the grounds that he was still a slave. But before Nelson received concurrence from his brethren for his opinion, additional developments took place. Justices John McLean and Benjamin Curtis announced that they would dissent. They claimed that free blacks were indeed citizens, that in some Northern states they exercised the franchise, and that the decision of the Missouri Supreme Court should be reversed. The response of the majority proslavery justices was to have Chief Justice Taney write a new opinion for the Court, confronting the points raised by the dissenters and going much further than Nelson's earlier draft.

Taney may have received encouragement for his determination to settle once and for all the admittedly divisive issue of slavery in the territories, as well as the status of blacks, from an unusual source—President-Elect James Buchanan. For reasons that remain unclear, Justice Catron had leaked hints as to how the Court might decide this closely watched litigation to Buchanan, and advised him to contact Justice Robert Grier, a fellow Pennsylvanian and old acquaintance of the incoming chief executive. He urged Buchanan to hint to Grier the importance of deciding the vexatious question of slavery in the territories once and for all. Buchanan did so. Unaware of Catron's correspondence with Buchanan, Grier responded that he also wanted to see an acceptable but authoritative majority opinion from the High Court (Gatell 1969, 878–879).

The result, however, was anything but what Grier desired. For his part, Nelson declined to withdraw or alter his original draft. Ultimately all nine members of the Court submitted opinions in the *Dred Scott* case. But Nelson's was the only concurrence that retained the judicial pronoun "we." It might be that Nelson still spoke for his colleagues even though he was not speaking for the Court.

By 1861, Nelson had come to accept the breakup of the Union. Incredibly, he failed to sense the passion that the issues of slavery and union had generated in many parts of the country. He wrote that it was now "too late in the age for men to fight without any useful purpose." Nelson did not see how the Union could be cobbled back together by bayonets. "Everybody agrees the Union can't be saved by this means" (Gatell 1969, 826). He spoke for the dissenters in the *Prize Cases*, although as a circuit justice he enforced the majority finding—Nelson declined to give the federal authorities "a free hand in seizing ships" (Cushman 1993, 145). As a conservative Democrat, Nelson found himself in grudging acceptance of the war's outcome, even as he rejected the methods employed by Lincoln's administration to bring it about.

Robert C. Grier

Like a number of his judicial brethren, Robert Grier had demonstrated unusual intellectual potential early in life. Grier was born in 1794, son of a minister and the oldest of eleven children. In 1806, the elder Grier was invited to head Northumberland Academy in Pennsylvania, so as a young man, Robert mastered Greek and Latin. Indeed, he insisted on reading the Bible in Greek throughout his life. He was admitted to Dickinson College as a seventeen-year-old junior in 1811 and returned to Northumberland to become the principal. Upon his father's death in 1815, Grier ran the academy—teaching, among other subjects, "mathematics, astronomy, chemistry, Latin and Greek . . . all while studying law on the side!" (Cushman 1993, 152). By 1817, he had been admitted to the bar.

Apparently, Grier's two judicial appointments—first to the Allegheny District Court and later to the U.S. Supreme Court—were more accidental than premeditated. Both actions involved convoluted Pennsylvania politics. He remained a state judge for more than a decade, and like Samuel Nelson, gained a reputation as a competent, capable, and noncontroversial jurist. When the "Pennsylvania Justice," Henry Baldwin, died in 1844, President Tyler was unable to fill the vacancy before his term expired, even though he offered the post to James Buchanan. President James Polk's first choice was rejected by the Senate. Polk next turned back to Buchanan, who expressed tentative interest but ultimately could not make up his mind. In August 1846, he finally came up with Grier's nomination, more than a year after he had assumed the presidency.

Again like Nelson, Grier concurred in the major Taney Court decisions involving commerce. He also demonstrated a tolerance for slavery typical of many Northern Democrats (Gatell 1969, 877). Alone among his brethren, in the *Dred Scott* case, Grier managed simultaneously to concur both with Taney and Nelson in an opinion of barely half a page. He believed that Nelson was correct in arguing that the Court should have followed the Missouri holding and that Taney was on target in his dismissal of the Missouri Compromise as unconstitutional. Tolerating slavery as a partial cost of union was one thing, as Catron and Wayne had previously noted. Like them, when it came to secession, Grier drew the line.

Although his colleague Nelson despaired of the future as war approached, Grier took a more aggressive stand in support of the Union. Upon learning that his son-in-law "was a secessionist," the justice concluded that he was "as insane as the others." As to the outcome of what he feared would become a "long war," Grier had no doubt.

Robert C. Grier (Mathew Brady, Handy Studios, Collection of the Supreme Court of the United States)

"We must conquer this rebellion or declare our republican government a failure" (Gatell 1969, 880). He spoke for the Court in its most important decision rendered as the war progressed, the *Prize Cases* (see Chapter 1). But as will be seen, Grier was less supportive of the government as the war turned into the process of Reconstruction. Moreover, mental infirmity clouded his last years on the Court.

Nathan Clifford

Nathan Clifford, the last of the prewar justices still sitting when Chase took his seat, was born in New Hampshire in 1803. He represents something of an exception to the early indications of intellectual ability prominent in the backgrounds of his brethren. He never went to college, and "he was to spend the rest of his life learning on his own" (Gillette 1969, 963). Clifford studied law and was admitted to the New Hampshire Bar before his twenty-fifth birthday. He moved to Maine, where he established both a large family and a successful law practice. By the age of 27, he had been elected to the Maine House of Representatives as a Jacksonian Democrat, and his fidelity to that party remained a given until his death. Clifford consistently opposed, for example, both high tariffs and a national banking system. After three terms in the Maine legislature (one as speaker of the House), he served two terms in Congress (Hall 1992, 161). In 1846, President James Polk selected Clifford as his attorney general, but Clifford later resigned from that position, so that he could heed Polk's request to participate in the final peace negotiations with Mexico. In 1858, Clifford's old friend James Buchanan appointed him to the High Court, where he did not hesitate to exercise his political predilections.

Described accurately as a real "doughface"—that is, a Northerner with Southern sympathies—Clifford's nomination was clouded by the ongoing slavery-abolition crisis in the Kansas territory, and he received Senate approval by the narrow margin of 26–23. His biases were predictable, consistent, and freely expressed. He favored strict constitutional construction, objected to the abolitionists, and opposed expanded federal power—even as events moved steadily in that direction. Like many Southerners, Clifford could denounce secession but fault Lincoln's imposition of a naval blockade in the *Prize Cases.* In the postwar period he agreed with his fellow Democrat Stephen J. Field in rejecting both state and federal imposition of test oaths as a means of reserving public office and the professions for "loyal" citizens. In the *Legal Tender Cases* he endorsed a ban on the continued use of paper money (greenbacks) as legal tender and angrily dissented when a new majority reversed this holding. In his later years, he demonstrated consistent concern with "extending federal authority" during and beyond the era of Reconstruction (Cushman 1993, 169).

As William Gillette noted, Clifford failed "to recognize that federal power was needed to impose national order" and that this process could only come about by

Nathan Clifford (Mathew Brady, Handy Studios, Collection of the Supreme Court of the United States)

"welcoming constructive change" (Gillette 1969, 973). A rigid prewar Jacksonian Democrat, Clifford was an anachronism. There is no doubt that Clifford was able to master fields of law as a justice that he had not encountered as an attorney in Maine. But these accomplishments were negated by his increasing petulance, failing health, absences, and absentmindedness. He refused to resign until a Democratic president could appoint his successor, and he died in 1881—an industrious hack, a monument to mediocrity (Gillette 1969, 973).

Noah H. Swayne

Serving as Lincoln's secretary of the treasury, Chase watched as Lincoln made four appointments to the High Court, beginning with Noah Swayne. Born in 1804 in Virginia to parents who were strict Quakers, Swayne had been introduced to antislavery views at a very early age. He was admitted to the Virginia Bar while still a teenager. Swayne moved to Ohio, where in 1829 he was elected to the state legislature as a Jacksonian Democrat. In 1830, Jackson appointed him to the post of U.S. attorney, a position Swayne retained for the next eleven years. Unlike Clifford, he grew increasingly uncomfortable with the Democratic position on slavery and by 1854 had joined the new Republican Party. A strong and consistent Lincoln supporter, in 1862 he enjoyed unanimous support from the Ohio congressional delegation as he solicited a Supreme Court appointment—even though he had no judicial experience.

The death of Justice John McLean in April 1861, as the Civil War began, left an opening for an Ohio appointment. Swayne sought it openly and vigorously. Well aware of the importance Ohio played in national politics, he lobbied Salmon Chase, just named to Lincoln's cabinet, and Senators Benjamin Wade and John Sherman—all important Republicans well known to Lincoln. Swayne's efforts on his own behalf included a trip to Washington. In the end he proved successful. Perhaps this was due as much to sustained pressure put on Lincoln by supporters of the candidate as to Swayne's success as an attorney. Occupied with the crisis over Sumter, Lincoln finally appointed Swayne in January 1862.

Swayne possessed what Lincoln understandably looked for in all his Court appointments: a clear and unmistakable commitment to the Union cause. He was among the most nationalistic justices in his reaction to the emergency precipitated by the Civil War; thus Swayne was consistent in supporting the war measures adopted by Lincoln's administration. He also endorsed the three constitutional amendments that resulted from the conflict. Indeed, Swayne's efforts to insure Ohio's ratification of the Fifteenth Amendment were important to that state's ultimate affirmative vote by a very narrow margin—one vote in the Senate and two in the House. On the other hand,

Noah H. Swayne (Mathew Brady, Handy Studios, Collection of the Supreme Court of the United States)

as will be seen, his support for the amendment itself was accompanied by endorsement of a judicial holding that minimized its import and impact.

As a justice, Swayne tended to support business and industrial expansion. In 1864, for example, he upheld the contractual rights of railroad bondholders, even in the face of repudiation sanctioned both by the Iowa legislature and state supreme court. Obligations sacred to law, he intoned, cannot be discarded simply because "a state tribunal has erected the altar and decreed the sacrifice" (Hall 1992, 327). Remaining on the bench until 1881, Swayne eagerly schemed to become chief justice whenever a vacancy occurred, as it did in 1864 and in 1873. Justice Samuel Miller ridiculed Swayne's efforts to convince President Grant to appoint him chief justice after Chase's death. Swayne, he noted, "artfully beslobbered the President" (Gillette 1969, 997). Always looking to his own advancement, Miller concluded that in dealing with people, including his fellow justices, Swayne manifested "an absence of any real sincerity and the presence of an ever watchful selfishness." He was, in short, one "whose ambitions far outstripped his abilities" (Gillette 1969, 999).

Samuel F. Miller

Lincoln's second appointment followed the passage of the Judiciary Reorganization Act of 1862, by which Congress created a new federal judicial circuit consisting only of states west of the Mississippi. It made good political sense that he select a justice from this area, and as with Swayne, one who enjoyed overwhelming support from his congressional delegation.

Samuel F. Miller was born in 1816 in Richmond, Kentucky. Ironically, he shared a personal characteristic, one that was comparatively rare among Supreme Court justices, with Justice Joseph Bradley, with whom he often disagreed. Both men were the sons of farmers and the products of families of modest means. Miller had no formal legal training and, again like Swayne, no prior judicial experience.

In 1838, at the age of twenty-two, he had received an M.D. degree from Transylvania University. He practiced medicine in Kentucky for almost ten years but taught himself the law. In 1847, having abandoned his medical career, he was admitted to the bar on motion of his office mate. Two years later, Miller moved to Iowa, where he established a very successful practice and turned to local politics. A staunch Republican and Lincoln supporter, Miller had numerous contacts in Congress once the new western circuit had become a reality in 1862. The right man in the right place at the right time with the right credentials, Miller was confirmed within half an hour after Lincoln submitted his name to the Senate (Cushman 1993, 177–178; Ross 2003, 11–138). Miller was the first Supreme Court justice "born west of the Appalachians, and appointed from west of the Mississippi River" (Cushman 1993, 179).

Samuel F. Miller (Handy Studios, Collection of the Supreme Court of the United States)

Possibly because he lacked judicial experience, Miller's opinions reflected a pragmatic approach to problems rather than a strictly logical application of legal doctrine. His legal insights were based more on experience than formal training. He also had a tendency toward moderation as he rendered his decisions, a trait that his brethren seem to have appreciated. By the time of Miller's death in October 1890, he had spoken for the Court more than 600 times. In this he went far beyond the legendary Chief Justice John Marshall, who until Miller's High Court tenure, had held the record for speaking on behalf of his brethren. Miller also demonstrated both a consistent reluctance to see his Court act as a censor of legislative policy and a tendency to seek a balance between federal and state lines of authority. He was a "progressive moderate" (Gillette 1969, 1012–1013). These qualities marked him as one of the more distinguished members of the Chase Court.

Miller played a key role in the Chase Court's treatment of the Reconstruction issues that came before it. In the *Legal Tender Cases*, for example, Miller led the ultimately successful effort to permit a rehearing on the legality of greenbacks. He took a cautious position concerning the extent to which the Civil War had changed traditional federalism. Miller had strongly supported the merging of abolition with the goal of maintaining and retaining the federal Union. But aside from protection for the ex-slave, he hesitated to endorse major alteration in the way states and the federal government had interacted. It fell to the ex-physician to speak for a bare majority in the most significant Reconstruction litigation cases to come before the Court, the famous *Slaughterhouse Cases* (1873).

Here the High Court interpreted the Fourteenth Amendment, enacted in 1866 and ratified in 1868, for the first time. As will be seen in the next chapter, Miller had no doubt that it had been intended to apply to the freedmen. But the case in front of the Court did not involve any ex-slaves at all. Rather, the dispute centered on the authority of the Louisiana legislature to pass a statute restricting the operation of slaughterhouses in New Orleans to a certain limited area. White butchers and stockmen claimed the protection of the new amendment. In essence, as William Gillette well put it, counsel for the butchers "tried to marry laissez-faire capitalism to the Fourteenth Amendment" but Miller "refused to perform the ceremony" (Gillette 1969, 1020). He was unwilling to believe that the drafters of this new provision had intended to transform the relationship between states and the federal government to the extent set forth by their lawyers.

David Davis

Lincoln's third appointment went to the first of two personal acquaintances he named to the High Court. Appointed in 1862, David Davis had been born in 1815 and was a

David Davis (Unknown, Collection of the Supreme Court of the United States)

graduate of Kenyon College in Ohio, which he had entered when he turned thirteen. By 1840 he had settled in Illinois as a young attorney with an interest in local politics. Indulging a talent for land speculation, which he practiced in Illinois and several other states, Davis developed valuable and lifelong business interests. He ran (unsuccessfully) for the state senate in 1840, but by 1844 had gained a seat in the Illinois House of Representatives. Davis spent the early part of his professional life as an itinerant lawyer, often in the company of another Illinois attorney, self-educated and self-taught: Abraham Lincoln. In 1848, Davis was elected to a seat on the state circuit court. Over the years Davis and Lincoln became fast friends. Davis supported Lincoln's losing effort in 1858 to defeat Douglas as Illinois senator and managed his successful presidential campaign two years later, in 1860.

Of all Lincoln's High Court selections, Davis appears to have enjoyed his tenure least, apparently finding the work tiresome and dull. In common with Lincoln's other appointees, Davis sustained various wartime measures the administration employed between 1861 and 1865, with one notable exception. This exception, however, resulted in one of the landmark cases arising from the Civil War and it provided Davis with the opportunity to write his most enduring and significant opinion. This case, *Ex parte Milligan*, decided in 1866, narrowed the authority of military commissions to try civilians in time of war.

Unlike a court-martial, whose authority was limited to members of the military, by 1865 there could be no doubt concerning the legality of military tribunals, as the Court had indicated in an 1864 opinion, *Ex parte Vallandigham*. But the *Milligan* case raised additional questions. A Democratic malcontent from Indiana, Lambdin Milligan was arrested late in 1864 by military authorities for several military offenses, tried by military commission, and sentenced to death. Shortly before his assassination, Lincoln had ordered the case returned to the military for "correction of errors," but instead Andrew Johnson reaffirmed the death sentence and even set a date for execution. Whereupon Milligan, aided by distinguished counsel, turned to the federal courts.

For reasons discussed in the next chapter, the Supreme Court waited until December of 1866 to decide that Milligan's trial had been unconstitutional. On that point, Davis spoke for a unanimous court. But Davis went further, and although only a bare majority of the Court agreed with him, he emphasized that when civilian courts were open and operational, under *no* circumstances could either the president or Congress order trial of civilians by a military commission. During the entire war, Indiana had never been an active war theatre, and its courts had never suspended operations. Indeed, the reason military authorities had decided to try Milligan by commission was based on that premise. They did not trust an Indiana jury to bring in the guilty verdict that they sought.

Stephen J. Field

Lincoln's fourth appointment to the Court reflected, once again, his dual concerns that the nominee be committed to the Union cause and that he represent a part of the country of major importance in terms of growth—both geographical and legal. A member of the California Supreme Court, Stephen J. Field filled these needs very well. Born in Connecticut in 1816, he was the sixth of nine children and was raised in Massachusetts in a strict Puritan environment by his father, David Dudley Field, a Congregationalist minister. Indeed, portraits of Justice Stephen Field seem to radiate a sense of rigid self-righteousness, confidence, and certainty. Field spent a number of his teenage years abroad, returning to Massachusetts to enter Williams College at the age of seventeen. He graduated at the top of his class in 1837 and promptly entered the New York law firm of his older brother, David Field, Jr., under whom he read law. The elder Field was well on his way to becoming one of the outstanding legal practitioners in the Eastern United States. But the younger sibling may have found working with his brother a bit confining, because in 1849 he moved to California, where he might build a legal career on his own.

Indeed, he did. Field plunged into legal practice and California politics, as well as a series of feuds and personal controversies that seemed to follow the young attorney. Elected to the legislature in 1850, he played a major role in the transformation of a bundle of statutes into a uniform body of civil and criminal law—a code based in part upon efforts by his older brother to construct such a piece of legislation for New York State. By 1857, Field had been elected to the California Supreme Court and became its chief justice two years later. A close friend of influential Republicans, such as Leland Stanford, and well versed in land and mining law, Field seemed the right choice for Lincoln, as he sought to bind California closer to the Union cause. Moreover, Field was a Democrat. By selecting him, Lincoln emphasized his desire to place national priorities above partisan political interests.

As a justice, Field's major opinions tended to reflect his values, which included veneration of property rights and hostility to state regulations, whether or not he could find a clear basis for them either in the Constitution or in judicial precedent. In his majority opinion in the 1867 *Test Oath Cases*, for example, Field held that "the theory upon which our political institutions rest is, that all men have certain and inalienable rights—that among these are life, liberty, and the pursuit of happiness; and that in the pursuit of happiness all avocations, all honors, all positions, are alike open to everyone, and that in protection of these rights all are equal before the law" (*Cummings v. Missouri* 1867). Even as Field wrote his opinion, a new constitutional provision, the Fourteenth Amendment, was awaiting state ratification. Later it would serve Field well as a foundation for his basic assumptions concerning government and society.

Stephen J. Field (Handy Studios, Collection of the Supreme Court of the United States)

Like John Marshall, Stephen Field had little difficulty in articulating such assumptions, regardless of a lack of precedent.

For a time Chase presided over a ten-member Court, as Congress—seeking to insure that Lincoln would have ample opportunity to appoint pro-Union justices—had added a tenth seat by the 1863 act. This newest vacancy was filled by Stephen Field. By 1867, however, two justices had died, and the struggle between Andrew Johnson and Congress resulted in Johnson being unable to make any appointments to the High Court, a fate shared thus far by only one other full-term president, Jimmy Carter (1976–1980). With President Ulysses Grant inaugurated in 1869, Congress restored the Court membership to nine, where it has remained ever since.

William Strong

Grant had moved promptly to fill two court vacancies by nominating his attorney general, E. Rockwood Hoar, and the former secretary of war, Edwin Stanton. But Hoar fell victim to partisan wrangling in the Senate, while Stanton—though appointed and immediately confirmed—died before he could take the oath of office. Again, Grant had two vacancies to consider. He moved to fill them on February 7, 1870. The date held special significance for "Court watchers." On this date, the Court handed down its decision in the first of the *Legal Tender Cases*, in which it held by a 4–3 vote that the continued use of paper money, popularly known as greenbacks, was unconstitutional *(Hepburn v. Griswold)*. In his opinion for the majority, Chief Justice Chase disavowed as unconstitutional a policy that, as secretary of the treasury, he had earlier endorsed and helped to implement. Invariably, the question of a rehearing on this case became linked to the question of where Grant's two nominees might stand on the issue of paper specie.

There was no doubt where one of them stood. William Strong, a native of Connecticut, had enrolled in Yale before he turned sixteen. He later received a master's degree from Yale Law School and was admitted to both the Connecticut and Pennsylvania Bars in 1832, at the age of twenty-four. He settled in Reading, became fluent in both German and local dialects, and built a very lucrative practice. By 1846 he had been elected to Congress as an antislavery Democrat and served two terms. Having returned to his law practice, and still a Democrat, Strong was elected to the Pennsylvania Supreme Court in 1857 for a fifteen-year term. His antislavery views and strong support of the Union resulted in his shift to the new Republican Party. Strong remained on the Pennsylvania bench until 1868 (Cushman 1993, 196–197).

One of his most important votes as a member of the Pennsylvania Supreme Court came when he joined his colleagues in affirming the constitutionality of the Legal Tender Act of 1862. A number of state courts had already so held, and indeed by 1870, at

William Strong (Mathew Brady, Handy Studios, Collection of the Supreme Court of the United States)

least sixty state justices had considered this issue, with only one Republican jurist opposing the use of paper money as legal tender. The initial decision of the United States Supreme Court on the Legal Tender Act, declaring the measure unconstitutional, came in February 1870, on the same day that Grant sent Strong's name to the Senate. This led some to accuse the president of seeking to pack the Court in order to gain a rehearing and a reversal of the High Court's holding. Although there is no convincing evidence that Grant had so conspired, there is no doubt that Strong's view on legal tender were well known. Indeed, within a year, he would write for the new five-member majority in overruling Chase's decision (*Knox v. Lee*).

Joseph P. Bradley

Grant's other nominee, Republican Joseph P. Bradley, graduated from Rutgers College in New Jersey and taught himself sufficient law to be admitted to the bar "at the relatively advanced age of twenty six" (Lurie 1986, 347). A voracious reader at home in several languages, also well versed in mathematics, the young attorney built a successful career in Newark. Along the way, he married the daughter of William Hornblower, New Jersey's chief justice. Given Bradley's later hostility to railroads, it is interesting to note that as a lawyer, one of his most important clients was the notoriously corrupt Camden and Amboy Railroad. (Four years after Chase's death, Bradley was the guiding light behind a famous decision, *Munn v. Illinois*, which affirmed the right of a state to regulate certain commercial enterprises, including railroads, in the public interest.) By 1868 he had become a strong supporter of Grant for the presidency and was one of New Jersey's presidential electors pledged to him, specifically supporting the Legal Tender Act.

The fact that Grant was probably well aware that both Strong and Bradley had publicly supported paper money prior to their nominations in no way renders him guilty of "court packing," an accusation often raised after 1871. There is no evidence that he intentionally sought out nominees in favor of paper money as legal tender. On the other hand, the government moved for reconsideration of Chase's decision only *after* Grant's two nominations had been confirmed. It requires no great mathematical skill to realize that three dissenters in the 1870 holding plus the two new appointments would make up a new majority.

During the early stages of the war, Bradley had emphasized that the overriding duty of the president was to "put down the rebellion cost what it may. . . . The rebellion must be put down. Nothing else must be thought of" (Lurie 1986, 349). The issue was not slavery. Rather, it was obedience to the Constitution, which should "stand just as it is, word for word and letter for letter." Bradley further added that as far as the South was concerned, "the Constitution gives us no power to meddle with them, no more than it gives them power to meddle with us." Like many in the North, including Lincoln, by 1865 Bradley had come to the inescapable conclusion that abolition must be joined with saving the Union as the twin goals of the conflict. But both his basic conservatism and racism remained unchanged.

Joseph P. Bradley (Vic Boswell, National Geographic, Collection of the Supreme Court of the United States)

Ward Hunt

Grant's third appointment, and the final appointee to the Chase Court, was Ward Hunt. Like several of his colleagues, Hunt had been a Jacksonian Democrat. A native of Utica, New York, born in 1810, Hunt studied law for a time at the famous Tapping Reeve School in Litchfield, Connecticut. By 1832 he had returned to Utica and established a successful law practice. Six years later he was elected to the state legislature, and in 1844 became Utica's mayor. Like some of his judicial brethren, Hunt found the Democratic Party's position on slavery increasingly unacceptable, with the result that in 1856 he joined in establishing the Republican Party in New York State. In doing so, Hunt became well acquainted with a leading power in state politics, Roscoe Conkling. This friendship would ultimately lead Hunt to the United States Supreme Court (Cushman 1993, 207–208).

In the meantime, Hunt had sought state judicial office, running unsuccessfully for a seat on the New York Court of Appeals. In 1853, he tried again, and again was defeated. After the war, and now well established as a Republican, Hunt tried for a third time and at last met with success. In 1865 he succeeded his mentor and former partner, Hiram Denio, on the state high court, and in 1868 he became chief justice. A state constitutional amendment required the reorganization of the court of appeals in 1869, but Hunt managed to stay on as commissioner of appeals.

In November 1872, Supreme Court Justice Samuel Nelson retired. Eighty years old and in poor health, Nelson had missed much of the Court's 1871–1872 term. President Grant, responding to an enthusiastic endorsement from now New York Senator Roscoe Conkling, named Hunt to succeed Nelson. Nominated on December 3, 1872, Hunt took his seat early in January 1873. He arrived just in time to participate in one of the landmark decisions of the Chase Court, the *Slaughterhouse Cases*. In less than six months, the chief justice was dead, and the Chase Court was a thing of the past. Yet, in barely nine years it had rendered a number of decisions that reshaped our constitutional history. They dealt with Reconstruction, with new forms of regulation, and with the changing nature of the federal Union.

References

Cushman, Claire. 1993. *The Supreme Court Justices: Illustrated Biographies, 1789–1993*. Washington, DC: Congressional Quarterly Press.

Gatell, Frank O. 1969. "John Catron." In Leon Friedman and Fred Israel, eds., *The Justices of the United States Supreme Court 1789–1969: Their Lives and Major Opinions*. 2 vols. New York: Chelsea House.

Ward Hunt (Mathew Brady, Handy Studios, Collection of the Supreme Court of the United States)

Gillette, William. 1969. "Noah Swayne." In Leon Friedman and Fred Israel, eds., *The Justices of the United States Supreme Court 1789–1969: Their Lives and Major Opinions.* 2 vols. New York: Chelsea House.

———. 1969. "Samuel Miller." In Leon Friedman and Fred Israel, eds., *The Justices of the United States Supreme Court 1789–1969: Their Lives and Major Opinions.* 2 vols. New York: Chelsea House.

Hall, Kermit, ed. 1992. *The Oxford Companion to the Supreme Court of the United States.* New York: Oxford University Press.

Hyman, Harold M. 1997. *The Reconstruction Justice of Salmon P. Chase:* In re Turner *and* Texas v. White. Lawrence: University Press of Kansas.

Labbe, Ronald, and Jonathan Lurie. 2003. *The Slaughterhouse Cases: Regulation, Reconstruction, and the Fourteenth Amendment.* Lawrence: University Press of Kansas.

Lurie, Jonathan. 1983. *Law and the Nation: 1865–1912.* New York: Alfred A. Knopf.

———. 1986. "Mr. Justice Bradley: A Reassessment." *Seton Hall Law Review* 16: 343.

Ross, Michael A. 2003. *Justice of Shattered Dreams: Samuel Freeman Miller and the Supreme Court during the Civil War Era.* Baton Rouge: Louisiana State University Press.

Urofsky, Melvin I., ed. 1994. *The Supreme Court Justices: A Biographical Dictionary.* New York: Garland.

3

Major Decisions

Although Chase served as chief justice for barely eight years, his tenure did not lack for significant cases. Early in his term and shortly before his death, his Court handed down two enduring landmarks in U.S. constitutional history; *Ex parte Milligan* (1866), and the *Slaughterhouse Cases* (1873). Sandwiched in between these dates, the justices decided other issues, as they reacted and responded to a turbulent era, described in Chapter 1. Approximately one dozen of them warrant discussion here.

Military Commissions: Ex Parte Milligan *(1866)*

This case arose in October 1864, even before Chase had been confirmed as Lincoln's choice to succeed the late Chief Justice Roger Taney. A Democratic partisan and strident critic of "Mr. Lincoln's war," Lambdin Milligan was arrested by order of the army general commanding the Indiana military district. By the end of the month he had been tried by a military commission and sentenced to death. As noted in Chapter 2, Lincoln ordered the record in Milligan's trial corrected for various unstated "errors." Meanwhile, a grand jury met for more than three weeks in Indianapolis and declined to hand down any indictment or presentment in Milligan's case. Indeed, no federal indictment was ever made against him by any grand jury. After Lincoln's murder, Milligan's problems took on renewed urgency as President Johnson affirmed the death sentence and ordered it be carried out on May 19, 1865.

Milligan's lawyers sought a writ of habeas corpus from the federal circuit court, but the two judges sitting in Indianapolis disagreed on the case and referred it to the Supreme Court, as provided by law. The resulting litigation involved some of the most distinguished lawyers of the day, including David Dudley Field (Justice Field's older brother) as well as a future president of the United States, James Garfield. Although the justices heard the case in March 1866 and reached a verdict in April, the written opinions were not released until the end of the year. When they were made available on December 17, the entire Court unanimously held that Milligan should be released. Agreement ended here, however, and other issues found the justices split 5–4.

Justice David Davis, Lincoln's former campaign manager, wrote for the Court, noting that Milligan's case "involves the very framework of the government and the fundamental principles of American liberty." Why had it taken so long to announce in public a case decided unanimously eight months before? Davis hinted at the answer early in his opinion. "During the late wicked Rebellion," he wrote, "the temper of the times did not allow that calmness in deliberation and discussion so necessary to a correct conclusion of a purely judicial question. Then, considerations of safety were mingled with the exercise of power. . . . Now that the public safety is assured, this question, as well as all others, can be discussed and decided without passion or the admixture of any element not required to form a legal judgment." In other words, now that sufficient time had passed since the end of the war and the Union Army had diminished remarkably in size since early in 1865, the Court could risk handing down a decision adverse to the military. Better a delayed decision than one ignored and dismissed by those to whom it is directed.

Davis explained that Congress had passed an act early in March 1863 suspending the writ of habeas corpus, and this at a time when "an armed rebellion against the national authority, of greater proportions than history affords an example of, was raging." Under its provisions, the president could and, on September 15, 1863, did suspend the writ. But the statute also directed that the federal courts be furnished a list of all parties not prisoners of war who were being held in federal custody, like Milligan, and who were citizens of states in which "the administration of the laws in the Federal tribunals was unimpaired." After such a list was furnished, if a federal grand jury failed to indict any person on the list, he was to be released. Even if the federal authorities declined to make such a list available, if twenty days had passed since his arrest and the termination of the grand jury, he was still entitled to his discharge.

Counsel for Milligan emphasized how their client met every condition just noted. He was detained under presidential order, he was not a member of the armed forces, he was a citizen of Indiana—a state never active as a theatre of war—and a grand jury had sat for more than twenty days after he had been arrested and had failed to file any indictment against him. He, therefore, had every right to seek a writ from the circuit court, and if that court disagreed on the merits of his position, the judges, in turn, had every right to certify it to the full Supreme Court, which is what had happened. The case was properly before the High Court. Therefore, Davis wrote, if "there was law to justify this military trial, it is not our province to interfere; if there was not, it is our duty to declare the nullity of the whole proceedings." No graver question, added Justice Davis, "was ever considered by this Court."

He went on to list a number of constitutional safeguards concerning due process found in the Bill of Rights, which, at the time of this case had been held to apply exclusively to the federal government. Anticipating the claim of military necessity as a justification for Milligan's treatment, Davis rejected it out of hand early in his opinion. The Constitution, he insisted, "is a law for rulers and people, equally in war and in peace, and covers with the shield of its protection all classes of men, at all times, and under all circumstances. No doctrine, involving more pernicious consequences was ever invented . . . than that any of its provisions can be suspended during any of the great exigencies of government." Where then, did the military commission that had tried, convicted, and sentenced Milligan get its authority?

Certainly not from Congress, which had not established such a tribunal. Nor from the president, "because he is controlled by law, and has his appropriate sphere of duty, which is to execute, not to make, the laws." There were indeed, Davis conceded, "laws and usages of war," accepted and well established. But "they can never be applied to citizens in states which have upheld the authority of the government, and where the courts are open and their process unobstructed."

Such in fact was an accurate description of Indiana during the Civil War. Its courts and grand juries, both state and federal, had been ready to act in any complaint concerning Milligan. Instead, military authorities had raised the justification of martial law. But "martial law cannot arise from a threatened invasion," Davis wrote. "The necessity must be actual and present; the invasion real, such as effectively closes the courts and deposes the civil administration. . . . [It] can never exist where the courts are open, and in the proper and unobstructed exercise of their jurisdiction. It is also confined to the locality of actual war."

Here, again, conditions in Indiana failed to meet this criteria. How could Milligan be treated as a prisoner of war when he had "lived in Indiana for the past twenty years," had been arrested there, and had never resided in any of the states in rebellion against the Union? He had not engaged in legal acts of hostility against the government, and only such persons who do so and are captured can legitimately be called prisoners of war. "If [Milligan] cannot enjoy the immunities attaching to the character of a prisoner of war, how can he be subject to their pains and penalties?" (1866). The Chase Court unanimously agreed that Milligan's military trial and death sentence had been unconstitutional, but beyond this point, unanimity ended.

As the above excerpts from Davis's opinion indicate, his majority opinion had gone much further than this. He had insisted that under *no* conditions could Congress authorize military tribunals in the circumstances as noted above. Speaking for the four dissenters, including three Republicans appointed by Lincoln, Chief Justice Chase denied this assertion. True, Congress had not authorized the tribunal that had prosecuted and punished Milligan. But it had *always* possessed and still retained *inherent* power to do so. "The fact that the Federal Courts were open was regarded by Congress as a sufficient reason for not exercising the power," Chase argued, "but that fact could not deprive Congress of the right to exercise it."

Chase observed that while no taint of disloyalty had attached to the Indiana courts, "it might have been otherwise. In times of rebellion and civil war it may often happen, indeed, that judges and marshals will be in active sympathy with rebels, and courts their most efficient allies." In other words, Congress had not acted here, but if it had or did so under similar circumstances in the future, there were no constitutional barriers to impede such action. The dissenters were unwilling, Chase concluded, "to give our assent by silence to expressions of opinion which seem to us calculated, though not intended, to cripple the constitutional powers of the government, and to augment the public dangers in times of invasion and rebellion."

Thus this first landmark decision of the Chase Court set forth a holding that has been widely praised as a landmark in the history of U.S. civil liberties. It should, however, be seen in its context. The decision did not ban the imposition of martial law. Further, it apparently applied only to states where civil courts and governmental procedures were in full operation. Therefore, it made no definitive pronouncement about the federal government's military authority within the defeated Southern states, contrary to the position taken by many Radical Republicans, who were very critical of the Court's decision. On the other hand, the *Milligan* case represents the first time in which the Supreme Court intervened by reversing a matter involving the administration of military justice. As such, it remains an extremely important precedent. Yet, as will be seen in the next chapter, *Milligan* has had troubling implications for the interplay between the courts and U.S. military action in World War II and in the wake of 9/11, as well as for constitutional protection of "traditional" U.S. civil liberties. In *Milligan*, Lincoln's five appointees were split: Davis and Field in favor; Swayne, Miller, and Chase opposed.

Test Oath Cases: Cummings v. Missouri *(1867)*

In post–Civil War politics, Democrats tended to favor limitations on governmental power to a greater extent than did Republicans. This tendency should be kept in mind as one considers the next significant Chase Court decisions, the loyalty or *Test Oath Cases*. In two separate decisions each by a 5–4 majority, Justice Field held loyalty oaths, whether imposed by the states or by the federal government, to be unconstitutional. Field was the only Democrat appointed to the Court by Lincoln. In the next two decisions to be discussed, he split from the other four Lincoln nominees and joined the four other Democrats on the Court. The remaining Lincoln appointees united in a dissent authored by Justice Miller. The *Test Oath Cases* involved two statutes; one enacted by the state of Missouri, and the other by Congress.

In 1865, although it had never formally seceded, Missouri adopted a new constitution. It included a loyalty oath that, as Justice Field later noted, contained "more than thirty distinct affirmations or tests." These various provisions were intended to go beyond specific acts against the Union and "to reach words, desires, and sympathies, also." Further, "no clergyman of any religious persuasion" could "teach, or preach, or solemnize marriages unless such person shall have taken . . . such oath." The penalty for the refusal of Father John Cummings, a Catholic pastor, to take this oath was a fine of $500 and imprisonment until the fine and associated trial costs were paid. Counsel for Cummings, including Justice Field's brother, insisted that the oath was in fact punishment rather than a legitimate test of one's fitness and qualifications for a particular occupation or calling (*Cummings v. Missouri* 1867).

Speaking for a bare majority, Justice Field agreed with his brother. Counsel for Missouri had argued that punishment meant only to be deprived of one's "life, liberty or property, and that to take from him anything less than these is no punishment at all." On the contrary, insisted the Court, "the deprivation of any rights, civil or political, previously enjoyed, may be punishment," as might be "disqualification from office . . . or from the pursuits of a lawful avocation." Even as Field wrote the opinion for the Court, the Fourteenth Amendment was before the states for ratification. But Field, in what would become a major tenet of his constitutional philosophy, did not need to wait for this step. With or without the new enactment, he emphasized that as part of certain inalienable rights, "all honors, all positions are alike open to every one, and that in the protection of these rights, all are equal before the law." Surely such a doctrine applied to Cummings.

Field argued that what Missouri had done with such an all-embracing test oath was to enact a bill of attainder, which he defined simply as "a legislative act which inflicts punishment without a judicial trial." The provisions of the oath "presume the guilt of the priests and clergymen, and adjudge the deprivation of their right to preach or teach unless the presumption be removed" by their taking the oath. In other words, the state "assume[s] the guilt and adjust[s] the punishment conditionally," and this it cannot do. The constitutional protections against bills of attainder and ex post facto laws were clear. Their intent was that "the rights of the citizen should be secure against deprivation for past conduct by legislative enactment, under any form, however disguised. If the inhibition can be evaded by the form of the enactment, its insertion in the fundamental law was a vain and futile proceeding."

Ex Parte Garland *(1867)*

The companion case, decided on the same day with the same majority and spokesman for the Court, essentially applied the reasoning in *Cummings* to a federal statute. But there were some interesting differences in the matter of *Ex parte Garland*. There could be no doubt of his conduct. An attorney, A. H. Garland, had served in both houses of the Confederate Congress, where he had represented one of the seceded states, Arkansas. Prior to outbreak of war, he had been admitted to the Supreme Court Bar and had taken the traditional oath required of all attorneys who appeared before that tribunal. In 1862, however, Congress enacted a loyalty oath statute and in 1865 amended it to bar any attorney from appearing in the federal courts unless he or she "shall have first taken and subscribed the oath" of 1862. In March 1865, the Court amended its own rules to conform to the congressional mandate.

In July 1865, however, Garland received from President Johnson a "full pardon and amnesty for all offences by him committed." Further, he took the new oath prescribed by the president before the pardon could be implemented. In due course, Garland appeared before the High Court seeking to resume his practice before it. He argued first that the congressional act of 1862 was unconstitutional, and second that even if the enactment was found to be legal, Garland was released from compliance with its provisions because of Johnson's full pardon.

Given his reasoning in *Cummings*, it is not surprising that Field sustained Garland's prime contention. He noted the third provision of the statute, which required the applicant to swear that "he has never sought, accepted, or attempted to exercise the function of any office whatsoever, under any authority . . . in hostility to the United States." Unless Garland was prepared to perjure himself, there was no way he could swear to such a provision. And, unless he subscribed to the oath in its entirety, he was barred from the practice of law. Field found this dilemma constitutionally suspect. In fact, he argued, Garland was excluded from "any of the professions or any of the ordinary avocations of life" as punishment in a manner prohibited by the fundamental law.

Further, Field refused to permit Congress to reduce the significance and impact of the presidential pardon. If the legislature could impose an oath to which an applicant could not swear, and then barred him from his chosen calling, of what use was the pardon? The process was an attempt to make sure that "the pardon may be avoided, and that accomplished indirectly which cannot be reached by direct legislation. It is not within the constitutional power of Congress thus to inflict punishment beyond the reach of executive clemency."

As was noted earlier, Chase was troubled by the loyalty oath issue—as indeed were all the other Lincoln appointments to the Court. Justice Miller spoke for them in dissent. He emphasized that an unconstitutional congressional act "should be so clear as to leave little reason for doubt, before we pronounce it invalid." Such was not the case here. Longstanding tradition required that all attorneys, as well as governmental authorities, must swear that they would bear faithful allegiance to the government. This was the purpose of the ceremonial oath by which lawyers were admitted to the bar. Miller could not resist implying that if "all the members of the legal profession" in the lately seceded states had remained true to their oaths pledging a loyal and faithful allegiance to the national authority, "we should have been spared the horrors of that rebellion" (*Ex parte Garland* 1867).

Further, Miller asserted that an individual who had "voluntarily given aid, comfort, counsel, or encouragement" to armed hostility against the government had "forfeited his right to appear in her courts and take part in the administration of her laws." What was wrong, he asked, with Congress requiring loyalty as a qualification for all who practice law in the national courts? How was this a punishment? Both state and federal constitutional history were replete with many examples of legal qualifications not attainable by all, and they could not be called punishments. Miller pointed to an age qualification, one that many "distinguished lawyers can never attain, and which effectively bars them from judicial office in many states." An attorney, he noted, could not receive judicial appointment beyond a certain age. Is this punishment? In the case at hand, is Garland's admitted inability to swear the oath a lack of appropriate qualification rather than a punishment? Because the enactments under attack here could not be shown to be intended as punishments, they could not legitimately be considered ex post facto laws or bills of attainder.

As is often the case in a closely divided court decision, the dissent may well have had logic on its side but not votes. Miller was uncomfortable with his position, all the more as by its terms his own brother-in-law, William P. Ballinger, would be barred from practice in the federal courts. Miller wrote to him, "I have felt bound by my clear conviction thus to vote and I am not sorry that the result is adverse to my opinion . . . because I think the requirement unnecessarily harsh at present" (Fairman 1971, 244). One suspects that the dissenting justice referred here to the context in which the loyalty oath cases had arisen.

Decided approximately one year after the *Milligan* decision, *Cummings* and *Garland* symbolized ongoing constitutional change during the course of Reconstruction. In the first place, *Garland* represented the first significant Chase Court holding to focus on *congressional* action, while *Cummings* apparently remains the first example of the Court declaring a part of a state constitution unconstitutional. In *Milligan*, the justices had confronted the military. In the *Test Oath Cases*, handed down even as the conflict between Johnson and Congress intensified, the Court weighed in on the side of civil liberties at the expense of both federal and state legislative authority.

In the second place, lurking within the arguments on behalf of Garland and Cummings—raised, it might be noted, by prominent Democratic counsel—could be found foundations for opposition to Reconstruction in general. Some hoped—ultimately in vain—that much of the proposed agenda for congressional action might meet the same fate. A possible weapon against congressional activism might be at hand in the guise of a new emphasis on legal formalism. David Dudley Field had specifically argued, and his brother Stephen had accepted the idea, of a property right inherent in practicing a chosen profession free from punitive restraints imposed by the legislature. Drawing on general "constitutional principles" rather than the more specific Fourteenth Amendment, not yet ratified by the states, Justice Field implied that such a right clearly warranted judicial protection. Finally, the elimination of loyalty oaths in Missouri could only enhance the "political strengths of Missouri Democrats" (Mauer 2001, 248). In turn, such a result reflected the political uncertainties that characterized Reconstruction in general.

Thus far, with the exception of the *Garland* case, the Chase Court had avoided direct confrontation with the executive and legislative branches of government. *Milligan* involved the army, and *Cummings* involved the state of Missouri. But Reconstruction occurred in an atmosphere of marked Southern-state antagonism toward congressional policies, as well as Northern racial and political ambivalence toward the Confederacy—defeated in battle yet defiant in practice. Faced with such intransigence from the South, as well as growing Northern disenchantment with both the prospects of black suffrage and a policy of harsh treatment toward the defeated Confederates, the Republican majority in Congress wavered. Late in 1867, Justice Miller took note of the new reality. "Negro suffrage in the North," he predicted (correctly), "will probably be abandoned as a party platform but the experiment of reconstruction on the Congressional basis will probably be adhered to . . . because it affords the only chance for a republican party in the South." Increasingly, Miller found the entire political picture unimpressive. "I feel more than I ever did in my life indifference to party success," and if it was desirable that a High Court jurist be nonpartisan, "I am as near possessing that qualification, as any man on the bench" (Fairman 1971, 402).

Encouraged by both Republican vacillation and Andrew Johnson's strident and persistent recalcitrance, the South resisted congressional Reconstruction with renewed vigor. Some ex-Confederates such as former Georgia Governor Joseph Brown urged a reaching out to the North. "We need capital and labor. Neither will come till our difficulties are settled" (Fairman 1971, 416). Others preached defiance toward the military leaders installed from Washington, be they native Southern Unionists or Northern renegades. "They are each and all infamous, cowardly, and abandoned villains who, instead of wearing shoulder straps and ruling millions of people, should have their heads shaved, their ears cropped, their foreheads branded, and their precious persons lodged in a penitentiary." So wrote the editor of the *Vicksburg Times*, one William H. McCardle, in November 1867. His words would have interesting consequences.

Congress and the Court: **Ex Parte McCardle** *(1869)*

Promptly arrested by the military on several charges, including "inciting insurrection, disorder, and violence," McCardle was scheduled for trial before a military commission. His lawyers sought a writ of habeas corpus from the federal circuit court sitting in Jackson. In his defense, they cited the recent case of *Milligan*, and this controversial precedent appeared to support their position. Nevertheless, in a thoughtful opinion, Judge Robert Hill denied the writ but allowed McCardle to remain free on bail. A federal law, enacted in February 1867, however, provided direct appeal to the U.S. Supreme Court. Intended "to enlarge the privilege of habeas corpus," and thus to insure "federal judicial intervention to protect newly liberated slaves," this is the statute upon which the white editor sought relief from Chase's Court. Hoping to avoid a decision on the merits, the government moved "to dismiss for want of jurisdiction" (Fairman 1971, 450–451). By a unanimous vote, the Court rejected the motion.

In fact, there was much more to the case than might appear from first glance. Mississippi in 1867 was not in the same position as Indiana in 1864. Once a seceded state within the Confederacy, it was now subject to the congressional plan of Reconstruction and, in the view of the Radical Republicans, had not yet been formally readmitted to the Union. Further, even as McCardle's lawyers pressed their case before the Supreme Court early in March 1868, relations between Congress and President Johnson had reached the crisis stage. The House of Representatives voted to impeach Johnson early in February. During arguments before the Court, Chief Justice Chase was summoned to appear before the Senate, which was about to convene as a court to try the beleaguered chief executive. Indeed, David Field's argument on behalf of McCardle was interrupted by the Court's sudden adjournment so that Chase could attend this Senate session.

Further, besides the specific matter of the impeachment lurking in the background, congressional Republicans were genuinely concerned about the "track record" of Chase's Court thus far. From their perspective—and it must be remembered that the period 1867–1868 was one of incredible tension in Washington—rightly or wrongly Radical Republicans saw the *Milligan* decision and the more recent *Test Oath* holdings as judicial assaults against their plans for Reconstruction. They feared that the justices might use the *McCardle* case as a vehicle for declaring the Reconstruction Act of 1867 unconstitutional. Since in 1867–1868 this statute was seen as *the* lynchpin for the entire program of congressional Reconstruction, such concern is understandable. For its part, the Court did not shy away from the importance of the case they had agreed to decide. The tribunal allowed six hours of arguments for each side, "three times the normal amount" (Fairman 1971, 451).

Counsel for McCardle essentially rehashed much of what had already been argued and decided in *Milligan*, emphasizing that even though some of that decision had carried by only a 5–4 margin, "it is now as binding on the conscience of those who did not concur as those who did." Counsel for the government, Senator Matthew Carpenter, sought to distinguish *Milligan* from the case at hand. Here, unlike Indiana in the earlier litigation, the state involved *had* seceded from the Union, and "Congress *had* authorized trial by military commission." More important, with an eye toward ongoing events in Washington, Carpenter warned Chase and his colleagues to be wary of excessive use of judicial authority. Although it may not have been necessary considering that the widely publicized impeachment proceedings against Johnson were in progress, Carpenter noted that "members of the bar had a duty, when occasions require, to admonish and warn, and that too whether courts will listen, or whether they will refrain" (Fairman 1971, 451–452, 453). Again, he did not mention the fact that even as he spoke, a bill awaited consideration by the Senate Judiciary Committee—one that would have acknowledged that congressional action in Reconstruction was "a power not subject to judicial control" (Fairman 1971, 454).

The Court took McCardle's petition under advisement on March 9, 1868. By the time it first reached this case in conference, apparently on March 21, Congress had already launched a preemptive strike against the Court. It took the form of a statute that simply repealed the earlier Habeas Corpus Act of 1867, which had permitted the High Court to hear appeals in such cases. The new measure awaited a certain presidential veto, to be followed by an equally certain override. By a vote of 7–2, Chase's Court decided, in conference, to postpone consideration of the case. But the vote, supposedly confidential, did not remain so for very long. The two leading Democratic justices, Grier and Field, had dissented, and before their protests were formally presented, word about the case "leaked out." Secretary of the Navy Gideon Welles, a Lincoln appointee still in Johnson's cabinet, noted in his diary that the Chase Court "had caved in, fallen through, failed in the McCardle case." Orville Browning, Johnson's secretary of the interior, wrote that "this exhibition of cowardice on the part of the Court, and their readiness to surrender . . . to the usurpation and tyranny of Congress is among the alarming symptoms of our times" (Fairman 1971, 467).

Of course Democrats opposed to Reconstruction hoped that the *McCardle* case would have served as a vehicle for a full frontal judicial assault against congressional action in this area. For his part, Justice Grier insisted that by postponing a decision on a case that had been fully, if not exhaustively, argued, the Court was subject "to the imputation that we have evaded the performance of a duty imposed on us by the Constitution. . . . I am not willing to be a partaker of the eulogy or opprobrium that may follow" (Fairman 1971, 474). The lawyer for McCardle was even more blunt. "This whole government," he wrote, "is so rotten and dishonest that I can only protest. . . . Though the Court might have done its duty in McCardle's case, it has not and will not. . . . The Court stood still to be ravished and did not even hallo while the thing was being done" (Fairman 1971, 478). And so Chase's Court put off *McCardle* until the next term, which began in December 1868, after Ulysses Grant had been elected to the presidency.

Finally, on April 12, 1869, Chase announced for a *unanimous* court that McCardle's case would be dismissed due to a new lack of jurisdiction. Field and Grier had objected not to the ultimate decision, but rather to what they considered to be an inappropriate postponement in reaching it. With impeachment a thing of the past, with Johnson out and Grant in, perhaps Chase, who had seen any possibility of his receiving the Democratic nomination in 1868 as hopelessly lost, found new courage. Although he readily acquiesced in congressional action to gut the Habeas Corpus Act of 1867, his opinion ended with an intriguing claim that such action was in fact based on a very narrow foundation. "Counsel seem to have supposed . . . that the whole appellate power of the court, in cases of habeas corpus, is denied. But this is an error. The act of 1868 does not exempt from that jurisdiction any cases but appeals from Circuit Courts under the act of 1867. It does not effect the jurisdiction which was previously exercised." In other words, appellate jurisdiction under statutes such as the famous Judiciary Act of 1789 was unchanged.

As if to reiterate its position, Chase's Court handed down a decision almost identical to *McCardle* in the case of *Ex parte Yerger*—decided on October 25, 1869. But the difference in the time period was significant. By the fall of 1869, congressional Reconstruction had lost both its novelty and, according to some critics, its sense of immediacy. Further, the Fourteenth Amendment was now part of the Constitution, the tensions and turmoil of impeachment were past, and Ulysses Grant was now the chief executive. There was, in short, much less urgency for Congress to feel that the Court was about to derail Reconstruction. Finally, once again speaking for his brethren, Chase utilized vigorous rhetoric but undercut it with lack of real follow-up.

The chief justice reiterated the grand intent of habeas corpus jurisdiction: "It is that every citizen may be protected by judicial action from unlawful imprisonment." This assumption was what had led Congress in the famous Judiciary Act of 1789 to so provide. As he had in *McCardle*, Chase ruled that in 1867 Congress had expanded certain judicial authority to issue the writ; further, that in 1869 it had repealed such expansion—something that the legislature had every right to do. But this repeal "did not purport to touch the appellate jurisdiction conferred by the Constitution. . . . They [the actions of Congress] reach no act except the act of 1867." Thus in this case, judicial authority to issue a writ "is affirmed." But the Court did not push the issue, a specific federal writ in the case of *Yerger* was *not* issued, and the case was quietly resolved. Once again, Chase had employed a judicial tactic often used in U.S. jurisprudence: to articulate boldly a general principle, even as one rejects its concrete application to the case at hand. Had the Republican majority in Congress examined the Chase Court's record in toto between 1865 and 1869, it would have seen that despite the holdings in *Milligan* and the *Test Oath Cases*, and unlike Andrew Johnson, the justices were far from seeking open confrontation with the legislature. Indeed, even before *McCardle* was accepted for argument, the justices had backed away from an opportunity to do just that.

Congressional Reconstruction and the Court: Mississippi v. Johnson *(1867)*

After passage of the Reconstruction Act in 1867, both Mississippi and Georgia sought Court intervention, hoping for a judicial finding that the new law was unconstitutional. Although President Johnson had vetoed the Reconstruction statute, as a matter of presidential authority he was more concerned over the effort by these two states to block executive implementation of it. He need not have worried.

In *Mississippi v. Johnson,* Chase dismissed the state's claim. The authority of the president under the Reconstruction acts was "purely executive and political." "Congress," he added, "is the legislative department of the government; the President is the executive department. Neither can be restrained in its action by the judicial department." In an intriguing example of prescience on Chase's part, he asked what might happen if the president refused to execute the acts of Congress: "Is it not clear that a collision may occur between the executive and legislative branches of the government? May not the House . . . . Impeach the President for such refusal?" This, of course, was precisely what would happen. In the case at hand, decided on April 15, 1867, Chase emphasized that "we are fully satisfied that this court has no jurisdiction of a bill to enjoin the President in the performance of his judicial duties."

Georgia v. Stanton *(1868)*

Although the Court dismissed Georgia's complaint on May 13, 1867, for reasons similar to those in *Mississippi,* the written decision was not released until February 1868, shortly before the House voted to impeach President Johnson. Perhaps the timing was a judicial attempt to lessen congressional concern over the Chase Court's apparent judicial activism. At any rate, Justice Nelson echoed Chase in the earlier holding. Contrary to what Georgia claimed, to warrant court intervention "the rights in danger . . . must be rights of persons or property, not merely political rights, which do not belong to the jurisdiction of a court." Indeed, the issues raised called for "the judgment of the court upon political questions, and, upon rights of a political character." Nelson concluded that his Court "possesses no jurisdiction over the subject matter presented" (76–77).

Thus, when put in perspective, after *Milligan* and the *Test Oath Cases,* the Chase Court avoided conflict with Congress. It did so by boldly proclaiming judicial independence as an operational principle, even as the justices abandoned it on several occasions as an operational practice. If there be any doubt of this trend, one can look again at *Texas v. White* (1869), which was also briefly discussed in Chapter 2.

Texas v. White *(1869)*

After it had seceded, Texas sold some state securities in an effort to raise money to help finance the Confederate cause. With the war over and Texas now under congressional administration, the new government installed by Andrew Johnson, in accordance with the statute, brought suit to recover the securities. The defendant argued that Texas was net yet readmitted to the Union from which it had withdrawn, and thus it had no standing to sue in federal court. In one fell swoop, Chase had an opportunity to offer important judicial insights "concerning secession, Reconstruction, and the nature of the federal union" (Hall 1992, 869).

There was, of course, no issue concerning Texas during the Civil War. She had seceded, and "relations of Texas to the Union were broken up." Drawing on his experience as a member of Lincoln's cabinet, Chase also found no difficulty in confronting a related issue: Could a state secede from the Union and yet conform to the federal Constitution? Like Lincoln, who had never wavered on this point, Chase had no doubt as to the answer. It could not. The early Articles of Confederation adopted during the Revolution spoke of a union "which was solemnly declared to be perpetual." Further, this conception was key to the later Constitution's preamble "to form a more perfect Union." It would be difficult "to convey the idea of indissoluble unity more clearly than by these words. What can be indissoluble if a perpetual Union made more perfect, is not?"

But, possibly reflecting on a number of cases his Court had recently considered, Chase emphasized that the states were indispensable to the federalism envisaged by the framers. "Without the States in union," he noted, "there could be no such political body as the United States." Chase went even further: "It may not be unreasonably said that the preservation of the States, and the maintenance of their governments, are as much within the design and care of the Constitution as the preservation of the Union and the maintenance of the National government." Chase, it might be noted, had little of the eloquence of his predecessor, John Marshall; nor did he have the sparkle of a Daniel Webster. But in *Texas v. White*, he managed to come up with one famous sentence that still resonates in contemporary constitutional law and history: "The Constitution, in all its provisions, looks to an indestructible Union, composed of indestructible States."

Therefore, Texas could not and did not ever leave the Union. Her ordinance of secession was "absolutely null." No matter what she said and did, "Texas continued to be a State, and a State of the Union: and her obligations as a member of the Union," and those "of every citizen of the State as a citizen of the United States, remained perfect and unimpaired." Yet, again like Lincoln, Chase had to accept the fact that four years of war and more than a half-million casualties were a matter of fact, not theory. Even though secession was impossible, all must "admit that during this condition of civil war, the rights of the State as a member, and of her people as citizens of the Union, were suspended." Texas and its citizens, "refusing to recognize their constitutional obligations, assumed the character of enemies, and incurred the consequences of rebellion."

One such consequence was the necessity for the United States to provide for the restoration of a republican form of government, as guaranteed to each state under the Constitution. Here Chase may well have had other issues in mind, namely the rights of the newly liberated freedmen. A republican form of government should, in theory at least, include these new Americans. The way in which this would occur was, he held, primarily one of "legislative power." Here, Chase indicated that Reconstruction retained a political and not a judicial character. And while the chief justice intentionally avoided any reference either to the constitutionality or to the illegality of military Reconstruction, Republicans assumed, correctly, that Chase's Court considered this program "within the scope of congressional power" (Hall 1992, 869). Finally, as Texas had never left the Union, its current leadership did indeed have access to the federal courts.

Justice Grier spoke for several members of the Court in dissent. He pointed to the ineluctable fact that whatever Chase might say, Texas was *not*—at the time of this litigation—represented in the Union. No Texas senators, he insisted correctly, were to be found in that chamber; nor were any members of the current House of Representatives from Texas. The state was under military occupation, not subject to the civil authority. "I am not," he concluded, "disposed to join in any essay to prove Texas to be a State of the Union, when Congress has decided that she is not. It is a question of fact, I repeat, and of fact only. *Politically,* Texas is not *a State in this Union.*" But such had been Chase's majority opinion.

Federalism—State and Federal: Crandall v. Nevada *(1868)*

Of course, not all major decisions of the Chase Court directly dealt with the war and its aftermath. The 1868 decision in the case of *Crandall v. Nevada* is of interest because it reflects judicial awareness of federalism in a different context. The case arose from an act passed by the newly admitted state of Nevada on March 8, 1865. In serious need of cash, the state authorities determined to levy a tax on every passenger leaving Nevada via railroad or stagecoach. The assessment was not much, apparently one dollar per person, yet state legislators projected a revenue of $10,000 from this new tax. Crandall, who apparently worked for a stagecoach company, declined to reveal how many passengers had left the state. Arrested by the local sheriff, Crandall later found himself before a justice of the peace, where he was sentenced to a jail term of one day. At this point he sought out a writ of habeas corpus, but ultimately the

Nevada Supreme Court sustained the statute. The stagecoach company apparently lost interest in the case, possibly because it was well aware of the imminent completion of the transcontinental railroad, but not Nevada.

It prepared to defend the statute before Chase's Court, even though as Charles Fairman noted, this case had a "dubious title" to be taken as a legitimate case or controversy (Fairman 1971, 1305). Nonetheless, it ultimately reached the Court for final argument in 1868. One wonders why the justices wished to decide this case even though one side was not represented. There were numerous precedents available, which indicated that Nevada's statute was of doubtful legality. Perhaps, in the context of 1868, the case should be seen as a possible opportunity for the justices to assert anew their primacy in the area of constitutional interpretation and adjudication—in a case devoid of the passion raised by some of the decisions noted above. In holding the Nevada statute unconstitutional, Justice Miller might have used the Commerce Clause as a basis for the decision. Instead he used an expansive reading of federal power based largely upon Chief Justice John Marshall's highly regarded *McCulloch v. Maryland* decision of 1819.

In the course of his opinion, Miller presented an eloquent description of Washington, D.C. "Here sits its legislature, composed of senators and representatives, from the States and from the people of the States. Here resides the President, directing through thousands of agents, the execution of the laws over all this vast country. Here is the seat of the supreme judicial power of the nation, to which all its citizens have a right to resort to claim justice at its hands." The federal government "has a right to call to this point any or all of its citizens to aid in its service," be they members of Congress, workers in the executive branch, or in federal courts. This right "cannot be made to depend upon the pleasure of a State over whose territory they must pass to reach the point where these services must be rendered . . . and no power can exist in a State to obstruct this right that would not enable it to defeat the purposes for which the government was established."

Here, Miller quoted extensively from Marshall and the *McCulloch* decision. By a unanimous vote, his Court had denied the authority of Maryland to tax a federal entity. The chief justice had not hesitated to employ the well-established legal technique (still used today, to say nothing of Chase's era) of the slippery slope analogy. "If the States may tax one instrument . . . they may tax any and every other instrument. They may tax the mail; they may tax the mint; they may tax patent rights; they may tax the papers of the custom house; they may tax the judicial process; they may tax all the means employed by the government to an excess which would defeat all the ends of government. This was not intended by the American people." As had Marshall, so Miller also denied that the amount or extent of the tax made any difference.

Rather it was the right to levy any tax of such a character. So, "in the case before us it may be said that a tax of one dollar for passing through the State of Nevada, by stage coach or by railroad, cannot sensibly affect any function of the government, or deprive a citizen of any fundamental right. But if the State can tax a railroad passenger one dollar, it can tax him one thousand dollars. If one State can do this, so can every other State. And thus . . . [they] may totally prevent or seriously burden all transportation of passengers from one part of the country to the other." Without specifically mentioning the point, Miller seemed to bring the right of travel under constitutional protection—an issue to which he would return in the famous *Slaughterhouse Cases*, five years in the future. Although the High Court unanimously rejected the Nevada statute, Chief Justice Chase joined Justice Clifford in rejecting Miller's rationale, arguing that congressional power to regulate interstate commerce clearly banned state action such as that at issue here.

But this decision did not mean that the states lacked all potency when it came to economic regulation—even in the context of an emerging national market. One year later, another unanimous decision made this point very clear.

In the wake of the Civil War a number of corporations began to market their products or services on a national level. This was especially true in the case of insurance companies. Invariably such practices of expansion brought these enterprises into competition if not conflict with local businesses. Responding to local pressures, numerous states began to impose taxes or license fees on "non resident or foreign" corporations that, for the most part, had been chartered in other states. The case of *Paul v. Virginia* arose when an agent representing a number of out-of-state companies refused to pay a fee for a license as mandated by the state of Virginia. His lawyers argued that such a license was an inappropriate burden on interstate commerce (Hall 1992, 625).

Even though the Court had unanimously barred an exit tax levied by Nevada, but on different constitutional grounds, in this case Justice Field had no difficulty sustaining Virginia's action. Lawyers for the out-of-state corporations argued that their policies and sales were in fact transactions in interstate commerce and thus not subject to state regulation. But in 1869, neither Field nor the Court was prepared to admit that corporations were in fact citizens and thereby entitled to constitutional protection from state action. Although they moved much further in this direction during the next twenty years or so, the justices have consistently held that in spite of its interstate nature, insurance regulation levied by the state remains constitutional (*Paul v. Virginia* 1869).

Veazie Bank v. Fenno *(1869)*

The Chase Court never seemed to lose sight of the fact that in delineating a balance between state and federal spheres of authority, each had its legitimate needs. Barely one month after the *Paul* case, Chase spoke for the Court in another federal-state dispute involving taxation. This one arose in the wake of the critical need for revenue as the Union fought a four-year civil war.

It will be recalled that as secretary of the treasury, Chase had much to do with the fiscal success achieved by the North. In 1866, Congress increased an already existing tax of 1 percent on state bank notes to 10 percent—a large increase. Officers of the Veazie bank in Maine refused to pay, setting up an interesting collision between state and federal fiscal authority. Counsel for the bank insisted that Congress could not use its taxing power to destroy a legitimate corporation, in part because the statute represented a "direct tax" and thus was forbidden under well-established Court holdings. Moreover, the federal measure represented an unfair and inappropriate tax on a state agency.

The former secretary of the treasury rejected all these arguments. Chase further added that while the tax might indeed be excessive, such a fact did not make it unconstitutional. Possibly concerned with lingering congressional fears respecting his Court's course, Chase added that in this case, the Court could not provide relief. This could only be gained through the political process, not a judicial edict. Indeed, the tax might be considered less a tax than a regulatory measure to control national currency, surely a legitimate responsibility of the federal government. "Without this power," Chase concluded, "indeed, its attempts to secure a sound and uniform currency for the country must be futile."

Collector v. Day *(1871)*

In 1871, as it entered its final phase under Chase's leadership, the High Court reflected once again its respect for state authority. A unanimous decision, handed down in 1842, had banned a state from imposing a tax on the income of a federal official. This holding had built upon the precedent set forth by John Marshall in *McCulloch v. Maryland*. Now, in what it considered the logical obverse to this edict, in *Collector v. Day* the justices banned the federal government from taxing the income of a state official. Holding both federal and state authorities as independent of each other—except when expressly indicated otherwise in the Constitution—Justice Nelson affirmed the legitimacy of state sovereignty. But the decision was not unanimous. Justice Bradley insisted that "no man ceases to be a citizen of the United States by being an officer under the State government." Where, he asked, "are we to stop in enumerating the functions of the State governments which will be interfered with by Federal taxation? [I] cannot but regard it as founded on a fallacy, and that it will lead to mischievous consequences." As will be seen in the concluding chapter, a later Court shared Bradley's concern.

Miller and Chase had been together in the *Test Oath Cases*, as well as in the dissent from the broad holding in *Milligan*. Moreover, with the exception of *Texas v. White*, the two justices had been on the same side in all the Reconstruction cases discussed above. And they both reflected a lack of interest in federal action to insure the black franchise beyond support for the Fifteenth Amendment, a position that—Miller had predicted correctly—would also be embraced by major elements in the Republican Party as congressional Reconstruction waned. But in the remaining four cases to be discussed below, Miller and Chase were on opposite sides. Indeed, in the *Legal Tender Cases*, they apparently were more than just opponents, as will be seen.

Chase was no stranger to the controversy involving paper money. As Lincoln's secretary of the treasury, he was the principal architect of the financial war waged by the North. Under his watch, the national bank system was revived, having been essentially dormant since the Jacksonians' war against the Bank of the United States. Further, at his request, Congress levied an income tax and authorized the sale of more than $1.5 billion in bonds, hawked largely by Jay Cooke. Chase also oversaw adoption of a heavy tax structure, which was ultimately felt on virtually all economic and recreational activities throughout Northern society. By the end of the war, these various taxes had raised more than a half-billion dollars in revenue. But in early 1862, Chase realized he could not wait for tax dollars to kick in.

Reluctantly, he turned to paper money. Like many Republicans, he had long supported hard money, based on gold and silver. But also, like many Republicans, in 1862 Chase saw little alternative, and his candor explained his unwilling but ultimately consistent support for paper money as legal tender. "Immediate action," he noted, "is of great importance. The treasury is nearly empty."

Chase's former senatorial colleague and successor as secretary of the treasury, William Pitt Fessenden, was equally blunt. "It shocks all my notions of political, moral, and national honor," he noted. There could be no doubt that "the thing is wrong in itself, but to leave the government without resources at such a crisis is not to be thought of" (McPherson 2001, 223–224). Emphasis on the immediate necessity of such a step obviated the need to agonize over the question of whether or not it was wise or otherwise desirable. But was such a step constitutional, and would the new "greenbacks" be valid as payment for debts incurred before they were produced? Realizing or perhaps rationalizing that these questions might be addressed after the war had been won, Chase saw the greenbacks succeed as legal tender that was accepted by the North, and without the terrible inflation experienced by the Confederacy.

During the war years, at least, his doubts were well concealed. In 1863, speaking to an Ohio political rally with an uncharacteristic sense of humor, Chase related what had transpired in terms of financing the war. "I went to work and made 'greenbacks,' and a good many of them at that . . . and as I like to get pretty near to the people, and as the engravers thought me rather good looking, I told them they might put me on the end of the one dollar bills." Chase concluded that his system of finance—a national banking system, bonds that would pay interest in hard specie, and greenbacks—represented "a very simple thing. It is common sense and courage—that is all" (Fairman 1971, 689–690). Yet Chase still believed that while necessity might give legal tender temporary validity, it was only temporary, and he welcomed the opportunity to eviscerate as chief justice what he had worked to enact as secretary of the treasury.

Starting in 1863, a number of state courts litigated the legality of the new currency. Between 1862 and 1869, at least fifteen state tribunals confronted this issue and, with only one exception, sustained its legality. The one exception became the most famous of the *Legal Tender Cases* decided in 1870, *Hepburn v. Griswold.* It represented, as Justice Nelson put it, "one of the most important measures growing out of the war, and difficult to deal with since." Beyond the problem of constitutionality was the murky judicial context in which the case was decided.

Legal Tender Cases: Hepburn v. Griswold *(1870)*

In an effort to blunt Johnson's potential for gaining a High Court sympathetic to his philosophy, during the summer of 1866 Congress had barred him from naming any new justices. This was accomplished through a statute that forbade new appointments until the "number of associates shall be reduced to six," not including the chief justice. At this point there were nine justices sitting on the ten-member Court, due to the death of Justice Catron in May 1865. When Justice Wayne died of yellow fever in July 1867, the Court remained at eight until Congress again intervened after Johnson had left the White House. In a statute that took effect in December 1869, Congress restored the number to nine where, in spite of President Franklin Roosevelt's ill-fated efforts to increase the number to fifteen in 1937, it has remained ever since. Thus Grant had one vacancy to fill, and it was still open when Justice Grier resigned, effective January 31, 1870. In declining health, both physical and mental, Grier's brethren had unanimously requested him to retire, especially as the new statute also provided salary for life to any justice who had served for ten years and had reached the age of seventy. Grier fit both criteria.

He had participated, however, in the arguments on *Hepburn,* and apparently when the first vote was taken on November 27, 1869, the Court was split 4–4. Confused about what he had decided, Grier changed his mind and joined those in favor of declaring legal tender unconstitutional, a 5–3 majority. Chase and Field were among this group, while the other three Lincoln appointments—Swayne, Miller, and Davis—consistently supported the paper currency. Impatient to get the case disposed of, Chase hoped to announce the majority decision on January 31, with Grier still on the bench until the end of the day. But the dissenting justices insisted on the opportunity to prepare a written explanation of their position.

Thus these important opinions came down on February 7, the same day that Grant made his two nominations to bring the Court to full membership. With the Court soon to contain nine justices, Chase's impatience had led him to articulate a major constitutional holding supported only by four of them. Charles Fairman concluded that delay in deciding would have been preferable "to declaring an Act of Congress invalid by the vote of a confused mind" (Fairman 1971, 719). He found the conduct of the chief justice even more egregious because Chase was well aware of the Court practice that "only by a majority of the full Court ought a constitutional question be decided." As will be seen however, Chase's victory was fleeting.

In a famous New Deal–era Supreme Court decision, Justice Roberts held that the only function of the Court was to compare the statute under attack with the Constitution's text (see *United States v. Butler* [1936]). Had he examined Chase's opinion for the Court in *Hepburn v. Griswold*, he would have read: "it is the plain duty of the court to compare the act with the Constitution, and if the former cannot, upon a fair construction, be reconciled with the latter, to give effect to the Constitution rather than the statute. This seems so plain that it is impossible to make it plainer by argument." Chase went on to insist that the disputed authority to "make notes legal tender" was not the same as the admitted "power to issue notes to be used as currency." Further, he saw the real issue as the government's power to declare greenbacks to be "legal tender in payment of preexisting debts." In other words, could a debt contracted *before* greenbacks were created be paid off by them as legal tender? Chase said no.

Of course Chase was well aware of his prior policies as secretary of the treasury. And probably with himself in mind, he wrote that in 1862, the year of crisis, "different views, never before entertained by U.S. statesmen or jurists were adopted by many. The time was not favorable to considerate reflection upon the constitutional limitations of legislative or executive authority." Again, "if power was assumed from patriotic motives, the assumption found ready justification in patriotic hearts." But that was then. Now, many who "insisted upon its necessity . . . have, since the return of peace and under the influence of the calmer time, reconsidered their conclusions, and now concur in those which we have just announced."

Miller responded in dissent. Within the Constitution, he noted, there were a number of subjects in which actions by the states were forbidden, including the provision that "no State shall coin money, emit bills of credit, or make anything but gold and silver coin a tender in payment of debts." But he emphasized that no such limitation applied to the federal government. In carrying out its constitutional mandates, Congress was empowered to coin money, issue bills of credit, and to regulate the value thereof. Although a state was barred from impairing the obligation of contracts, such a ban could not apply to Congress.

How else, for example, could it adopt uniform bankruptcy rules, which could only impair obligations of existing contracts? On no less than three occasions, Congress had done so, and each time "it operated on contracts made before it was passed." Never had there been any question raised as to the constitutionality of such measures. He reminded Chase's majority of John Marshall's words that "Congress must possess the choice of means, and must be empowered to use any means which are in fact conducive to the exercise of the power granted by the Constitution."

As Chase had done, Miller also recalled conditions in1862. It was a time when "a general collapse of credit, of payment, and of business seemed inevitable, in which faith in the ability of the government would have been destroyed, the rebellion would have triumphed . . . and the people [would have been] impoverished. The National government would have perished, and with it, the Constitution which we are now called upon to construe with such nice and critical accuracy." And what of the Congress, the president, and the fifteen state courts? All of them had endorsed the constitutionality of the legal tender enactments. Are we now, asked Miller, "to reverse their action, to disturb contracts, to declare the law void because the necessity for its enactment does not appear as strong to us as it did to Congress, or so clear as it was to other courts? Such is not my idea of the relative functions of the legislative and judicial departments. Where there is a choice of means, the selection is with Congress, not the court."

Even as the Chase Court demonstrated its deep division on this issue, Grant moved to return the bench to its accustomed size. Indeed, he had already nominated two distinguished lawyers to the two seats in December 1869. One was his attorney general, E. Rockwood Hoar, the other was Edwin Stanton, the former secretary of war and, next to Lincoln himself, the civilian most responsible for its successful outcome. But Hoar fell victim to partisan bickering in the Senate, caused in large measure by the firmness with which he declined to participate in Republican politics of the day; Stanton, confirmed on the same day he was nominated, died suddenly four days later, a victim of exhaustion and stress. Again Grant had two vacancies to fill, and he announced them on the same day as Chase announced the decision of the Court in *Hepburn v. Griswold.* By March 21, his two nominees, William Strong and Joseph Bradley, were confirmed, and Rockwood Hoar, still attorney general, wasted no time in reviving the issue.

Four days later, Hoar sought reversal of the legal tender decision, which caused some additional rancor within the Court. Although Chase did all he could to prevent re-argument, Miller wrote a very candid account of how *Hepburn v. Griswold* had been decided. It mentioned that "an aged and infirm member of the Court had changed his vote, and had subsequently been advised to resign." But Miller went even further in his statement, which was signed by the three original dissenters plus Strong and Bradley (and thus a majority of the Court): "Of Grier, we do not say he did not agree to the opinion. We only ask, of what value was his concurrence, and of what value is the judgment, under such circumstances?" (Fairman 1971, 739). Miller deleted this section from the "revised draft" but preserved it in his papers.

On March 31, 1870, the Court agreed to hear Hoar's motion. Referring to Grier, Hoar mentioned that the "deciding judge" had switched his vote. Thus, "it would come down to the point that on the differing opinions at different times of his life, of a single man, the whole constitutional power of Congress . . . was to be subverted and set aside" (Fairman 1971, 741). The matter was continued until April 11, when Hoar apparently reiterated his request for an early hearing and decision, "because the country is disturbed and will continue to be disturbed until the whole question at issue is settled." According to a newspaper account of the session, Chase interrupted "with evident feeling," and Miller replied "with equal feeling," while Nelson came to the rescue of Chase, and Davis "spoke up, saying he concurred" with Miller. It was "a very lively scene . . ., the oldest lawyers practicing there having witnessed nothing like it" (Fairman 1971, 742). Finally, on April 30, the Chase Court announced that another legal tender case would be set down for re-argument during the new term, beginning in October 1870.

Miller described part of this episode in a letter to his brother-in-law dated April 21, 1870. "We have had a desperate struggle in the secret conference of the Court for three weeks over two cases involving the legal tender question. The chief justice has resorted to all the stratagems of the lowest political trickery to prevent their being heard, and the fight has been bitter in the conference room. . . . The excitement has nearly used me up. It has been fearful; and my own position as a leader in marshalling my forces, and keeping up their courage, against a domineering Chief, and a part in Court who have been accustomed to carry everything their own way, has been such a strain on my brain and nervous system as I never wish to encounter again" (Fairman 1971, 744–745). But more delay lay ahead for those justices who, like Miller, awaited an opportunity to reconsider *Hepburn.* Although the Court had announced in April that the new case would be argued in the fall of 1870, it would be almost a year before the case was actually reached.

Chief Justice Chase suffered the first of an ultimately fatal series of strokes in late summer of 1870. He did not return to the bench until April 17, 1871, the day before the *Legal Tender Cases* were called. But when he rejoined his brethren, it was as "an old man." In November 1870, Miller wrote that whether Chase "will be able to serve efficiently may remain doubtful." Besides the stroke, Chase faced continuing burdens as chief justice: He was not highly regarded as a lawyer, he was without prior judicial experience, he was unable to inspire affection and deep respect from his peers, and all of his extremely able and ambitious colleagues felt that they were better qualified than he to serve as chief justice. One can understand why Miller believed that Chase could probably be little more than a "figurehead to the Court" (Fairman 1971, 752–753). In addition to Chase, Field was ill for a number of weeks, as was Nelson, who also was absent from Court to assist in a diplomatic mission at the request of President Grant. Finally on April 18–19, a full bench heard re-argument on the legal tender issue.

Knox v. Lee *and* Parker v. Davis *(1871)*

In some respects, re-argument seemed a bit anticlimactic. The three dissenting justices in *Hepburn* were now joined by Strong and Bradley, whose support for legal tender was common knowledge. Further, few if any new arguments were raised. Thus the lawyer seeking that *Hepburn* be affirmed anew essentially repeated what Chase had noted in his majority opinion. But Clarkson Potter emphasized the danger to the Court's reputation if it changed its mind. "Should you affirm [*Hepburn*], you would indeed settle [the question;] but should you overrule that decision without change in the opinions of the justices who have heretofore passed upon the question, how then will you have settled it? What can then result but to leave this question open for the future, and destroy the consistency and influence of the Court?"

Potter was offended by the imminent possibility that the Court would reverse itself only because two new justices had been appointed. To "so gratuitously and needlessly review an abstract constitutional question so solemnly decided; to review it, not because of changes or doubts on the part of those who shared in the decision, but through a change in the composition of the Court, is to divert the regard of the people from the Court itself to the personnel of those who compose it; and . . . in effect to abdicate the highest function with which your honors are entrusted." Why, he wondered, had the Court even agreed to rehear the case, when none of the majority had changed their minds?

Attorney General Amos Ackerman, Hoar's new replacement (and like his predecessor, soon to lose his job due to Republican political machinations), focused on the old means-and-ends argument. He had no doubt of the legitimate ends served by the issuance of the new currency: "Insurrection could not be suppressed, armies could not be raised and supported, and a navy could not be provided and maintained," without a currency. It was not up to the Court to reject the means once it had endorsed the ends. "This court may consider the question of congressional power, but not the question of congressional wisdom. If Congress may issue a currency [and none denied that it could] as an appropriate means to lawful ends, it may, in its discretion, give to that currency few, many, or all the faculties of money."

Chief Justice Chase had argued in *Hepburn* that this type of reasoning "goes very far." Ackerman agreed. "It leads," he wrote "to the conclusion that that Congress has a great deal of power. A government without power is contemptible." Moreover, a statute that worked well, as legal tender did, cannot now be termed unconstitutional. The question of constitutionality "ought to be decided now as it would have been decided in 1862. The Constitution is not variable. Where Congress had the choice of means, the validity of its actions cannot be affected by the correctness or incorrectness of its judgment in choosing."

Ackerman could not resist concluding with a reference to the famous rhetoric of Daniel Webster, who had long insisted that Congress had no power to make paper a legal tender and had been freely cited by Ackerman's opponents. That eminent but fallible man "is clearly wrong," Ackerman wrote. Those who enacted the 1862 statute "had an experience in public necessities which was wanting to him."

A similar sense of the anticlimactic also hung over the Court as the decisions finally were read on January 15, 1872, all the more as they had been announced in May of the previous year. Speaking for the new five-member majority, Justice Strong needed only half of his first paragraph to indicate that *Hepburn* would be overruled. "It would be difficult," he noted, "to overestimate the consequences which must follow our decision." Indeed, "they will affect the entire business of the country, and take hold of the possible continued existence of the government." Strong meant, of course, a decision that reaffirmed the unconstitutionality of legal tender—something he knew was not about to happen.

> If it be held . . . that Congress has no constitutional power, under any circumstances, or in any emergency, to make treasury notes a legal tender for the payment of all debts (a power confessedly possessed by every independent sovereignty . . .), "the government is without those means of self preservation which, all admit, may . . . become indispensable, even if they were not when the acts of Congress . . . were enacted." Moreover, if the Court was to so hold, "our decision must cause throughout the country, great business derangement, widespread distress and the rankest injustice." Like it or not, "legal tender treasury notes have become the universal measure of values." To disregard them now means that "ruinous sacrifices, general distress, and bankruptcy may be expected. These consequences are too obvious to admit of question." (1871)

Of the five-member bloc in this case, it is interesting that only the two new members, Strong and Bradley—the justices most responsible for the new alignment—handed down written opinions for the majority. In his concurrence, Bradley spelled out what Strong had merely implied: "When the [*Hepburn*] decision is recent, and is only by a bare majority of the court, and during a time of public excitement on the subject . . . I consider it our right and duty to subject it to a further examination, if a majority of the court are dissatisfied with the former decision." Such had happened in this case. "With all deference and respect for the former judgment of the court, I am so fully convinced that it was erroneous, and prejudicial to the rights, interests, and safety of the general government, that I, for one, have no hesitation in reviewing and overruling it."

By the time the Court finally released these opinions, in January 1872, Chief Justice Chase had returned to the bench but in an inexorably accelerating state of declining health. Indeed, he would be dead in barely a year. At the same time, however, his tribunal had begun an era of marked judicial vigor. Even as the *Legal Tender Cases* were resolved, attention focused on two of the three new Reconstruction amendments, especially the Fourteenth.

Adopted by Congress in 1866 and ratified in 1868, the Fourteenth Amendment had been strongly opposed by then–President Andrew Johnson. A sort of omnibus amendment with multiple objectives, for our present purposes we need focus only on its first section. Seeking to insure that the definition of citizenship put forth by the Civil Rights Act of 1866 would be protected from executive or even congressional interference, the framers adopted a dual definition of citizenship for the first time: "All persons born or naturalized in the United States . . . are citizens of the United States and of the State wherein they reside." The section went on to forbid the states from making any law that would abridge the privileges and immunities of United States citizens, depriving any person of life, liberty, or property without due process of law, and denying to any person within its jurisdiction the equal protection of the laws.

As the Court finally disposed of the legal tender issue, the equally significant questions both of congressional intent and ultimate meaning of these citizenship provisions now claimed the attention of the justices. A source of bitter contention from the beginning, the amendment's ultimate ratification became an integral part of congressional Reconstruction between 1866 and 1868. But it was not until 1872 that the Court had heard major argument on these questions. The vehicle in which they arrived was a statute adopted by Louisiana in 1869, approved by a white governor, and litigated by a white former U.S. Supreme Court justice on behalf of clients who were also white—all ironic developments in a case replete with irony. Yet it furnished the Court with its first opportunity to interpret the Fourteenth Amendment.

State Police Power and the Fourteenth Amendment: Slaughterhouse Cases *(1873)*

The *Slaughterhouse Cases* began with a series of lawsuits filed in New Orleans in 1869, following enactment of a law by a racially mixed Louisiana legislature—itself a new product of Reconstruction—elected largely by the votes of newly enfranchised blacks. The statute concerned the location of a central slaughterhouse, but it should be seen not so much as a product of Reconstruction as the fulfillment of a sustained and determined effort by public health advocates in New Orleans to reform sanitary conditions. In 1860, one writer had noted "the utter destitution of the city in every essential of sanitary regulation necessary to health or even to decency and public self respect." Another observer, a doctor, wrote that between 1796 and 1869, sanitary conditions in New Orleans represented "one long, disgusting story of stagnant drainage, foul sewerage, environing swamps, ill and unpaved streets, no sanitary regulations, and filth, endless filth every where" (Labbe and Lurie 2003, 35). Efforts to confine slaughterhouses to one part of the city had been ongoing for more than half a century. Indeed, a statute very similar to the one enacted in 1869 had been adopted just before the outbreak of the Civil War but never went into effect.

In 1869, during the relatively brief era of Republican Reconstruction in Louisiana, the legislature adopted a slaughterhouse statute. The new law was immediately assailed, in part because it was the product of a racially mixed legislature, convened or imposed, depending on point of view, by an outside occupying force. Further, by 1869 the butchers of New Orleans had become a well-organized group, whose political influence had been a factor in preventing sanitary reform during the past half-century (Labbe and Lurie 2003). They immediately attacked the measure.

The statute awarded a group of seventeen individuals the exclusive right to build a "grand slaughterhouse," which would have to be large enough to accommodate all the butchers in the city. After a certain date, slaughtering could *only* be done at this new facility, and its proprietors could charge only the fees listed in the statute. The white butchers were quick to denounce these provisions as a blatant contribution to a corrupt monopoly, sanctioned by a corrupt legislature, with support from an equally corrupt administration. Absent from this type of rhetoric was mention of two additional provisions found in the law. One mandated that *any* butcher could either use the facility to butcher his own beef *or* pay to have it done for him. He was then free to sell it wherever and whenever he wished, but the actual slaughtering could only be carried out in the facilities of the Crescent City Live Stock Landing and Slaughterhouse Company. Further, if the company refused to accept healthy beef from a butcher or denied him use of the facility, it was subject to heavy penalties also specified in the statute. For more than three years, the company and the butchers slugged it out in a spate of suits, first within Louisiana, and ultimately before the High Court, where the case was argued in 1872 and re-argued in 1873.

Representing the butchers was a man who, if it had not been for the vicissitudes of war, might very well have heard the case as a member of the Supreme Court. Born in Georgia in 1811, John Campbell graduated "with first honors" from Franklin College (better known today as the University of Georgia) at the age of fourteen. He went to West Point but had to withdraw before he could graduate, due to the sudden death of his father. At the ripe old age of eighteen, he was admitted to the bar and began to practice law, first in Georgia and later in Alabama, where his career flourished. By the time he turned forty, Campbell was arguing cases before the Alabama Supreme Court and turned down two nominations to that court. In 1853, responding to the unanimous request from the Supreme Court justices that he appoint Campbell to the bench, a quiescent President Franklin Pierce readily acquiesced. Campbell served on the High Court until he resigned to follow his seceded state in 1861. As an assistant secretary of war in the Confederate cabinet, he negotiated with Lincoln, awaited the arrival of Union troops in Richmond as that city surrendered, and was thrown into a federal prison for four months after Lincoln's death. Pardoned by Andrew Johnson, Campbell returned to New Orleans, where he had moved in 1861. There he sought with great success to rebuild his law practice. Among his clients in 1869 was the group of white butchers.

By 1869, the state police power was a long established and freely endorsed state legislative prerogative (Novak 1996). In spite of this fact, in an effort not only to get relief for his butchers but more importantly to undercut Reconstruction itself, Campbell relied both on the Civil Rights Act of 1866 and the Fourteenth Amendment. Defeated in the Supreme Court of Louisiana, he turned to the federal courts, citing federal law—an irony not lost on contemporary observers. "Few observers," noted the *Daily Picayune*, "would have dreamed . . . it necessary to appeal to the Civil Rights Bill to protect the rights of the people in this or any other Southern city from invasion." But the only hope apparently lay in the federal courts, and there employing "poison as an antidote for poison" (Labbe and Lurie 2003, 143).

Argued first in 1872 before the Chase Court, the justices found themselves split 4–4. When Ward Hunt took his seat as the newly appointed ninth justice in 1873, the *Slaughterhouse Cases* were re-argued before the full tribunal. By now Campbell had rehearsed his points thoroughly. Again, they reflected a significant duality of purpose. Of course he wanted to gain a victory for his clients. But even more important for this "bitter, hate-filled man" was his desire to strike at the overall process of Reconstruction, one he regarded as a vindictive course of action that had enabled a supposedly corrupt governor and legislature in Louisiana to enact the bill in the first place (Ross 2003, 241).

Campbell based his appeal on both the Thirteenth and Fourteenth Amendments, even though it was surely a stretch to apply the amendment that ended slavery to a group of white butchers! He insisted, however, that being forced to butcher only in a certain place and under certain conditions represented a form of involuntary servitude that was forbidden under the new enactment. Too able an attorney not to realize that this argument was less than convincing, he placed much greater emphasis on the Fourteenth Amendment. Ignoring the reasons that had led to its adoption, he focused on what the implications of the new enactment were for the now permanently altered federal Union.

The former slave owner and states rights enthusiast noted that the new Reconstruction amendments "go very far to determine that the Constitution creates a national government and is not a federal compact." Now, "the sovereignty of the State government is reduced—and wisely reduced by the Constitution—to a very limited extent." Railing against the evils of universal suffrage—although it had nothing to do with his case—Campbell noted that "whatever ambition, avarice, usurpation, servility, licentiousness, or pusillanimity needs a shelter will find it under its protecting influence." Besides the abuses resulting from universal suffrage, in the wake of the war "there had been an effusion over the whole land of an alert, active, aspiring, overreaching, unscrupulous class, the foulest off spring of the war," including, he probably believed, those who had engineered the slaughterhouse statute. Such individuals with their vicious monopolies "sought money, place and influence in the worst manner and for purposes entirely mischievous."

The key to preventing the evil results of all this was, of course, the Fourteenth Amendment, to be interpreted by a vigilant federal judiciary. Gathered within its protective shield, intoned Campbell, can be found "the hope of the laboring man; the confidence and trust of the merchant; the stability, success and profit of the agriculturist; the leisure and inspiration of the student; and the peace, the comfort, the enjoyment of the family and home." This enactment "is not confined to any race or class. It comprehends all within the scope of its provisions. . . . The mandate is universal in its application to persons of every class and every condition of persons." For this former prison inmate, "the signs of the time show that the protection has not been extended too soon" (Labbe and Lurie 2003, 188, 192–193).

Counsel for Louisiana emphasized what Campbell had ignored: the main purposes of both the Civil Rights Act and the Fourteenth Amendment. They resulted only from the war and its aftermath. Without this awesome conflict, they never would have been deemed necessary. Further, their intent was to protect the ex-slave, to insure that he enjoyed the fundamental rights of citizenship long held by whites—and nothing more. Finally, they pointed out that accepting Campbell's position would result in the Court having to oversee all types of state legislation, to become, in effect, a censor over state initiatives. Such a transformation of federalism, they concluded, had not been the intent of Congress when it adopted these new measures.

Chase's Court split 5–4 over the issues raised in the *Slaughterhouse Cases*. Speaking for the majority, Justice Miller—a former physician familiar with epidemics—rejected Campbell's arguments. He pointed to the fact that under the Louisiana statute, no one was denied the right to follow the occupation of a butcher. Only the location of slaughtering was restricted, an action clearly within the traditional perimeters of the police power. Troubled, however, by the great emphasis Campbell had placed on the Reconstruction amendments, Miller conceded that under certain conditions they might indeed apply to other than the newly liberated slaves. But he also recalled events of the last ten years "which are familiar to us all" and insisted of the new enactments that "no one can fail to be impressed with the one pervading purpose found in them all . . . and without which none of them would have been suggested; we mean the freedom of the slave race, the security and firm establishment of that freedom, and the protection of the newly made freeman from the oppressions" of his former masters. As lawyers for those defending the statute had argued, to discern the meaning of the amendments, one had to look beyond its words to the events that had inspired them. So Miller felt it necessary "to look to the purpose which we have said was the pervading spirit of them all, the evil which they were designed to remedy."

Applying a narrow meaning to the Fourteenth Amendment, all the more perhaps because in the case before him the plaintiffs were white butchers bickering over where they could slaughter beef in a crowded municipality—Miller emphasized that newly liberated blacks might indeed look to the federal government for protection from inappropriate state conduct. But privileges and immunities for the rest of the citizenry remained where they had always been, within the hands of the states. Campbell's butchers might indeed have a legitimate beef, but they were in the wrong judicial forum. Finally, Miller pointed to the lack of a clear intent from Congress that the new amendments were to introduce fundamental changes in the federal system. In short, with the possible exception of the ex-slave, the Union is as the Union was. The traditional balance between federal and state remained unchanged (Labbe and Lurie 2003, 214–220).

Too ill to write a dissent, all Chase could do was to concur silently in the opinion filed by Justice Field. As was seen in the *Test Oath Cases*, Field had already indicated his conviction that the Constitution protected basic privileges and immunities rightfully held by U.S. citizens. Now the new amendment specified what Field had earlier inferred: It now protected them from state interference. To argue otherwise, as had Miller, would show that the Fourteenth Amendment "was a vain and idle enactment, which accomplished nothing, and most unnecessarily excited Congress and the people on its passage." In fact, Field concluded, the privileges protected by it "are those which of right belong to the citizens of all free governments." This surely included the right of the butchers "to pursue a lawful employment in a lawful manner" (Labbe and Lurie 2003, 223–227).

Thus by a 5–4 vote margin, the Chase Court declined to find any major changes in federalism intended by Congress. Since *Slaughterhouse* was one of the most significant decisions of the Chase Court, we will briefly return to it again in the next chapter. But one day after this landmark ruling was announced, Miller handed down yet another decision concerning the Fourteenth Amendment's scope. This one involved a white female from Illinois.

Bradwell v. Illinois *(1873)*

Myra Bradwell sought a license to practice law from the Supreme Court of Illinois. The Illinois statute in question provided "that any adult person of good character and having the requisite training, was eligible for admission to the bar" (Hall 1992, 82). Although no one denied that Bradwell fit both criteria, the state court denied her application because of her gender. Upon rejection of her request, she appealed to the High Court. The issue she raised focused on the question of whether a female properly trained and concededly qualified to practice law could claim that a right and privilege to do so was protected by the new enactment. It might have been reasonable to expect, after the vigor with which the dissent in *Slaughterhouse* had just emphasized the equality of rights and privileges to follow one's chosen calling, that the justices would have voiced some support for her position. Quite the opposite occurred.

Anticipating the position taken by Justice Field, Bradwell's attorney argued that the Fourteenth Amendment "opens to every citizen of the United States, male or female, black or white, married or single, the honorable professions as well as the servile employments of life; and that no citizen can be excluded from any of them." There are many cases, added Matthew Carpenter, "in which the silver voice of a woman could accomplish more than the severity and sternness of man might achieve." And indeed, "the broad shield of the Constitution is over them all, and protects each in that measure of success which his or her individual merits may secure" (135–137). It did not bode well for Bradwell's cause that Illinois felt it unnecessary to have counsel defend the position assumed by her high court.

Again Miller spoke for the Court, and again he reflected a narrow view of the Fourteenth Amendment's scope. Just as the privileges and immunities claimed by the white butchers did not warrant federal protection, neither could Bradwell's request find sanction there. Relying on the reasoning he had employed the day before, Miller found that the right to practice law did not depend on federal citizenship. States were forbidden under the amendment to interfere with those privileges and immunities belonging to citizens of the United States, "and it is these and these alone which a State is forbidden to abridge." The right to regulate and control granting of licenses to practice law remained where it always had been, in the hands of the state. Miller at least was consistent. But the same cannot be said for Field, Bradley, and Swayne—all of whom concurred with Miller in this case, yet had denounced his *Slaughterhouse* opinion with vigor. What was the difference between the right to practice law and the right to maintain a butcher shop?

Of the three, only Bradley chose to add a written concurrence, which bristled with Victorian platitudes about the role of women. "Man is, or should be," he noted, "woman's protector and defender." Female natural and proper timidity and delicacy belonging to the female sex "unfits it for many of the occupations of civil life." As a matter of fact, "the paramount destiny and mission of wom[e]n are to fulfill the noble and benign offices of wife and mother. This is the law of the Creator." According to one observer, "Bradley's opinion seemed to cause no little amusement upon the Bench and on the Bar" (Lurie 1986, 365).

Chief Justice Chase, in one of his very last appearances, could only dissent "from the judgment of the Court, and from all the opinions." He alone, apparently, saw the link between the dissents in *Slaughterhouse* and the consistency of Bradwell's position. His illness, however, rendered impossible his writing a dissent. Three weeks later, on May 7, Chase passed away. The legacy of his term as chief justice is discussed in the following chapter, but brief comment about his own career is appropriate here. In noting contemporary assessments about him, one senses a consistent tone of ambiguity.

Chase's tenure as chief justice capped an eventful life that saw a successful law practice and service as governor, senator, and cabinet officer. His ambitions, however, apparently ran ahead of his accomplishments. Commenting on Chase's death, *Harper's Weekly* noted that it is "not so much the chief justice or the eminent politician, the lawyer . . . for whom the country grieves, as for the friend who sustained it in its moment of trial. . . . And in return, if he have faults, the country hides them in a decent veil, and dwells tenderly upon his patriotic services." His old acquaintance and later successor as Ohio governor, as well as a recipient of the presidency that had always eluded Chase, was equally circumspect, but critical.

Rutherford Hayes observed in his diary that Chase "possessed noble gifts of intellect" as well as "great culture and a commanding presence. When this is said, about all that is favorable has been said. He was cold, selfish, and unscrupulous. . . . Political intrigue, love of power, and a selfish and boundless ambition were the striking features of his life and character." E. R. Hoar, who was well acquainted with Chase and had served as Grant's attorney general with such integrity that it cost him his appointment to the High Court, was even more candid. Chase was "insincere, selfish and intriguing, and did more than anyone else to degrade and ruin the office of chief justice" (Fairman 1971, 1474–1476). Justice Miller recalled that Chase's considerable strengths were "warped, perverted and shrivelled by the selfishness generated by ambition." Nevertheless, Miller added, Chase "was a great man and a better man than public life generally leaves one" (White 1996, 38, 45).

As will be seen, the word *ambiguity* may well describe the legacy left by the Court over which Chase presided, in addition to being an apt description of the man himself.

References

Fairman, Charles. 1971. *Reconstruction and Reunion, 1864–1888*. New York: Macmillan.

Hall, Kermit, ed. 1992. *The Oxford Companion to the Supreme Court of the United States.* New York: Oxford University Press.

Labbe, Ronald, and Jonathan Lurie. 2003. *The Slaughterhouse Cases: Regulation, Reconstruction, and the Fourteenth Amendment.* Lawrence: University Press of Kansas.

Lurie, Jonathan. 1986. "Mr. Justice Bradley: A Reassessment." *Seton Hall Law Review* 16:343.

Mauer, John Walker. 2001. "The Test Oath Cases." In John W. Johnson, ed., *Historic U.S. Court Cases.* 2nd ed. New York: Routledge.

McPherson, James. 2001. *Ordeal by Fire: The Civil War.* 3rd ed. New York: McGraw-Hill.

Novak, William J. 1996. *The People's Welfare: Law and Regulation in Nineteenth Century America.* Chapel Hill: University of North Carolina Press.

Ross, Michael A. 2003. *Justice of Shattered Dreams: Samuel Freeman Miller and the Supreme Court during the Civil War Era.* Baton Rouge: Louisiana State University Press.

White, G. Edward. 1996. "Salmon Portland Chase and the Judicial Culture of the Supreme Court in the Civil War Era." In Jennifer M. Lowe, ed., *The Supreme Court and the Civil War.* Washington, DC: Supreme Court Historical Society.

4

Legacy and Impact

As was hinted as the last chapter concluded, ambiguous may be the best adjective to describe the legacy of the Chase Court. In the case of its members—all of whom had been a part of the Civil War era, probably the most cataclysmic event in their experience—the passage of time invariably affected both their perceptions of constitutional law and the roles they played in its later course. Rancor and recrimination receded as reconciliation and reunion came into vogue. But as David Blight has demonstrated so brilliantly, the freed African Americans were omitted from this vast exercise in national harmony. Indeed, the slaves had been liberated, but the blacks were marginalized, ignored, and increasingly isolated as the Gilded Age came to an end along with the nineteenth century. After Chase's death, the Supreme Court contributed in no small measure to this tragedy.

Further, in what may have been his last important case—even though he could not do more than articulate his one-sentence dissent—the dying chief justice saw his brethren refuse to apply the Fourteenth Amendment to women excluded from the practice of law, even though a rationale for such a position had been clearly expressed in the *Slaughterhouse* dissents. But the constitutional protection extended to white male butchers apparently did not extend to a white female seeking to work as an attorney (*Bradwell*), even though none denied that she was qualified. Perhaps Chase sensed, as he indicated his total disagreement with the decision, that his colleagues had rejected his broad view of the Fourteenth Amendment. In retrospect, however, *Bradwell* was just the beginning.

As the previous chapters indicate, the Chase Court dealt with some critical issues in the eight years Chase served as chief justice. Some of the cases caused by tensions between Congress and Andrew Johnson in the course of Reconstruction are of relatively slight interest today. But issues dealing with the Fourteenth Amendment, which the Chase Court interpreted for the first time, serve as important benchmarks against which—for better or for worse—later court decisions can be compared. At least two key areas—state action as related to the Fourteenth Amendment and the ultimate significance of the *Milligan* case for constitutional rights in wartime—invite contemporary comparison with what the Chase Court undertook.

Chief Justice Chase's passing in the spring of 1873 took place as the death throes of Reconstruction itself became apparent. Within one year, the Democrats—long opposed to congressional Reconstruction—would control the House of Representatives. In the middle of Grant's second term, committed radicals such as the late Thaddeus Stevens or Charles Sumner, had been or would be replaced not by politicians of a similar viewpoint, but rather by men who reflected the current conservative weariness with Reconstruction. Although the Fifteenth Amendment had been ratified, and some additional legislation intended to protect African Americans had been enacted by Congress, by 1874 the mood of the country was shifting. In a series of decisions, the Court took notice of this shift—even as it welcomed its new chief justice, Morrison R. Waite, who was described perhaps a bit unfairly as a "respectable mediocrity," a man with "every requisite except repute" (Lurie, 351). A little-known attorney from Ohio, Waite was Grant's fourth choice to fill Chase's seat. Among his earlier choices had been Roscoe Conkling, a well-known politician rather attorney, and one quite comfortable with the dubious political practices common in the Gilded Age. It remains unclear to what extent the Court "follows the election returns," but under Waite's leadership, the Supreme Court demonstrated both an increased tolerance for state regulation and a lack of interest in whatever "rights" African American citizens were supposed to have, with a few exceptions.

State Authority

If the Chase Court had sustained some major pieces of national Reconstruction law, the Waite Court was more circumspect. In Waite's first year as chief justice, the Court unanimously reaffirmed the narrow view they had adopted in the *Slaughterhouse Cases*. In the case of *Minor v. Happersett*, the new chief justice considered the question whether a female denied the right to vote under state law could raise the Fourteenth Amendment as a basis for federal judicial relief. Given the recent holding in *Bradwell*, the answer was simple: of course not. The state of Missouri was so confident concerning the legality of its refusal to allow Minor to vote purely on the basis of her gender that it did not even bother to submit briefs in the case.

Chief Justice Waite held that the granting of citizenship in no way included the right to vote. In the American context, he insisted, citizenship and suffrage had always been two separate attributes of sovereignty. One could clearly be a citizen without possessing the right to vote, as evidenced by Virginia Minor. Thus the Fourteenth Amendment was neither a source of "a substantive federal suffrage right" nor a federal limit on what a state might decide concerning the franchise (Hall 1992, 192). The unanimous opinion was joined by all the *Slaughterhouse* dissenters still on the bench.

Nor did the adoption of the Fifteenth Amendment, which supposedly insured federal protection of the right to vote, fare any better under the Waite Court. In the case of *United States v. Reese* argued early in 1875, Chief Justice Waite gutted key provisions of an enforcement act passed by Congress to support the final Reconstruction Amendment. He claimed that this new enactment conferred no right on any person. Rather, it simply forbade discrimination against voters on racial grounds. What good, it might be asked, was such a stilted interpretation if one did not have the right to vote in the first place? In dissent, Justice Ward Hunt noted that "the intention of Congress is too plain to be discussed." He chided his colleagues for their willingness to misconstrue a statute so that "good sense is sacrificed to technical nicety."

Yet Hunt joined in a subsequent decision that reiterated the nit-picking relied upon in *Reese*. This case arose out of a bloody race riot in Louisiana, one that resulted in the deaths of more than one hundred blacks. Using the Federal Enforcement Act of 1870, also known as the Ku Klux Klan Act, federal prosecutors secured indictments against three whites who had been involved in the violence. They were indicted under a section of this law that "forbade conspiracies to deny the constitutional rights of any citizen."

But Waite could not find any legitimate grounds for federal intervention in this case. Emphasizing the *Slaughterhouse* distinction between state and federal authority, he found numerous procedural violations in the indictments and virtually negated the effectiveness of the act for future federal enforcement. This was true even though the Court ignored the issue of the Enforcement Act's constitutionality (Goldman 2001, 106). By insisting that primary responsibility for such conduct lay in state rather than federal jurisdiction, Waite insured that at least in the Southern states, inaction would result in the freedmen being slighted by the legal and judicial process, a move in which the North quietly acquiesced (*United States v. Cruikshank* 1874).

Another example of the inconsistency that the High Court demonstrated in civil rights cases concerned the question of excluding African Americans from juries. Now that the Fourteenth Amendment supposedly had provided equal protection as well as citizenship for the former slaves, action by Southern states seeking to restrict jury service as they had long known it became an important issue. In 1880, the Court handed down several decisions dealing with this subject. In *Strauder v. West Virginia*, the dispute appeared very clear "because a state statute specifically limited jury service to all white male persons" (Wiecek 1998, 296). The Court held that if the Fourteenth Amendment meant anything, it certainly applied in this instance. Such a statute violated the Equal Protection Clause, a position it reaffirmed in two similar cases. (See *Strauder v. West Virginia* 1880.) It appeared that a transformation in federal protection of civil rights was at hand.

Such was not the case. In yet another decision on the same subject, handed down shortly before *Strauder* (indeed, it follows directly in the printed volume of the decisions), the Court apparently reversed itself. Paul Kens well notes that the promise of this case "was short lived. It began to lose its way on the same day it was decided" (Kens 1997, 185).

In *Virginia v. Rives*, the facts appeared similar to *Strauder*, in that the defendants were black and had been tried before an all-white jury. But there was a crucial difference between the two cases. Virginia, although it had employed an all-white jury, had no statute mandating such a practice. In theory, blacks were technically eligible, even though apparently none "had ever been allowed to serve." Further, the county judge had selected the jury, and his action, rather than a Virginia statute, had been the cause of the alleged discrimination. Defendants, insisted Justice Strong, could appeal to the Virginia appellate courts, and if they still were unsatisfied—in theory, again—they might then move their case into federal court. His decision reflected a widespread view that "enforcement of criminal law was very much a province of the states" (*Virginia v. Rives* 1879). This decision represented yet another example of where the real needs of newly liberated blacks collided with long-held traditions of federalism (Kens 1997, 186–187). Such cases bring to mind Philip Paludan's insightful observation that "the black man might be deprived of equal protection . . . not because he was hated, but because constitutionally established federalism was loved" (Paludan 1975, 13).

A little more than a decade after the first major *Slaughterhouse* decision, the High Court confronted its sequel. Much had happened since 1873. The state of Louisiana had been "redeemed," Reconstruction had ended, and an all-white legislature had repealed the original twenty-five-year monopoly granted to the Crescent City Company. Now it was the company's turn to claim that such legislative conduct was unconstitutional. Again, no blacks appeared to have been involved in the litigation, and again Justice Miller spoke for the Court, but this time on behalf of a unanimous bench. Just as the Louisiana legislature had seen fit in 1869 to grant an exclusive franchise, so too at a later date might it move to repeal the earlier enactment. The legislature could give, but it could also take away (*Butchers' Union Co. v. Crescent City Co.* 1884).

In both instances, the state police power justified such action, which, according to Miller, was all that had been decided in the 1873 decision. In 1873, the butchers had claimed in vain that the Fourteenth Amendment protected their calling. In 1884, the company claimed in vain that the Fourteenth Amendment protected its charter from state revocation during the life of the grant. On the surface it appeared that the Court still followed the narrow track set out in 1873. But in fact, the Court had shifted ground, and Miller had shifted with it.

Only four years after *Slaughterhouse I*, Chief Justice Waite handed down the opinion in the case of *Munn v. Illinois* (1877). Under heavy pressure from their agrarian constituents, the Illinois legislature had enacted a statute limiting the price grain elevator operators might charge for their services. One of the more sleazy operators among this group—indeed he had already been expelled from the Chicago Board of Trade—Ira Munn challenged the new law on the grounds that his right to charge what he wished for his services, free from state interference, was protected by the Fourteenth Amendment. By a 7–2 vote, the Supreme Court sustained a prime example of what would become known as the Granger Laws. It is interesting to note that both Miller and Bradley, who had been on opposite sides in *Slaughterhouse*, strongly supported Waite's majority decision in this case.

Essentially, Waite argued that if one offers to serve the public, he must submit to regulation on behalf of the public he seeks to serve. "When private property is devoted to a public use, it is subject to public regulation" (*Munn v. Illinois* 1877). If a proprietor such as Munn objects to this kind of a statute, "for protection against abuses by legislatures the people must resort to the polls, not the courts." One wonders if Miller had any idea of how far he and the Court had moved in barely four years since *Slaughterhouse*. In *Munn*, Waite made no mention of the limiting characteristics assumed in the Fourteenth Amendment that Miller had deemed so important, such as its history and his contention that it was primarily intended to apply essentially to the ex-slave. At no point did Waite even hint that it was improper for Munn to emphasize the Fourteenth Amendment, even though Munn was no more an ex-slave than had been any of the white butchers in the earlier litigation. Moreover, one suspects that even though he lost, the High Court accepted Munn's major premise; that the Fourteenth Amendment did ban certain types of state-imposed regulations concerning private business. Unfortunately for Munn, however, *this* statute just was not one of them.

In spite of his concurrence in *Munn*, Miller still believed in a limited application of the Fourteenth Amendment. One year after this case, he found in the growing body of due process litigation coming before the Court "abundant evidence that there exists some strong misconception of the scope of this provision." Further, Miller lamented its use as a new method of testing the "merits" of legislation. But he spoke more of what had been rather than what was to come. By the time of his death in 1890, the Court had taken the first step toward the application of judicially generated standards concerning substantive due process in relation to state legislation. The case generated a vigorous dissent from Justice Bradley, as well as a concurrence by Miller that reflected—as he acknowledged—marked hesitation. (See *Chicago, Milwaukee, and St. Paul Railroad v. Minnesota* [1890].)

The development of substantive due process really took off after the Chase Court era had passed, following the *Milwaukee* rate case just noted. But it had a beginning in *Slaughterhouse*, specifically in Justice Field's dissent, where he had pointed to an inherent right to practice any lawful calling without undue interference from the state. By 1897, this supposed right became a full-blown constitutional privilege known as freedom or liberty of contract. The facts of *Allgeyer v. Louisiana* (1897) are of less significance than the unanimous holding that it was unconstitutional for any state to adopt a statute that deprived an individual of the right to enter into contracts. Indeed, the right to voluntarily enter into a lawful contract, though nowhere mentioned in the Constitution, had somehow now become a liberty protected by the Due Process Clause of the Fourteenth Amendment. In an age of unparalleled American industrialization, courts and lawyers increasingly relied upon liberty of contract as a means to block statutes dealing with minimum wages or maximum working hours.

Eight years later in *Lochner v. New York*, by a one-vote margin, the High Court invalidated a New York statute that limited the hours of work that a baker might undertake to sixty per week or ten per day. In so doing, the five-member majority used a form of judicial supervision to interject its views into the relationship between employer and employee, regardless of what the New York legislature had concluded. In 1905, Justice Rufus Peckham conceded the legitimacy of the state police power in the areas of "public morals, health, safety, peace and good order." But to limit a baker who had voluntarily chosen to work a stated number of hours in agreement with his employer to an arbitrary number of hours was not acceptable. Since when, Peckham asked, had baking been considered an unhealthy trade? Moreover, if the legislature in its wisdom could limit hours of work for a baker, why not those of a lawyer or doctor? One had to be careful to insure that the legislature, under the sneaky cover of the police power, was not in fact interfering with constitutional rights that the Fourteenth Amendment had placed beyond such interference. Responsibility for the exercise of such judicial oversight was a special obligation for the Court.

Writing in dissent, Justice Harlan had no difficulty accepting Peckham's invoking liberty of contract. Nor did he disagree that his brethren were obligated to look beyond the wording of a statute to see if its intended effect was legitimate. Having undertaken to do just that in his indignant dissent, however, Harlan insisted that in *this* instance, New York had ample justification to enact a law limiting bakers' hours. He cited reports dealing with public health as well as scholarship on the diseases associated with contaminated flour and sanitary conditions of the "modern" bakery. Finally, he emphasized the applicability of the presumption of constitutionality doctrine to the statute under attack in this case.

If Peckham had embraced certain of Field's ideas in his opinion, ideas that had emerged during the Chase Court era, one other dissent echoed Miller's earlier position in *Slaughterhouse*, handed down as that era had come to a close. In *Lochner*, the recently appointed Justice Oliver Wendell Holmes declined to join Harlan's dissent and instead added a very short statement of his own. It not only undercut the basic premise for the majority opinion but also dismissed the judicial methodology that both

Peckham and Harlan had utilized, albeit to reach very different conclusions. In language that is still cited, Holmes insisted that it was not a proper judicial function to second guess a legislature, which in its wisdom chose to enact such a statute. The Fourteenth Amendment, he reminded his brethren, does not "embody Herbert Spencer's Social Statics." Personal judicial predilections for laissez-faire doctrines should not be engrafted onto the Constitution, which was not "intended to embody a particular economic theory" (Kens 1998, 162). As Miller had done in 1873, so Holmes in 1905 vindicated the right of a legislative majority to adopt a regulatory measure it deemed appropriate (*Lochner v. New York* 1905). Although liberty of contract survived into the 1920s, it was swept aside by the jurisprudential express of the New Deal after 1937.

A final example of what state action had come to mean in the post-Chase era is the 1883 decision in the *Civil Rights Cases.* Largely as a tribute to Charles Sumner, who had died while his proposed civil rights bill was pending, Congress passed a watered down version that outlawed discrimination in various public facilities such as theaters, skating rinks, and restaurants. Conspicuously absent from the list of proscribed institutions were the public schools. Not until 1883 did the Court confront the constitutionality of the measure. During the eight years that had elapsed since the bill was enacted, much had happened. These developments indicated that concern about rights for the ex-slave had declined to a level of minimal national significance.

In the first place, the Democratic nominee for the presidency in 1876, a squeaky-clean New York attorney named Samuel Tilden, received more popular votes than his Republican counterpart, an equally respectable three-term governor of Ohio. But electoral votes from Oregon as well as several Southern states still under Reconstruction were disputed. Hayes would have to win all of them in order to gain the White House. Because control of Congress was split, a potential stalemate threatened to cause a deadlock over who should count the electoral votes—the House, which was controlled by the Democrats, or the Senate, which was in the hands of the Republicans. This potential crisis was averted by congressional creation of a fifteen-member panel to decide this question. It would consist of five members drawn from the House (three Democrats and two Republicans), the Senate (three Republicans and two Democrats), and the High Court (two Republicans, two Democrats, and one truly independent jurist—David Davis). But Davis, possibly with a real sigh of relief, resigned to accept election to the Senate from Illinois. In his place, the Court selected Justice Joseph Bradley, a Republican from New Jersey. Not surprisingly, he voted with the Republicans, giving Hayes an 8–7 margin and all the contested electoral votes.

But before the House acquiesced in such an outcome, a number of quasi-secret negotiations took place. They resulted in a number of "understandings." Among them Hayes had to agree that Reconstruction would end, that all federal troops would be withdrawn from the South, and that a Southerner would be appointed to his cabinet, with enhanced opportunities for Southern patronage. At first, the long-term costs to the Republican Party appeared more significant than did any lasting benefit for Hayes. Although he did serve one term as president, a self-imposed limitation, acceptance of these conditions meant an end to Republican efforts to gain a lasting political presence in the South, which from 1876 to 1968—with one exception—became a solid Democratic voting bloc. But in reality, by 1876 and thereafter, the Republicans had garnered sufficient support in the East and Midwest to make loss of Southern support irrelevant. Not until the era of Richard Nixon and his "Southern strategy" in 1968 would this trend change. As with so much of Reconstruction, the real losers were the ex-slaves.

It was in this context that Joseph Bradley spoke for the Court in 1883. By a vote of 8–1, the Court declared much of the 1875 Civil Rights Act unconstitutional. Bradley insisted that the Fourteenth Amendment barred *only* state acts of discrimination. "It is state action of a particular character that is prohibited." Therefore, unless and until "some state law has been passed or some state action . . . has been taken," Congress is powerless to enact any federal legislation under the Fourteenth Amendment. Bradley could have stopped there. But he added several comments that indicated how well the High Court had followed the election returns as ultimately determined by the commission on which Bradley had served. "It would be running the slavery argument into the ground," he wrote, "to make it apply to every act of discrimination which a person may see fit to make as to the guests he will entertain, or as to the people he will take into his coach or cab or car, or admit to his concert or theater." Further, "when a man has emerged from slavery . . . there must be some stage in the process of his elevation when he takes the rank of a mere citizen, and ceases to be the special favorite of the laws." For most of the High Court, that time had come (*Civil Rights Cases* 1883).

Not so however, for Justice John Harlan, a former slaveholder who had been named to the Court by President Hayes to replace Justice Davis. Harlan denounced Bradley's opinion as one in which the Reconstruction Amendments "have been sacrificed by a subtle and ingenious verbal criticism." Well aware of the irony in that the pen and inkwell with which Harlan wrote this dissent had been used by Roger Taney in the "infamous" *Dred Scott* decision of 1857, he insisted that Congress possessed ample authority to enact the Civil Rights Law of 1875. He emphasized, however, that personal discrimination based on race was acceptable. "Whether one person will permit or maintain social relations with another is a matter with which government has no concern." But in this case, private proprietors licensed by the state had discriminated. Taking a cue from *Munn v. Illinois*, and it may be that Harlan knew how strongly Bradley had supported that decision, he insisted that it applied here. Indeed, Harlan invoked the essence of Waite's holding based on a British precedent, which Bradley had called to Waite's attention. Although his dissent showed several examples of modernity, in 1883, Harlan spoke alone.

Due Process in Wartime

Ex parte Milligan remains one of the most famous Chase Court decisions. The reaction in the twentieth century to the 1866 holding, however, has been much more favorable than that accorded it when first announced. Fearing, mistakenly, that the decision would interfere with congressional Reconstruction in the South, many Republicans were very critical of the holding. In time, however, it came to be regarded as a landmark decision in American civil liberties. Nevertheless, in the wake both of World War II as well as the more recent tragedies of 9/11 and their aftermath, its lasting significance may be uncertain.

It will be recalled that the gist of the *Milligan* holding was simply that military tribunals could not try an American citizen who was not in the military *if* civilian courts were open and operating. But a bare majority of Chase's Court had gone further and ruled that under *no* circumstances could Congress establish military tribunals as it had done in Indiana during the Civil War, with both state and federal courts open and operating throughout the conflict. There could be, of course, no doubt that Milligan was a citizen, even though federal citizenship had not yet been defined in 1866. World War II provided an intriguing backdrop for a revisit to the *Milligan* case. Yet there were very important contextual differences between 1864 and 1942, when the High Court considered the case of the eight Nazi saboteurs—two of whom were American citizens. Some background information is necessary to understand why the *Milligan* case assumed new importance in 1942 when the Court wrestled with *Ex parte Quirin.*

Upon reading an account of the eight misfits, who were landed on the east coast from two German submarines in June 1942, identified to the FBI by one of their number, and apprehended before any acts of actual sabotage had occurred, the observer today might wonder why there was such an uproar after their arrests. From landing to incarceration had only taken two weeks. However, one needs to consider the national attitude in the context of 1942, with the Japanese attack on Pearl Harbor only six months past, with the U.S. Navy in disarray, and with the country facing a two-front war, a challenge the country had never confronted before in its entire history. In February and March, the United States had moved to intern Japanese Americans on the west coast, another indication of the unease, if not hysteria, affecting the country in the wake of Pearl Harbor.

Originally, the saboteur who had "fingered" the rest of his group assumed that he at least would be tried in a civilian court. However, once word of the arrests had reached the press, Roosevelt's administration turned toward trial before a military commission—a procedure apparently unused in the United States since 1865. There were a number of reasons for resuscitating this type of trial, including the secrecy under which it could be held. Since the arrests had been widely publicized, why did the government want to keep prosecution a secret?

The press applauded the skill and rapidity with which the FBI had rounded up the eight saboteurs. But in fact, the truth was more prosaic. Until one of the eight had voluntarily turned himself in to the FBI and identified the rest of his gang, the bureau apparently knew nothing about the entire episode. It wasn't skill and hard work on the part of FBI investigators at all—a fact that, from Washington's viewpoint, need not be made public. From a different perspective, Roosevelt might not have wanted it widely known how easy it had been for two German submarines to land two separate groups of saboteurs in America undetected. Far better to keep the proceeding secret and let the Nazis assume that the United States had a vast network that could easily catch would-be saboteurs.

There were additional reasons why trial by a military commission might be preferable. Whatever the acts of sabotage that the accused had *intended* to carry out, they had done nothing. Although there was an existing federal statute dealing with sabotage, the burden of proof for the government would be a heavy one. How could one prove attempted sabotage when no attempt had been made, and no act had been committed? There was also a federal statute dealing with conspiracy to commit crimes, but the maximum penalty for conviction under it was a three-year prison term (Fisher 2003, 47).

As the authorities considered trial by a military commission, they found it more and more appealing. The trial could be held in secret, and like many instances of military justice, could operate with rapidity as well as rigor. Even more important, using the nebulous "laws of war" as a basis, a commission could be much more flexible in its procedures. It would have a number of options open to it, including imposition of the death penalty. A court-martial, on the other hand, was compelled to follow the Articles of War, a far more specific statute and one permitting much less discretion. And even though past military commissions had been expected to follow the practices of courts-martial, this was more a tradition than a statutory requirement.

Less than one week after the would-be saboteurs had been arrested, acting under his powers as commander in chief, FDR ordered not only that the eight be tried by military commission, but that they have no access to any other civil court, state or federal. Further, the suspects were to be tried under the more general "laws of war." The commission would thus be able to pick and choose from existing precedents as it went along. Furthermore, Roosevelt stipulated that two-thirds of the seven-member tribunal would be sufficient for "conviction or sentence," unlike a court-martial, where a death sentence requires a unanimous vote. Finally, the president ordered that the complete trial record be turned over directly to him, thus bypassing even the traditional review within the military justice system. In several key areas, then, FDR rejected existing practice, as would another chief executive at the turn of the millennium. In both instances, such conduct represented real departures from well-established American traditions of due process (Fisher 2003, 52–53). And both have been subject to well-deserved criticism.

Before the commission could get very far in its work, one of the military lawyers detailed to represent the alleged saboteurs challenged the constitutionality not only of the commission, but also of Roosevelt's directive establishing it. The observer is struck by the determination and resourcefulness demonstrated by this young lawyer, Kenneth Royall, who later would become secretary of the army. Taking very seriously his responsibility to "guard the accused's interests by all honorable and legitimate means known to the law," he sought to move the case into civil court. Because FDR's original order setting up the commission also included Royall's appointment as counsel, Royall found himself in the unique situation of having to ask the commander in chief for permission to question his own order. Word came back from an aide that he should use his own judgment. Counsel did, and on July 29–30, with the commission almost in the concluding phase of the trial, the Supreme Court ordered a pause—as it began an extraordinary two days of hearings devoted to Royall's request for a writ of habeas corpus from the High Court. The shadow of *Milligan* hovered over the arguments in *Ex parte Quirin.*

Royall insisted that the *Milligan* precedent clearly applied to his clients for three reasons: (a) there had been no presidential proclamation of martial law; (b) the courts in New York were open and operating; and (c) in 1942, New York could hardly be considered an active theatre of war. Even though this apparently satisfied the three-part test in *Milligan,* Royall raised some additional points. Why was the administration so eager to execute his clients? What specific crimes had they committed? It was one thing to accuse them of intended sabotage. It was quite another to execute them for what they may have planned to do but failed to accomplish. Preparation to undertake a criminal act was not the same as committing it. Indeed, Royall urged that the commission "not let the fact of war absolutely change the character of what [the alleged saboteurs] have done. Give it weight, yes; but do not let it destroy our entire perspective of just exactly what has happened" (Fisher 2003, 72). Finally, Royall argued that FDR had gone beyond his constitutional authority in setting up the commission and giving it powers superior to those granted by the Articles of War, a federal statute.

As if to indicate the unusual character of this trial, the administration was represented both by FDR's Attorney General Francis Biddle, as well as the judge advocate general of the army. Biddle insisted that *Milligan* had to be confined to its context and holding. In all essentials, what happened in 1866 was very different from what happened in this case. The intended saboteurs had been landed in America, currently at war with Germany, and had been wearing German military uniforms. These admitted facts surely distinguished the accused from *Milligan.* Further, he added, "individuals ordered by the enemy to destroy American industries and lives . . . can hardly be in a position to claim constitutional rights, privileges and immunities from the Nation which they seek to destroy" (Fisher 2003, 92).

But Biddle was too shrewd a lawyer to seek an overruling of the 1866 holding. Nor did he deny that the High Court could hear petitioners' request for a writ of habeas corpus. Instead he implied that hearing the case was fully appropriate—as long as the justices ultimately declined to issue the writ! Judicial intervention, in other words, would be acceptable, as long as nothing came of it. This way, a possible clash between Court and commander in chief could be conceded but not confronted. Biddle assumed, and hoped, that the Court would see it his way. He need not have worried.

After these two days of hearings, in which the justices could not see any of the commission's papers, on July 31, the Court issued a very brief per curiam opinion, holding that the military commission had jurisdiction over the eight saboteurs. Thus their petition for a writ of habeas corpus was summarily dismissed. The Court promised a full opinion in due course, noting that it "necessarily will require a considerable period of time for its preparation."

Free to continue, the commission finished the case one day later, and after some internal deliberation unanimously recommended that all eight defendants be sentenced to death. FDR received a 3,000-page transcript on August 4. He could not have spent much time on it, because the jailer was informed on the same day that six out of the eight were to be electrocuted. When asked on August 7 if he had finished the review, FDR told reporters he "hadn't finished reading it." The six were put to death on August 8.

What was left of the Chase Court's "landmark ruling," and why did the justices cave in so completely to administrative pressure? The second part of the question is much easier to answer than the first. Given 1942, one should not be surprised that the Court acquiesced in what were clearly dubious procedures concerning the eight accused saboteurs. Reeling from the worst naval attack it had ever received, the country was at war with two major powers, with both of its coasts in possible peril. Victory was by no means assured as the saboteur episode unfolded. The Court could not have been blind to these realities. In *Milligan*, the Chase Court did not announce a decision until early 1866 and did not publish the actual opinions until December 1866. For all the majestic rhetoric of Davis's opinion, the Court had delayed almost a year before its release; well after the Union Army was being demobilized and the immense emotional impact of the Civil War had lessened. In 1942, the High Court may have assumed that it could not afford the luxury of delay.

Aside from the urgency of the time, another factor should be noted—unspoken but very much in the minds of the justices. The critical tensions between FDR and the Court during the mid-1930s had culminated in his famous court-packing plan. Although some argue that the Court had actually begun to change course *prior* to FDR's announcement in 1937, there is no doubt that ultimately it did change, dramatically shifting in favor of the administration. In 1942, with the only third-term president ever elected safely ensconced in the White House, were any of the justices seriously inclined to pick a fight with the commander in chief—and this only a matter of months after Pearl Harbor? Further, it cannot be denied that the Court, as one scholar noted, "carried water for the administration, and would do so again" (Fisher 2003, 122).

In the saboteurs' case, the Court allowed itself to be pushed aside by the army and the administration, even as Chief Justice Stone piously insisted that the Supreme Court "in time of war as well as in time of peace" would "preserve unimpaired the constitutional safeguards of civil liberty." Similarly, Stone noted the denial of access to the federal courts in Roosevelt's proclamation, but reiterated that in no way could Roosevelt bar judicial consideration of the proclamation itself. This had taken place, and while the Court had refused to intervene, it had, at least, listened to the saboteurs' request for a writ of habeas corpus. On the other hand, the justices declined to consider the saboteurs' guilt or innocence, their purview in the case was very narrow, and they avoided getting into murky constitutional questions.

In the unanimous *Quirin* opinion for the Court filed almost three months after the executions, Chief Justice Stone cited *Milligan* several times. He managed to claim it as a viable source for constitutional protection, even as he narrowed its reach and thus placed its holding beyond the grasp of the accused saboteurs. Stone reiterated that his Court was not concerned with their guilt or innocence. That issue had been left to the military commission. Nevertheless, "constitutional safeguards for the protection of all who are charged with offenses are not to be disregarded in order to inflict merited punishment on some who are guilty." Here, Stone paraphrased Justice Davis in the *Milligan* case. But he immediately added that "the detention and trial of [the saboteurs]—ordered by the President . . . [as] Commander in Chief of the Army in time of war and of grave public danger—are not to be set aside by the courts without the clear conviction that they are in conflict with the Constitution" (*Ex parte Quirin* 1942, 25).

Stone further referred to the heavy emphasis placed on the 1866 decision by counsel for the accused. Although he in no way denied *Milligan*'s applicability, he questioned its relevance in the present context. "We construe the [1866] Court's statement as to the inapplicability of the law of war to Milligan's case as having particular reference to the facts before it." That decision "is inapplicable to the case presented by the present record." But Stone refused to explain exactly how or why. "We have," he stated, "no occasion now to define with meticulous care the ultimate boundaries of the jurisdiction of military tribunals to try persons according to the laws of war." The accused "were plainly within those boundaries," and their resulting trial by military commission was in accord with the Constitution. In spite of this finding, there was still some life left in *Milligan*.

Milligan had emphasized the fact that the defendant was a civilian, unlike any of the Nazi saboteurs. And it is in this area that Davis's 1866 holding continues to have constitutional relevance. In 1955, for example, the High Court ruled that a former serviceman could not be tried by a military tribunal. Once a civilian, he was, in theory, beyond the reach of such courts (*Toth v. Quarles*, 1955). Two years later, the justices extended such protection when they ruled that "dependents of military personnel overseas 'could not constitutionally be tried by military authorities'" (Fisher 2003, 158). In a more contemporary context, even the Bush proclamation of November 13, 2001, establishing military commissions in the wake of September 11, 2001, paid some heed to *Milligan*. His order focused on individuals who are not United States citizens, who may be suspected of various terrorist connections. As of this writing, no American citizen has been tried by a military commission acting under Bush's original order.

Conclusion

In a number of instances, American legal and constitutional development has moved far beyond the purview of Chase's Court. The Fourteenth Amendment took on a new life, relying not on privileges and immunities but on the Due Process Clause and, later, the Equal Protection Clause. Although it emphasized deference to the states, in one case, the almost unanimous holding of the Chase Court was summarily overruled. In *Collector v. Day*, over the objections of only Justice Bradley, the Court had held that the federal government could not tax "essential instrumentalities" of the state. This decision was specifically overruled in the case of *Graves v. New York* (1939). Constitutional interpretation can never be permanently shielded from the winds of change. In some instances, however, the process can be unsettling.

The Chase Court as well as the Stone Court of a later era faced unusual pressures from the military in a time of war, and it can be argued that both knuckled under rather than resisted. It can further be argued that our much vaunted glorification of our civil liberties rings hollow if they are inoperable when they are needed most—in wartime, when there may be much disagreement over their legitimacy and legality. Our history, however, does not offer many examples where the Court stood firmly on the side of civil liberties in a time of war.

Assessing the Chase Court as well as the Stone Court in the wake of war invites us to reconsider why this should be so. One likes to believe that the American tradition of "equal justice under law," to quote the phrase inscribed on the front of the Supreme Court's majestic building, is strong enough to provide due process in all contexts and under all conditions. If so, why are we apparently afraid to test this belief even as we glorify the enduring reliability of our constitutional safeguards? All too often, it is a refusal to attempt that which seems unattainable that actually makes it so. This is why the Chase Court legacy remains one of ambiguity. Understanding why such is the case perhaps represents the ultimate lesson, which an examination of the Chase Court from 1865 to 1873 can teach us.

References

Blight, David W. 2001. *Race and Reunion: The Civil War in American Memory.* Cambridge, MA: Belknap Press of Harvard University Press.

Fairman, Charles. 1971. *Reconstruction and Reunion, 1864–1888.* New York: Macmillan.

Fisher, Louis. 2003. *Nazi Saboteurs on Trial: A Military Tribunal and American Law.* Lawrence: University Press of Kansas.

Goldman, Robert M. 2001. *Reconstruction and Black Suffrage: Losing the Vote in* Reese *and* Cruikshank. Lawrence: University Press of Kansas.

Hall, Kermit, ed. 1992. *The Oxford Companion to the Supreme Court of the United States.* New York: Oxford University Press.

Kens, Paul. 1997. *Justice Stephen Field: Shaping Liberty from the Gold Rush to the Gilded Age.* Lawrence: University Press of Kansas.

———. 1998. Lochner v. New York: *Economic Regulation on Trial.* Lawrence: University Press of Kansas.

Lurie, Jonathan. 1986. "Mr. Justice Bradley: A Reassessment." *Seton Hall Law Review* 16: 343.

Paludan, Philip S. 1975. *A Covenant with Death: The Constitution, Law, and Equality in the Civil War Era.* Urbana: University of Illinois Press.

Wiecek, William. 1998. *The Lost World of Classical Legal Thought: Law and Ideology in America, 1886–1937.* New York: Oxford University Press.

PART TWO

Reference Materials

Key People, Laws, and Events

American (Know-Nothing) Party

The Know-Nothing, officially called the American Party, was a short-lived organization formed in the late 1840s in response to massive immigration. It was an umbrella for a number of nativist groups arising in the 1840s, when immigration from West Europe, particularly Germany and Ireland, was largely unrestricted. In addition to favoring strict regulation of immigration and a lengthening of the naturalization period to over twenty years, the Know-Nothings also advocated prohibiting foreigners and Roman Catholics from holding public office. The party got its name because many of its members came from secret anti-immigrant organizations, such as the Order of the Star-Spangled Banner in New York City. When asked about the organization, party members who were instructed not to reveal anything about the party, would typically respond by saying, "I know nothing." The Know-Nothings nominated only one presidential candidate, the former president Millard Fillmore, who was the American Party's standard-bearer in 1856. Although the party was successful in a number of congressional contests because the Democrats were so badly split, Fillmore's presidential candidacy failed. As was true for other parties of the period, the American Party fragmented and self-destructed over the issue of slavery. The party's members sought other political outlets, and many joined the newly formed Republican Party.

Black Codes

The Black Codes were laws enacted after the Civil War by former slave states. The codes resembled the prewar slave codes and were designed to relegate blacks to a state of social inferiority comparable to their status before emancipation. The codes forbade blacks from pursuing certain occupations or professions, owning weapons, or congregating in groups. They also restricted blacks from living in certain areas and required them to carry passes when traveling. Interracial marriage was prohibited and blacks were excluded from jury service, holding public office, and voting. Some Black Codes contained provisions that segregated public transportation and schools on the basis of race. These statutes provided a legal basis for "forcing blacks to work, restricting their occupational mobility, and providing harsh systems of forced black labor, sometimes verging on peonage" (Davis and Graham 1995, 12).

Many Northerners, including congressional Republicans, saw the codes as thinly disguised attempts to restore prewar conditions. Most white Southerners, on the other hand, insisted that emancipation did not itself create civil status for freedmen comparable to that enjoyed by whites. The Black Codes acknowledged the blacks' free status but provided them with severely truncated freedom. The writers of Southern state constitutions after the war acknowledged that blacks should enjoy privileges of free status such as having the right to convey real and personal property and make contracts. Nonetheless, the Black Codes largely re-created the worst features of the slave codes. In addition, some Northern states enacted "attenuated counterparts" of the Southern codes during the same period. The codes typically prohibited the access of blacks into segregated public facilities. Nonetheless, the Southern codes profoundly offended the Northern ideal of equality before the law because of their "overt, comprehensive racial discriminations extending to almost every area of civil and criminal conduct." In effect, the Black Codes made ex-slaves roughly equivalent to the free blacks of slave times (Hyman and Wiecek 1982, 319–320).

Booth, John Wilkes (1838–1865)

Booth was an actor of prominence during the Civil War era. He was born in Harford County, Maryland, on May 10, 1838. Although his actor father discouraged his children from theatrical careers, all three sons followed him to the stage. Booth was fanatically opposed to abolition and abolitionists. He once left a performing company mid-tour to attend the execution of John Brown, who led the Harper's Ferry raid. He joined a secret society called the Knights of the Golden Circle, whose members believed the North was unjustly oppressing the South. Following the election of 1860, Booth routinely denounced President Abraham Lincoln. As the Civil War progressed, his passion for the Confederate cause intensified. At one time, he planned to kidnap Lincoln and use him to ransom all Confederate prisoners of war. Booth learned that Lincoln would attend a play at Ford's Theater on April 14, 1865. While Booth assassinated Lincoln, his coconspirators were to assassinate Vice President Andrew Johnson and Secretary of State William Seward. Seward was severely but not fatally wounded, and no attempt was made on Johnson's life. Booth escaped from the theater after shooting Lincoln, but broke his leg in the process. After having his leg attended to, he hid in a Maryland forest for six days and then in the tobacco barn of a Virginia farmer. Three days later, on April 26, federal troops surrounded the barn and set it afire. In the moments that followed, Booth was fatally shot, although it is not clear whether the shot that killed him was fired by one of his pursuers or by Booth himself.

Bradwell, Myra Colby (1831–1894)

Bradwell was a publisher and political activist. She was born in Manchester, Vermont, on February 12, 1831. She attended schools in Wisconsin and Illinois as she prepared to become a teacher. She married in 1852 and spent two years teaching in Memphis, Tennessee, before returning to Chicago. Her husband was admitted to the state bar and eventually became a state trial judge and served in the state legislature. Reared as an abolitionist, she raised funds during the Civil War for the survivors of Union soldiers. In 1868 she established the *Chicago Legal News*, which became a widely circulated law journal. With the assistance of her husband, she secured exemption from the Illinois law preventing married women from entering into contracts. The exemption enabled her to function as both the editor and business manager of the *News*.

Bradwell was committed to elevating the status of women. She used the *News* to urge gender equality in such matters as property ownership and law school admission, and she offered editorial support to women across the country seeking licensing to practice law. She used her influence to secure the passage of laws designed to enable married women to have greater control over property.

In August 1869, even though she was found qualified to practice law in Illinois, the state supreme court denied her application. The following year the court again denied her application solely on the basis of gender. Bradwell contested the court's ruling in the *News* and also petitioned for review by the U.S. Supreme Court. Senator Matthew Hale Carpenter represented her before the Chase Court and argued that Bradwell was entitled under the Privileges and Immunities Clause of the Fourteenth Amendment to practice law. The Chase Court took a narrow view of the clause and ruled against Bradwell. While her case was pending, Bradwell assisted in drafting legislation that prohibited the exclusion of women from various professions. A year later, a woman was licensed to practice law in Illinois. For the next twenty years, Bradwell was active in the woman's suffrage movement. After a lengthy period as an honorary member, Bradwell became the first woman formally admitted into the Illinois Bar Association. Bradwell did not again seek her law license following the Court's ruling. The Illinois Supreme Court, however, approved her two-decade-old application in 1890 and in March 1892, two years before her death, she was admitted to the Illinois Bar.

Browning, Orville Hickman (1806–1881)

Browning was a prominent Kentucky-born lawyer and politician. He graduated from Augusta College before pursuing his legal career. He was admitted to the bar in 1831 and began his law practice in Quincy, Illinois. He won election to the state senate in 1836 as the candidate of the Whig Party and served four years. In 1842 he was elected to the Illinois House but was defeated by Stephen A. Douglas in a bid for Congress the following year. Browning strongly opposed extending slavery into the territories and opposed the Kansas-Nebraska Act adopted in 1854. Within two years, Browning had joined the Republican Party and was instrumental in building support for Abraham Lincoln at the 1860 nominating convention. Although Browning wanted a seat on the Supreme Court, he was appointed to the U.S. Senate to fill the seat opened by the death of Stephen Douglas.

Browning initially supported vigorous prosecution of the Civil War, but eventually broke ranks with the so-called Republican "Radicals" over measures he believed unlawfully confiscated the property of Southern slaveholders. Unlike many Republicans, he believed the slavery issue should be resolved by each state and opposed Lincoln's Emancipation Proclamation. Although he remained steadfast in support of the Union, he was troubled by the influence of the Radicals in determining war policy and withheld his support of Lincoln in the presidential election of 1864. He strongly supported President Andrew Johnson and his vetoes of the Freedman's Bureau and Civil Rights Act of 1866. He believed these measures impermissibly encroached on state sovereignty. Similarly, he opposed the Reconstruction Act of 1867 and the Fifteenth Amendment. Browning served as Johnson's interior secretary for two and a half years. In 1868, when Johnson's attorney general resigned to assist in Johnson's defense against impeachment charges, Browning became acting attorney general for several months. Browning resumed his legal career in 1869 and represented the Chicago, Burlington and Quincy Railroad in one of the *Granger Cases* before the Supreme Court.

Buchanan, James (1791–1868)

Buchanan was the fifteenth president of the United States. Born in Mercersburg, Pennsylvania, on April 23, 1791, he graduated from Dickinson College in 1809 and became an attorney. Buchanan served in the Pennsylvania legislature before serving five terms in the U.S. House. Although initially a Federalist, he supported Andrew Jackson in 1824 and served two years as Jackson's minister to Russia before serving eleven years in the U.S. Senate.

Buchanan did not believe in slavery but sided with the South in sectional controversies and strongly denounced the abolitionist movement. He lost the Democratic presidential nomination in 1844 to James K. Polk and then served as Polk's secretary of state. He opposed the Wilmot Proviso, which would have prohibited slavery in any territory acquired from Mexico, and favored extending the line established by the Missouri Compromise to the Pacific. He failed to secure the Democratic nomination in 1848 and retired to private life at the end of Polk's term. After Franklin Pierce was elected in 1852, Buchanan was named minister to Great Britain. Buchanan resigned the post in 1856 to once again seek the presidential nomination. His two main rivals for the nomination were Pierce and Stephen A. Douglas, both of whom were damaged by their advocacy of the Kansas-Nebraska Act (1854). The party rejected its own incumbent president and turned to Buchanan as a compromise. Buchanan was elected in a three-way race, although he won only a plurality of the popular vote.

Buchanan believed secession by the Southern states was a real danger and sought to defuse sectional conflicts and resolve the issue of slavery in the territories. He tried to sectionally balance his cabinet, but it was "South heavy" and contained no supporters of Stephen Douglas, with whom Buchanan disagreed on most policy issues. The most critical of these issues was slavery in the territories. Buchanan hoped the Supreme Court would resolve the question in the *Dred Scott* case. In it, the Court ruled that Congress could not ban slavery in any territory, and Buchanan thought the territorial problem was resolved. Instead, the ruling was more like gasoline on a smoldering fire. Buchanan's position was further damaged by an economic recession that continued throughout his presidency. He also vetoed a number of measures that drove conservative Northerners to the Republican Party.

Buchanan had two opportunities to make Supreme Court nominations, but the Senate approved only one. Justice Benjamin Curtis left the Court after the *Dred Scott* ruling. Buchanan decided to replace Curtis, who was from Massachusetts, with someone from New England. He chose his old political ally Nathan Clifford from Maine. Clifford, however, defended the institution of slavery and met strong opposition from abolitionists. After a lengthy and acrimonious confirmation battle, Clifford was confirmed by a 26–23 vote. A second Court vacancy occurred in May of 1860 with the death of Justice Peter Daniel. Members of the Senate prepared for another confirmation fight, but Buchanan delayed until after the election of Abraham Lincoln. He eventually nominated Jeremiah Black of Pennsylvania. Black failed to gain support of Northern Democrats, and many Republicans wished to hold the vacancy for Lincoln. As a result, Black's nomination was defeated by a 25–26 vote (Abraham 1999, 85–86).

The party fragmented during Buchanan's presidency. The full dimensions of the intraparty conflict were evident at the nominating convention of 1860. Southern Democrats wanted to prevent Douglas's nomination and demanded congressional protection of slavery in the territories. Northern Democrats disagreed, believing such action would destroy the party in free states. As a result, the Southern and Northern Democrats both placed candidates in the race, enabling Abraham Lincoln to win easily. After Lincoln's election, seven Southern states began the process of seceding.

Buchanan blamed the dissolution of the Union on the abolitionists and Northern interference on the slavery issue. Buchanan did not favor secession but felt there was no constitutional means to avoid it. His decision not to abandon Fort Sumter in Charleston, South Carolina, prompted secessionist members of his cabinet to resign. Buchanan retired to Pennsylvania when his presidential term ended and supported the Union war effort. He died on June 1, 1868.

Calhoun, John C. (1782–1850)

Calhoun was vice president, secretary of state, and a member of the U.S. House and Senate. He was born in Abbeville, South Carolina, on March 18, 1782, the son of a prosperous farmer who owned many slaves. After graduating from Yale in 1804, he studied law. Although his associates were mostly Federalists, Calhoun was an outspoken defender of Jeffersonian Republicanism. He briefly practiced law but chose a career in public service. He was elected to the South Carolina legislature in 1808 and to the U.S. House as a Jeffersonian Republican in 1810. He was a congressional "War Hawk," favoring war with Great Britain in 1812. Calhoun resigned his seat in the House in 1816 to become secretary of war in the administration of James Monroe. In 1824, on the expiration of Monroe's second term, Calhoun was considered for the Republican presidential nomination but, unable to compete with the likes of Andrew Jackson, Henry Clay, and John Quincy Adams, he settled for the vice presidential nomination.

Calhoun claimed original sovereignty for the states. Indeed, he viewed the federal government as a mere agent of the states. At the request of the South Carolina legislature, Calhoun drafted resolutions threatening nullification of federal law deemed adverse to any vital state interests. Both Calhoun and Martin Van Buren served in Andrew Jackson's cabinet. After a period of discord between the two, the cabinet was reconstituted and Calhoun was ousted. With Van Buren effectively designated as next in line for the presidency, Calhoun was in effect purged from the Democratic Party. He resigned the vice presidency and was elected to the Senate from South Carolina. Nullification advocates controlled South Carolina politics and the state legislature adopted a nullification ordinance that affirmed the right of a state to nullify a federal statute.

Calhoun believed that protecting the institution of slavery was the most urgent priority of his time. Indeed, it defined the remainder of Calhoun's political life. He served in the U.S. Senate for almost twenty years, briefly holding the cabinet post of secretary of state in the Tyler administration. There he vigorously supported the annexation of Texas, believing that it would provide additional slave territory. He returned to the Senate in 1845 and strongly opposed war with Mexico, now fearing that the vast additional territories to be gained from Mexico would harm slavery interests. His fears were borne out when Congressman David Wilmot introduced an antislavery rider providing that any territory gained from Mexico would be a free territory. Calhoun vigorously defended slavery and advocated dissolution of the Union if Southern interests were not accommodated. Calhoun unsuccessfully led efforts to block the Missouri Compromise of 1850, which eased sectional tensions, albeit briefly, and delayed Southern secession. He died in Washington on March 31, 1850, several weeks after the measure was enacted.

Campbell, John A. (1811–1889)

Campbell was a distinguished lawyer and Supreme Court justice. Born to a wealthy Georgia family on June 24, 1811, he was extraordinarily precocious; he enrolled at the University of Georgia at the age of eleven. He graduated with honors at the age of fourteen and continued his studies at West Point. He then returned to Georgia, studied law, and was admitted to the bar in 1829 at the age of eighteen. He then moved to Alabama and established a successful law practice. Campbell was elected to the Alabama legislature in 1836 and moved to Mobile, Alabama, the following year. He twice declined appointment to the Alabama Supreme Court. A vacancy occurred on the U.S. Supreme Court in 1852, but President Millard Fillmore could not gain Senate confirmation for a replacement. Franklin Pierce, Fillmore's successor as president, nominated Campbell, and the Senate confirmed him on March 25, 1853.

Campbell joined the Court's majority in *Dred Scott v. Sandford* (1857), which struck down the Missouri Compromise and held that blacks were not citizens of the United States. Campbell believed that slavery and secession were issues for the states to decide, but he had emancipated his own slaves when he joined the Court. He was considered a possible Democratic presidential candidate in 1860, but the nomination went to Stephen Douglas instead. Campbell opposed Southern secession, yet felt it his duty to resign from the Court when Alabama seceded from the Union in 1861. When the war began, Campbell became assistant secretary of war for the Confederacy. Having lost his property during the war, he relocated to New Orleans to practice law. His practice was highly successful, and he argued more than forty cases before the U.S. Supreme Court, including his representation of the New Orleans butchers' association in the *Slaughterhouse Cases* (1873). These cases represented the Chase Court's first important opportunity to consider the new Fourteenth Amendment. Campbell maintained his New Orleans practice until his wife died in 1884, at which point he retired and moved to Baltimore, Maryland, where he resided until his death in 1889.

Carpenter, Matthew Hale (1824–1881)

Carpenter was a lawyer and politician born in Moretown, Vermont, on December 22, 1824. At the age of fourteen, he began the study of law before entering West Point. He remained at West Point for two years before resuming his legal studies. After being admitted to the bar, he moved to Wisconsin and established a practice in Beloit. He developed a reputation as an excellent attorney, involving himself in local Democratic politics and winning election as county district attorney. He was an outspoken advocate of states' rights. Carpenter gained statewide attention when he defended Wisconsin's Democratic governor, William Barstow, against claims that his appointees had engaged in vote fraud. His performance in the Barstow case put him in line for a number of high-profile cases. Soon thereafter, Carpenter moved to Milwaukee and joined the practice of Edward Ryan, an influential Democrat. Although Carpenter was a Democrat, he fully supported Lincoln's war policies. He also was among the first to favor emancipation. He later appeared before the Supreme Court in cases involving issues stemming from Reconstruction, representing Augustus Garland in a challenge of the test oaths in *Ex parte Garland* (1866) and serving with Lyman Trumbull as counsel in support of Reconstruction in *Ex parte McCardle* (1869). Carpenter was elected to the U.S. Senate the same year as the *McCardle* decision. He favored federal supervision of the former Confederate states rather than legislatively imposed readmission conditions. He supported woman's suffrage, citizenship for Chinese immigrants, and the Ku Klux Klan Act adopted in 1871. Two years later, he represented Louisiana and argued for a narrow interpretation of the Fourteenth Amendment in the *Slaughterhouse Cases* (1873). Although consistent with his long-held states' rights views, the decision had direct consequences for Reconstruction by making vulnerable federal protective initiatives on behalf of freed slaves. Carpenter lost his Senate seat in 1875 but remained active in politics. He argued for Democrat Samuel Tilden's claim for Louisiana's electoral votes in the disputed presidential election of 1876. Although in poor health, he returned to the Senate in 1879, serving until his death on February 24, 1881.

Civil Rights Act of 1866

The Civil Rights Act of 1866 was a primary component of the moderate Republican Reconstruction policy. The law, as amended, continues to be the foundation for the nation's most important civil rights laws. The law addressed the citizenship status of freedmen by declaring that "all persons born or naturalized in the United States and not subject to any foreign power, except Indians not taxed," were citizens of the United States. The act provided that citizens of the United States, irrespective of race, color, or previous condition of servitude, should have the same right in every state "to make and enforce contracts, to sue, be parties, and give evidence, to inherit, purchase, lease, sell, hold, and convey real and personal property," and to enjoy the "full and equal benefit of all laws and proceedings for the security of person and property, as is enjoyed by white citizens." The act further provided that any person who "under color of any law, statute, ordinance, regulation, or custom deprived any inhabitant of rights secured by the act" was subject to criminal penalty. The act gave federal courts exclusive jurisdiction over crimes in violation of the law, as well as civil and criminal cases involving persons unable to enforce in state courts the rights secured by the act (Kelly, Harbison, and Belz 1991, 330).

The Republican Congress that passed the act recognized the idea of dual citizenship in the sense of mutually reinforcing rights—national citizenship overlapped state citizenship and secured general rights like those enumerated by the Civil Rights Act. State citizenship was concerned with the entitlements derived from state law. More problematic than the attribution of citizenship was congressional delineation of civil rights. Particularly troublesome to conservatives was language in Senator Lyman Trumbull's original bill stating that "there shall be no discrimination in civil rights and immunities." Trumbull argued that the Thirteenth Amendment gave Congress authority to secure civil rights in this categorical fashion, but most Republicans disagreed and struck the "no discrimination" clause.

More controversial was the scope of federal power employed in the act. As the Black Codes indicated, the chief threat to freedmen's rights at this time came from the restored state governments. The expansion of federal jurisdiction contemplated by the act was considerable, since persons discriminated against under state laws could transfer their cases to federal courts. Republican moderates believed that this provision would compel states to abandon discriminatory laws in order to retain jurisdiction over matters that had been historically and exclusively theirs. President Andrew Johnson echoed states' rights objections and vetoed the bill. On April 9, however, Congress overrode his veto. Although the Democratic minority and a scattering of Republicans continued to support his administration, the Republican majority henceforth passed all subsequent Reconstruction measures over his veto (Kelly, Harbison, and Belz 1991, 331–332). Nonetheless, enough doubts persisted in the minds of many congressmen, even the Radical Republicans, that Congress decided to "incorporate the gist of the Civil Rights Act into a new constitutional amendment (Fourteenth) that would make explicit the power of Congress to legislate on behalf of African Americans" (Urofsky and Finkelman 2002, 442–443). The extent to which it actually did that, however, remains very much subject to debate.

Civil Rights (First and Second Enforcement) Acts of 1870 and 1871

State action was the chief threat to black rights in the early postwar period. After 1868, however, the main danger came from private sources—from individuals and groups attempting to keep blacks from their newly won freedom. Aided by "tactics of intimidation," conservatives regained control of several Southern states in 1870 and threatened to drive Republicans from power elsewhere in the South. To meet the danger presented by these actions, Congress passed additional civil rights laws known as the Enforcement Acts. The purpose of the new laws was to enforce the Fourteenth and Fifteenth Amendments.

The First Enforcement Act of 1870, adopted in May of that year, was designed to enforce the Fifteenth Amendment. It prohibited state election officials from "discriminating among voters on the basis of color in the application of local election laws." It also made bribery and intimidation of voters by individuals a federal crime and, in a section directed at terrorist groups, outlawed conspiracies that prevented citizens from exercising federal constitutional rights (Kelly, Harbison, and Belz 1991, 348).

The Second Enforcement Act was enacted on February 28, 1871. Commonly known as the Civil Rights Act of 1871, it amended the First Enforcement Act and granted federal courts jurisdiction over supervisors of elections. The statute, now known as 42 U.S.C., Section 1983, also authorized civil suits for damages against anyone depriving other persons of their civil rights. More recently, the provisions of this statute have been broadly interpreted and Section 1983 actions now represent a significant portion of dockets of contemporary federal courts.

Civil Rights Act of 1875

The Civil Rights Act of 1875 was the most far-reaching civil rights legislation of its time. In an attempt to foster the loyalty of Southern blacks, as well as to pay tribute to the recently deceased Senator Charles Sumner, the lame-duck Congress passed the 1875 measure. Originally introduced by Sumner in 1870, the law prohibited discrimination in the enjoyment of accommodations, inns, public conveyances on land and water, theaters, and other places of amusement. The laws punished any person who denied others equal access to these places. Although its focus on social, as opposed to political and legal, discrimination gave the bill a "radical appearance," language prohibiting segregated schools was removed. Furthermore, the provisions of the statute were generally thought to be unenforceable.

Although the act dealt with private denials of rights, Republicans upheld the act on the theory that the prohibited discrimination was in effect carried out under state authority—by businesses or institutions "created or regulated by state law or in which the state had a substantial interest" (Kelly, Harbison, and Belz 1991, 350). In the *Civil Rights Cases* (1883) the Supreme Court struck down the Civil Rights Act of 1875 because it was directed against private rather than state discrimination. In the Court's view, the Fourteenth Amendment did not "invest Congress with power to legislate upon subjects which are within the domain of state legislation" or "authorize Congress to create a code of municipal law for the regulation of private rights" (*Civil Rights Cases* 1883, 11). The Court also rejected the contention that denial of equal access to public accommodations was a "badge" of slavery that Congress could prohibit (Kelly, Harbison, and Belz 1991, 357).

Civil War

The Civil War, also known as the War Between the States, started on April 12, 1861, when Southern troops fired on Fort Sumter, a U.S. military post in Charleston, South Carolina. The war ended four years later, on April 9, 1865, when Confederate General Robert E. Lee surrendered to Union General Ulysses S. Grant in the small Virginia settlement of Appomattox. The war was fought between the Northern states, dedicated to ending slavery, and the Confederate States of America, a group of eleven states that had seceded from the Union with the objective of preserving the institution of slavery. In 1861, the United States consisted of thirty-four states, nineteen of which were free states. Although slavery was the principal impetus for the war, long-standing sectional differences between North and South aggravated the conflict. These divisions had their origins in colonial times and resulted from several factors. The most important factor was economic—the South quickly established a rural way of life supported by an agricultural economy based on slave labor. By the mid-1800s, the sectional divisions had widened enormously. The United States had expanded all the way to the Pacific Ocean and was rapidly becoming a major industrial and commercial nation. Although Northerners looked forward to a rapidly evolving future, Southerners tried to preserve their agricultural economy and way of life.

The Southern states strongly opposed efforts to block the expansion of slavery and feared that the North's stance would eventually endanger existing slaveholdings in the South. Some Northerners had begun calling for the abolition of slavery, while several Southern states threatened to secede from the Union as a means of preserving their right to keep slaves. When Abraham Lincoln, the candidate of the antislavery Republican Party, was elected president in late 1860, eleven Southern states seceded. The Confederacy, under President Jefferson Davis, counted on the proslavery fervor and the international importance of cotton to win its war against the Union. The Northern states, under President Abraham Lincoln, had more than twice the population of the Confederacy and great advantages in manufacturing and transportation capacity. The North was better able to sustain a lengthy war. Its victory over the Confederacy resulted in both the restoration of the Union and the abolition of slavery.

Clay, Henry (1777–1852)

Clay was a noted U.S. statesman born in Hanover County, Virginia, on April 12, 1777. His formal schooling was limited, but when he was fifteen, he gained a position in the state chancery office in Richmond. His extraordinary potential was noticed by Chancellor George Wythe, who had employed Clay as a secretary. Wythe was a professor of law and classics at the College of William and Mary and the teacher of Thomas Jefferson and John Marshall, among others. Under Wythe's direction, Clay completed his legal training and moved to Lexington, Kentucky. Clay was a Jeffersonian Republican and remained committed to republicanism, states' rights, and Jefferson's Party. In 1803 he was elected to the lower house of the Kentucky legislature and selected U.S. senator by the legislature in 1806. Clay returned to the Kentucky legislature in the following year and became its Speaker. In 1810, he was elected to the U.S. House and was chosen House Speaker. As Speaker, Clay assigned the so-called War Hawks to all the important committees so that war advocates controlled the House. He interrupted his House service to serve on the commission negotiating with Britain to end the War of 1812. He resumed the House speakership and advocated his so-called American System agenda, which included a protective tariff, a strong central bank, and government-sponsored public works.

Missouri's application in 1819 for admission to the Union as a slave state precipitated a crisis that nearly led to civil war. The primary issue was whether Congress had the authority to restrict slavery in the territories. Largely through Clay's efforts, the Missouri Compromise of 1820 was enacted and the volatile issue of slavery in territories was contained, at least for three decades. After a brief period away, Clay again became House Speaker in 1823 and began campaigning for the presidency. His 1824 bid against Secretary of State John Quincy Adams and Tennessee Senator Andrew Jackson resulted in no candidate receiving a majority of electoral votes. The election was resolved in the House when Clay threw his support to Adams. He later became Adams's secretary of state. Jackson defeated Adams in the election of 1828, and Clay once again retired to Kentucky. He resumed his law practice and began preparing for another presidential bid. The Kentucky legislature elected Clay to the U.S. Senate in 1831, where he served for most of the next 20 years. The 1832 presidential campaign centered on the national bank issue, and Clay was easily defeated by Andrew Jackson, who opposed the bank. Within two years, Jackson's opponents formed the Whig Party, and Clay, along with Daniel Webster and John C. Calhoun, were the party's leaders in the Senate. Clay was the Whig presidential nominee in 1844 against Democrat James K. Polk. Clay appeared to take both sides on the Texas annexation issue, and it cost him the election. The defeat ended Clay's quest for the presidency. With the end of the Mexican War came renewed conflict about slavery in the territories. Despite owning slaves, Clay detested slavery and urged gradual emancipation of all slaves. In one last attempt to avert secession and war, Clay proposed a series of resolutions dealing with a number of issues, including slavery, slavery in the territories, slave trade in the District of Columbia, and fugitive slaves. The "omnibus" package of resolutions was defeated, although each was separately reintroduced by Stephen Douglas and adopted. The Compromise of 1850 prevented secession, at least for the short-run. Clay died on June 29, 1852.

Compromise of 1850

The Compromise of 1850 was a collection of measures passed by Congress in hopes of relieving the sectional crisis existing in 1850. Admission of California to the Union intensified the long-standing conflict over slavery. California was seized by the United States during the Mexican War and was quickly settled. It immediately sought admission to the Union as a free state. But there were other matters intertwined with California. There was a border dispute between Texas and New Mexico. A more difficult problem was what to do with the rest of the territory acquired as a result of the Mexican War. Those lands had to be organized into territories, which required determination of whether slavery would be permitted. Furthermore, there was the troublesome question of whether slave trading would continue in the District of Columbia. Finally, the Southern states were demanding a stronger fugitive slave law.

The late 1840s produced a number of proposals addressing these questions. Some of these proposals were compromise measures while others were attempts to advantage either the North or South. Henry Clay, who had delivered the Missouri Compromise thirty years earlier, proposed a new compromise in an effort to preserve the Union. In an "omnibus" bill, the North won immediate admission of California as a free state, an end to the slave trade in Washington, D.C., and a favorable Texas boundary. The South gained the stronger fugitive slave law it sought, with assurances that it would be aggressively enforced. In addition, the proposal permitted slavery in the Utah and New Mexico territories.

Despite Clay's best efforts, the proposal was not passed in the Senate. Stephen Douglas revived the compromise, however, by putting together coalitions for each component of Clay's original proposal. The Compromise of 1850 reduced sectional tensions and was greeted with relief by many people in the country. Indeed, President Millard Fillmore called the compromise a "final settlement" of the crisis. As it turned out, the so-called "final settlement" would fall apart soon after it was implemented. In the end, the "series of laws that created the compromise might more properly be called the Armistice of 1850" (Kelly, Harbison, and Belz 1991, 380–381). Its incorporation of the concept of "popular sovereignty" opened the possibility of "nationalizing slavery." Because federal law had never established slavery as such, the institution was viewed as a local practice. The adoption of popular sovereignty seemed to suggest a policy that tolerated slavery in the yet unorganized territories. "As the movement for territorial expansion proceeded in the 1850s, this question became the focal point of sectional conflict over the place of slavery in the American republic" (Urofsky and Finkelman 2002, 262).

Confederate States of America

The name taken by Southern states when they organized their own government at Montgomery, Alabama, in February 1861. These states seceded from the Union, fearing that the election of Abraham Lincoln might lead to limitations on, if not complete abolition of, slavery. South Carolina was the first state to leave the Union, on December 20, 1860. Mississippi, Florida, Alabama, Georgia, and Louisiana seceded in January 1861, with Texas joining them the following month. Virginia, Arkansas, North Carolina, and Tennessee seceded later in 1861, bringing the total number of states joining the Confederacy to eleven. Several slave states, the so-called "border states," were located between the North and the Deep South. The Union and the Confederacy both sought to secure their allegiance. Ultimately, the borders states of North Carolina, Virginia, Arkansas, and Tennessee joined the Confederacy, while Delaware, Maryland, Kentucky, and Missouri remained in the Union. The Confederate states had briefly entertained the possibility of peaceful secession. All hopes of that ended with the attack on Fort Sumter on April 12, 1861, and the Civil War commenced.

The Confederacy was grounded on the principle of states' rights and the principle that any state had the right to withdraw from the Union whenever it wished, because the individual states had created the Union in the first place and retained the option to dissolve or withdraw from it. Organization of a government for the Confederacy began when delegates from the seceded states met in Montgomery, Alabama. The Constitution of the Confederacy was modeled after the United States Constitution, although there were some differences, such as six-year terms for the president and vice president. Under its new Constitution, Jefferson Davis of Mississippi was elected president of the Confederacy, and Alexander H. Stephens of Georgia was chosen vice president. Montgomery was the initial capital of the Confederacy, but after Virginia seceded, the capital was moved to Richmond. When Union forces took Richmond on April 3, 1865, Danville, Virginia, became the Confederate capital. The war ended when the Army of Northern Virginia surrendered on April 9, 1985, at Appomattox.

Dana, Richard Henry (1815–1882)

Dana was an attorney born in Cambridge, Massachusetts, on August 1, 1815. He interrupted his education at Harvard because of eyesight problems and took a lengthy voyage around Cape Horn to California, working as a crewman. He resumed studies at Harvard in September 1836 and graduated the following year. After studying law for three years, he was admitted to the bar in 1840 and began a successful practice of admiralty law. Meanwhile, Dana wrote the classic *Two Years before the Mast*, which was published in 1841. Dana was an antislavery activist and in 1848 helped found the National Free-Soil Party. He vigorously opposed the Fugitive Slave Law of 1850 and represented many who were prosecuted for violating the law. President Abraham Lincoln appointed him U.S. district attorney for Massachusetts in 1861, a position he held for five years. During the war, he successfully represented the Lincoln administration before the Supreme Court in the so-called *Prize Cases* (1863). After the war, Dana was elected to the Massachusetts legislature and was retained by the Andrew Johnson administration to recommend whether criminal punishments be imposed on Confederate President Jefferson Davis. He proposed dropping high treason charges against Davis, a course of action supported by other Republican moderates. The recommendation lost him support among the Radical Republicans in Massachusetts, however, and he lost his bid for the U.S. House in 1868. In 1876, he was nominated by President Ulysses S. Grant to be minister to England, but the Senate refused to confirm him. He retired from public life and spent the last years of his life in Europe. He died in Rome on January 6, 1882.

Davis, Henry Winter (1817–1865)

Davis was a congressman born in Annapolis, Maryland, on August 16, 1817. He graduated from Kenyon College in 1837 and studied law at the University of Virginia Law School. Davis established a law practice in Alexandria, Virginia, before moving to Baltimore after his wife's death in 1849. Davis had been interested in politics since college and joined the Whig Party when he settled in Maryland. When the Whigs collapsed, Davis joined the Know-Nothing (American) Party and was elected to Congress four times. In Congress, Davis was a voice of moderation at a time when slavery was dividing the nation and became a powerful figure in the antisecessionist movement in Maryland. He cast the decisive vote in the contest for House Speaker by supporting the Union Party candidate John Bell. His support of Bell cost him Republican support, and he was defeated in 1861. Reelected to Congress in 1863, Davis became a critic of Lincoln's suspension of habeas corpus and challenged Lincoln's presidential emancipation of slaves.

Davis chaired the Select Committee on the Rebellious States and introduced a plan for Reconstruction known as the Wade-Davis Bill, a more punishing plan than the one proposed by Lincoln. The differences between the Davis and Lincoln positions indicated a growing conflict between the president and Congress—a conflict that would become fully manifest during Andrew Johnson's administration. Wade-Davis was the primary expression of those who opposed executive control of Reconstruction. The proposal was ultimately pocket vetoed by Lincoln, and the negative reaction to it in Maryland led to Davis losing his congressional seat. Davis would later support enfranchising black males, Lincoln's reelection, and the execution of Confederate President Jefferson Davis. He lived only briefly after the Civil War, passing away in Baltimore on December 30, 1865.

Davis, Jefferson (1808–1889)

Davis was a U.S. senator and president of the Confederate States of America. He was born in Christian County, Kentucky, on June 3, 1808, but lived in the Louisiana Territory and Mississippi in his youth. He was appointed to West Point in 1824. After graduation, Davis served six years as a lieutenant in the infantry. In 1835, Davis resigned the military and returned to the family plantation in Mississippi. He developed ambitions for public office and became a committed states' rights advocate. He ran unsuccessfully for the state legislature in 1843 but won a seat in Congress two years later. By the 1840s, he was an established politician who strongly favored territorial expansion. When war with Mexico began, he went to Mexico as a colonel with the First Regiment of Mississippi Volunteers. His military exploits made him a hero in Mississippi, and in August 1847, he was elected to the U.S. Senate by the state legislature, where he became a leading spokesman for slavery and Southern interests in the territories. In his view, the territories belonged to the states collectively and decisions about slavery could not be made before statehood. He favored extending the Missouri Compromise line to the Pacific Ocean. He resigned his Senate seat in 1851 to run for governor of Mississippi. Although he made the contest close, he lost and briefly considered leaving politics. A year later, however, he joined the administration of Franklin Pierce as secretary of war, where he was a very influential pro-South voice.

Davis returned to the Senate in 1857 and resumed his role as defender of the South and slavery interests. He wanted to develop solutions that were not only favorable to the South but would also preserve the Union. He tried to unify the Democrats behind this effort, but the party remained badly divided and Abraham Lincoln was elected president in 1860. Once elected president of the Confederacy, Davis tried to form a strong and effective government. He believed he had executive authority sufficient to meet the demands of wartime, including the power to suspend habeas corpus as a means of dealing with those disloyal to the Confederacy. Davis's strong leadership notwithstanding, the quality of life for most in the South deteriorated markedly during the war. There was also resentment over the inequitable distribution of the costs of the war—the war was largely fought by the sons of poor families while the sons of the rich were able to avoid combat. This resentment brought about wholesale desertions from the Confederate armies. Davis was largely insensitive to these concerns, and his failure to take necessary action led to a corresponding decline in the performance of the Confederate military. The Confederate states surrendered in 1865. After the war, Davis was arrested and imprisoned for two years, although he was never brought to trial.

Davis spent the remainder of his life occupied with business ventures in Louisiana. He died in New Orleans on December 6, 1889.

Democratic Party

The Democratic Party had its origins in a congressional caucus begun by Thomas Jefferson in 1792. Its original purpose was to counter the Federalist Party and the policy proposals of Alexander Hamilton, including the incorporation of a national bank and protective tariff. The party was renamed the Democratic-Republican Party in 1798, with the core of its support coming from agrarian communities in the South and Mid-Atlantic states. Two years later Jefferson was elected president as the party's nominee. In addition, the Democratic-Republicans captured control of both the U.S. House and Senate. Following Jefferson's election, the party dominated presidential politics into the 1820s. The period during which Jefferson, James Madison, and James Monroe were president is often referred to as the "Era of Good Feeling." During this same period, the party maintained substantial congressional majorities. The party divided into several factions after the 1824 election of John Quincy Adams. With the party divided, Andrew Jackson was able to take control. Jackson was a charismatic war hero, but he also understood that organization won elections. The Jacksonian Democrats reunified the party by winning the White House in 1828 and 1832. Under Jackson, the party became the first broad-based, popular party in the country's history—labeled as the party of the "common man." In general, the party represented the less-privileged voters and welcomed new immigrants into its ranks. Its name was officially changed to the Democratic Party at its national convention in 1844.

Douglas, Stephen A. (1813–1861)

Douglas was a U.S. senator from Illinois and a three-time presidential candidate. He was born in Brandon, Vermont, on April 23, 1813. As a young man, he was drawn to the politics of Andrew Jackson. After moving to upstate New York, he graduated from Canandaigua Academy and studied law with a local attorney. He moved to Jacksonville, Illinois, was admitted to the Illinois Bar in 1834, and began his legal and political careers. He served as Illinois attorney general and a term as a state legislator before losing a bid for Congress. Following his tenure as Illinois secretary of state, Douglas served two years on the state supreme court. He was elected to Congress in 1843 and was sent to the U.S. Senate in 1847. Called the "Little Giant" for his small stature (he was about five feet tall) and extraordinary determination, Douglas became an influential player on the national stage. He was a leading expansionist and advocate of war with Mexico and chaired the powerful Committee on Territories, which had jurisdiction over territories seeking statehood. Douglas personally opposed slavery, but was unwilling to risk the destruction of the Union to abolish it. On the other hand, he strongly believed in white racial supremacy, and had little awareness of the growing moral revulsion against slavery in the North. He and Henry Clay submitted to Congress a package of legislation designed to strike a compromise on slavery but failed to secure its passage. Douglas then unpacked the component measures and shepherded each to adoption. Douglas thought popular sovereignty was the way to handle the problem of slavery in the territories. He was the principal force behind the controversial Kansas-Nebraska Act of 1854, which organized the two territories and allowed each to make its own determination about whether or not to allow slavery. The result of this measure was to foster migration of both pro- and antislavery groups to the territories. The act precipitated a change in the U.S. party system, with the Whig Party being replaced by the antislavery Republican Party. Douglas unsuccessfully sought the presidency in 1852 and 1856. He broke with his party's president, James Buchanan, when Buchanan supported the proslavery minority in Kansas. He sought reelection to the Senate in 1858 and engaged his opponent, Abraham Lincoln, in a series of historic joint appearances known as the Lincoln-Douglas debates. Douglas won the election, but Lincoln emerged as a national figure. In 1860, the Democratic Party was fatally divided over the issue of slavery in the territories and could not unite behind a candidate for president. The Southern delegates left the convention and nominated John Breckinridge for president. The remaining convention delegates, all from the North, nominated Douglas. The division in the Democratic ranks resulted in the election of Lincoln. Douglas continued to work for a way to avert civil war. When the war actually began, he supported Lincoln. While on an extended trip to rally the midwestern and border states, Douglas contracted typhus and died on June 3, 1861.

Dred Scott v. Sandford (1857)

The Court ruling that blacks were not citizens of the United States. *Dred Scott* was one of the Court's first major rulings on civil rights. It explored the nature of citizenship, the institution of slavery, and was a factor in precipitating the Civil War. Scott was a slave from Missouri who had been taken to the free state of Illinois and then to the Louisiana Territory, an area designated "free" under terms of the Missouri Compromise of 1820. Scott ultimately returned to the slave state of Missouri, where he brought suit, claiming that his residency in free areas had ended his slave status. The Missouri Supreme Court held that Missouri law governed, despite Scott's previous residence elsewhere. Scott then pressed his suit in federal court. The case could have been resolved by simply adhering to precedent and ruling that Scott's status was determined by Missouri law. The Supreme Court chose to address the slave issue, however, largely because of the extremely powerful antislavery arguments from dissenting Justices Curtis and McLean. The remainder of the Court decided against Scott, with each member of the Court entering a separate opinion.

In what is commonly viewed as the most controversial opinion, Chief Justice Roger Taney said that Scott was not a citizen because he was black and a slave, and thus not able to sue in federal court. Taney contended that at the time the Constitution was written, blacks were regarded as "beings of an inferior order and altogether unfit to associate with the white race, either in social or political relations." Instead, blacks were property. Taney invoked the concept of "dual citizenship" to foreclose Scott's claims. Federal citizenship is conferred only through federal action, and no state can "introduce a new member into the political community created by the Constitution of the United States"; no state can make him a "member of this community by making him a member of its own." Neither can a state "introduce any person, or description of persons, who were not intended to be embraced in this new political family, which the Constitution brought into existence, but here intended to be excluded from it." Scott was also a noncitizen because he was still a slave. Taney asserted that Scott had never achieved free status under provisions of the Missouri Compromise because that enactment was unconstitutional. In the Court's view, Congress did not have the authority to designate territories as free. To do so would deprive slaveholders of their due process property rights. The two dissenters, Curtis and McLean, split from the Court on every issue in the case. Curtis in particular disputed Taney's proposition that blacks were not citizens at the time the Constitution was ratified. The citizenship issue in *Dred Scott v. Sandford* was rendered moot by the ratification of the Fourteenth Amendment in 1868.

Emancipation Proclamation

As early as 1849, Abraham Lincoln believed that slaves should be emancipated, and advocated a program by which they would be freed gradually. In 1862, Lincoln tried to persuade Congress to free slaves gradually and proposed that slaveholders be compensated for giving up their "property." He failed to get congressional approval, however. In September 1862, the Union's victory at Antietam prompted Lincoln to issue a preliminary order declaring that unless the rebellious states returned to the Union by January 1, 1863, slaves living in those states would be freed. The order left room for compensated emancipation. No Confederate states took the offer, however, and Lincoln issued the Emancipation Proclamation. The proclamation declared that "all persons held as slaves" within the states of the Confederacy "are, and henceforward shall be free." The proclamation applied only to states that had seceded from the Union and left slavery undisturbed in the border states that did not secede. The proclamation did not immediately free any slaves, but it changed the character of the war—it announced the acceptance of black men into the Union military. By the end of the war, almost 200,000 black soldiers and sailors had fought for the Union. The proclamation also underscored the moral mission increasingly pursued by the Union forces.

Evarts, William Maxwell (1818–1901)

Evarts was a lawyer and politician born in Boston, Massachusetts, on February 6, 1818. He graduated third in his class at Yale and spent two years at Harvard Law School before completing his legal study with an attorney in New York City. He was admitted to the bar in 1841 and started his own firm the following year. Evarts supported Whig Zachary Taylor for president in 1848, and Taylor appointed him assistant district attorney for the Southern District of New York a year later. As part of the administration, Evarts supported both the Compromise of 1850 and the strengthened Fugitive Slave Law but lost his job when the Democrats won the White House in 1852. The Kansas-Nebraska Act prompted Evarts to participate in organizing the Republican Party of New York, and within a year he was a leader of the state party. He backed William H. Seward for president in 1860 but led the nominating convention to unanimously support Lincoln. Evarts represented the government in the *Prize Cases* and successfully argued to the Supreme Court that because of the state of war, the ships running the Union blockade were legitimate war prizes. He was also sent to Britain as part of a mission to stop Confederate ships from leaving British shipyards.

Evarts resumed his law practice in 1864 and was considered for the chief justiceship following Chief Justice Roger Taney's death. Lincoln selected Salmon P. Chase instead. Evarts disapproved of President Andrew Johnson's lenient Reconstruction policy and instead joined the Radical Republicans. Nonetheless, he was part of the defense team at Johnson's impeachment trial. Once Johnson was acquitted, Evarts joined his administration as attorney general. While attorney general, Evarts chose not to prosecute former Confederate President Jefferson Davis for treason and developed the administration's legal arguments in the *Legal Tender Cases* (1871). He resumed his law practice at the end of Johnson's tenure. Although considered, he was never nominated for the Supreme Court. The outcome of the 1876 presidential election was disputed, and Congress formed a commission to determine whether the Republican, Rutherford B. Hayes, or the Democrat, Samuel J. Tilden, would win the presidency. Evarts was Hayes's chief counsel and became Hayes's secretary of state and one of his most trusted advisers. In January 1885, Evarts was elected to the U.S. Senate. His record in the Senate was modest, but he introduced the Court of Appeals (Evarts) Act of 1891, which created intermediate appeals courts in the federal judicial system. Among the benefits of the act was the elimination of the need for Supreme Court justices to preside over circuit courts and the reduction of the number of appeals to the

Supreme Court. Evarts suffered ill health during his last years in the Senate and retired to New York City, where he died on February 28, 1901.

Federalist Party

The Federalist Party was the first U.S. political party and was produced by the debate at the Constitutional Convention in Philadelphia in 1787. It was not until the congressional debates over the Jay Treaty of 1794 that the substantive definition of the party's priorities emerged, however. The Federalists advocated a substantially stronger central government than was found under the discarded Articles of Confederation. Washington was nominally a Federalist, but the most important policy initiatives of the Federalists came from Treasury Secretary Alexander Hamilton. The most controversial of his proposals included the assumption of state debts by the central government and the chartering of a national bank. It is not surprising that support of the Federalists came from merchants, landowners, and established families of wealth and status. The principal opposition to Hamilton and the Federalists came from the followers of Thomas Jefferson. Federalist John Adams was elected president in 1796, but that would be the last national victory for the Federalists. During his one term as president, Adams faced opposition from the Hamilton faction of the party. With the Federalists irreparably split, Jefferson's Democratic-Republican Party captured the White House in 1800 and held it for the next two decades. Indeed, after the election of 1800, the Federalists were no longer viable at the national level. The Federalists attempted to maintain control of the federal judiciary while rebuilding electoral support. Although the Supreme Court under staunch Federalist John Marshall reflected Federalist values for a number of years, the Federalists did not put forth a presidential candidate and ceased to exist as a national party.

Fessenden, William Pitt (1806–1869)

Fessenden was a U.S. senator and Abraham Lincoln's treasury secretary. He was born in Boscawen, New Hampshire, on October 16, 1806. He was admitted to Bowdoin College at the age of thirteen and graduated in 1823. He studied law in Portland, Maine, and was admitted to the bar in 1827. He also got involved in politics, first with the Republicans and later with the Whigs. He was elected to the Maine legislature in 1831 but was defeated in his bid for reelection. He resumed his law practice, but after another term in the state legislature, he won election to Congress in 1840. Fessenden left Congress in 1843 and returned to his law practice. He served two additional terms in the Maine legislature, and in 1854 was elected to the U.S. Senate. Strongly opposed to extending slavery into the territories, Fessenden joined the Senate in time to vote against the Kansas-Nebraska Act. His abolitionist views prompted him to leave the Whigs for the Republicans, and his opposition to slavery in Kansas made him the political adversary of Stephen Douglas.

Fessenden was reelected to the Senate and urged President Abraham Lincoln to do anything necessary to prevent secession of the slave states. He was selected to chair the Senate Finance Committee and, working with Treasury Secretary Salmon P. Chase, played a crucial role in designing the plan for financing the war. When Chase was appointed chief justice in 1864, Fessenden was named to replace him as treasury secretary. He held the post until the beginning of his third Senate term the following year. Once the Civil War ended, Fessenden emerged as a leader of Senate Republicans, where he expressed disagreement with President Lincoln over Reconstruction policy. Lincoln proposed that former Confederate states could be readmitted if 10 percent of the state's population was repentant for the war and pledged loyalty to the Union. Fessenden believed Reconstruction was a legislative rather than an executive matter and insisted on indications of loyalty from at least a majority of a state's population.

Differences over postwar policy continued when Andrew Johnson succeeded Lincoln as president. Johnson's veto of the Civil Rights and Freedman's Bureau bills in 1866 produced a permanent split with the president. Fessenden chaired the Joint Committee on Reconstruction and provided a moderating influence on postwar policy. This was particularly apparent in the crafting of the Reconstruction Act of 1867 and the Fourteenth Amendment. When Johnson removed Secretary of War Edwin Stanton, impeachment proceedings were brought against the president. Although he was not a political ally of Johnson, Fessenden concluded that the president's actions were insufficient to warrant impeachment, and he played a decisive role in Johnson's Senate acquittal. Fessenden supported the presidential candidacy of Ulysses S. Grant but died in 1869, before he could stand for reelection to the Senate.

Field, David Dudley, Jr. (1805–1894)

Field was born in Haddam, Connecticut, on February 13, 1805. He was the son of a prominent clergyman, and one of his five brothers, Stephen J. Field, was one of the greatest justices to sit on the U.S. Supreme Court. After graduating from Williams College in 1824, Field read law and joined a leading legal practice in New York City, where he practiced until 1835. His wife died following childbirth, as did the child. Beset by depression, he left his practice and lived in Europe for a year. During his time abroad, he studied the legal systems of several European countries. Field returned to his practice in 1837 and was joined the following year by his brother Stephen, who remained his partner until leaving for California in 1849.

Legal reform became the focus of Field's work, a subject that occupied him for the remainder of his professional life. Field's answer to the demands of modern society was the codification of both substantive and procedural law. Field opposed slavery and joined the fledgling Republican Party in 1856, and he was instrumental in the nomination of Abraham Lincoln for president in 1860. His support of Lincoln contributed to Lincoln's nomination of his brother to the Supreme Court. After the war, Field argued three major cases before the Court. The first was *Ex parte Milligan* (1866), which challenged the use of military tribunals to try civilian defendants in the North; the second, *Cummings v. Missouri* (1867), challenged a state loyalty oath; and the third, *Ex parte McCardle* (1869), challenged military trials of civilians in the South while civil courts were open and functioning. Field was successful in the first two cases, and Congress removed the Court's appellate jurisdiction in the third. Subsequently, Field represented such clients as railroad giant Jay Gould and William "Boss" Tweed, head of the Tammany Hall political machine in New York City. Throughout, Field continued to work for legal reform. The penal code he crafted became law in New York in 1881, while his proposed civil code passed the New York legislature on several occasions but was vetoed by the governor each time. Field died on April 13, 1894.

Fifteenth Amendment

One of the three so-called "Civil War amendments," the Fifteenth Amendment provides that the "right of citizens of the United States to vote shall not be denied or abridged by the United States or by any state on account of race, color, or previous condition of servitude." A second section of the amendment empowers Congress to pass appropriate enforcement legislation. The amendment was proposed on February 26, 1869, and took effect on March 30, 1870. The Fifteenth Amendment did not extend the right to vote as such, but instead prohibited racially discriminatory actions by the states that would diminish the right to vote. The amendment left the states in control of administering elections, including setting voter qualifications, although early decisions of the Supreme Court acknowledged that federal power could be exercised if citizens were denied the opportunity to vote in state elections on the basis of race. It was not until World War II, however, that the Court used the Fifteenth Amendment to reach the more invidious discriminatory techniques, such as the racially exclusive white primary and literacy and other qualifying tests. Congressional initiatives based on the Fifteenth did not appear until the Voting Rights Act of 1965. The Warren Court unanimously upheld the 1965 statute in *South Carolina v. Katzenbach* (1966) and clearly established broad federal power over voting practices in the United States.

Fillmore, Millard (1800–1874)

Fillmore was the thirteenth president of the United States. He was born in Cayuga, New York, on January 7, 1800, son of a farmer on New York's western frontier. Fillmore had little formal education and spent much of his youth working in a local textile mill. He read extensively and essentially educated himself. Encouraged by a judge to study law, Fillmore prepared for a legal career and was admitted to the bar in 1823. He opened a law office in nearby East Aurora, New York, and was elected to the state assembly as the candidate of the Anti-Masonic Party. Fillmore spent three terms in the assembly but decided not to seek reelection in 1831. In 1832, he was elected to a single term in Congress. Fillmore was a founder of the Whig Party and returned to the Congress as a Whig in 1836. In 1844 he was the unsuccessful Whig candidate for governor of New York. At that point, serious division developed between William H. Seward's faction and Fillmore's more conservative faction. The party split notwithstanding, Fillmore was elected state comptroller in 1847. The following year, he was nominated as presidential candidate Zachary Taylor's running mate and became the vice president when the ticket won. Much of Fillmore's time was spent contesting Seward's faction for patronage appointments in New York, but that changed in 1850. On July 9, Taylor suddenly died, and Fillmore became the thirteenth president. His first major issue was dealing with the sectional crisis that threatened the country. Fillmore gave his support to Henry Clay's Omnibus Bill and worked for its approval in Congress. In doing so, he made changes in the cabinet to obtain members who endorsed Clay's compromise measure. When Clay's bill was defeated, Fillmore supported Senator Stephen A. Douglas's strategy of separately introducing the components of Clay's bill. When all of these proposals passed, Fillmore mistakenly announced that the new laws represented the "final settlement" of the slavery issue.

Fillmore's first opportunity to nominate a Supreme Court justice came in late 1851, when Justice Levi Woodbury died. Fillmore was concerned about abolitionist criticism of the Court's decisions on slavery and the fugitive slave issue, and he gave considerable thought before naming Woodbury's successor. He sought a young, New England Whig for the position and found such a nominee in Benjamin Robbins Curtis of Massachusetts, who came highly recommended and "enthusiastically backed by the still enormously influential Daniel Webster" (Abraham 1999, 82). The Senate abolitionists briefly delayed the vote on Curtis's nomination, but he was easily confirmed. Curtis would serve only six years on the Court. His belief that the Taney Court had "permitted political expediency to govern in the *Dred Scott* decision" was one of the factors prompting him to resign from the Court in 1857. In Henry Abraham's view, Fillmore "could be proud of his one appointee." Justice John McKinley died in July 1852, giving Fillmore his second opportunity to nominate a justice. He attempted to fill the vacancy quickly because the upcoming presidential election of 1852 did not look promising, either for him or for the Whigs. He submitted three names but none were confirmed, and McKinley's replacement was named by Fillmore's successor, Franklin Pierce (Abraham 1999, 82–83).

Whigs were not pleased with Fillmore in 1852 and refused to renominate him, though he was the incumbent president. After Fillmore left the White House, both his wife and daughter died. Despite his grief, he remained involved in politics. The American (Know-Nothing) Party wanted Fillmore as its presidential candidate in 1856. Despite its nativist agenda, the party was dedicated to preserving the Union, stressed patriotism and national unity, and believed that Fillmore's pro-Union position might allow him to resolve the sectional crisis. Initially reluctant, he consented to the nomination. The campaign, however, did not go well, and he won only 20 percent of the popular vote. His defeat marked the end of both the Know-Nothings and his political career. He supported the Union cause throughout the Civil War, although he did not support Lincoln's reelection in 1864. Fillmore engaged in philanthropic work until his death in Buffalo on March 8, 1874.

Fourteenth Amendment

The Fourteenth Amendment, one of the three constitutional amendments added to the Constitution after the Civil War, was designed to expand the basis of federal civil rights authority and to secure Southern compliance with newly established political rights for blacks. The amendment was proposed on June 13, 1866, and took effect on July 28, 1868. The provisions of Section 1 constitute the heart of the amendment. It begins by declaring that "all persons born or naturalized in the United States, and subject to the jurisdiction thereof, are citizens of the United States and the State wherein they reside." This language reversed the citizenship holding in *Dred Scott v. Sandford* (1857). The privileges and immunities provision, which follows, was intended to combat the effects of the Black Codes and to allow federal authority to protect and advance the civil rights of black citizens. The *Slaughterhouse Cases* (1873), however, neutralized this objective by using the dual citizenship doctrine. The doctrine allowed the Court to attach civil and political rights of importance to state citizenship. Section 1 also provides that "no state shall deprive any person of life, liberty, or property without due process of law." The Due Process Clause ultimately allowed the Court to extend most Bill of Rights guarantees to the states through a process known as incorporation. The clause also enabled the Court to engage in substantive review of state policies, particularly those regulating private property rights. Section 1 concludes by saying that "no state shall deny to any person within its jurisdiction the equal protection of the laws." The function of this provision is to prohibit classification bases that might be discriminatory. Section 5 empowers Congress to "enforce by appropriate legislation, the provisions of this article." Early attempts to do so were unsuccessful because the Court held that congressional power could be used only in a remedial fashion in cases in which the state itself was responsible for or an active participant in impermissible discrimination.

The amendment brought a federal presence to the protection of civil rights, but early interpretations of the amendment, such as the Chase Court's ruling in the *Slaughterhouse Cases*, preserved a dominant role for the states on most issues.

Freedman's Bureau

Soon after the end of the Civil War, Congress passed the Freedman's Bureau Act. The law created a federal agency with authority to provide relief and protection to freed slaves. The bureau began functioning in May of 1865 and became involved in providing legal protection for freed slaves in special military courts. The bureau found itself at "odds with the civil governments" restored under Reconstruction. President Andrew Johnson was displeased with the bureau's work, seeing it as unconstitutional meddling in the affairs of the Southern states. As a result, he blocked the agency's distribution of abandoned lands to freed blacks. When local law enforcement officials continued to discriminate against blacks, bureau officials requested "stronger legislative authorization for protecting the liberty and rights of the freedmen" (Kelly, Harbison, and Belz 1991, 328). As part of its Reconstruction policy, Congress enacted a second Freedman's Bureau bill in February 1866. Introduced by Senator Lyman Trumbull of Illinois, the bill extended the life of the bureau indefinitely. More importantly, it "placed Negro civil rights in the seceded states under federal military protection." Any person in any of the formerly seceded states charged with "depriving a freedman of his civil rights was to be tried by a military tribunal or a Freedman's Bureau agent in accordance with martial law." Congress sustained Johnson's veto by a narrow margin (Kelly, Harbison, and Belz 1991, 329). The bureau was disbanded in 1872.

Free-Soil (Liberty) Party

The Free-Soil Party, the successor of the Liberty Party, was a single-issue party—the abolition of slavery. The party was founded in 1847 to oppose the extension of slavery into the territories acquired from Mexico. The congressional battle over the Wilmot Proviso facilitated the development of the party by bringing together members of the Liberty Party, the "Barnburners" (the radical agrarian faction of the New York Democrats), and antislavery Whigs. At the party's first nominating convention in Buffalo, New York, former Democratic president Martin Van Buren was chosen as the party's standard-bearer. In addition to the slavery issue, the Free-Soilers advocated a homestead law and a comprehensive program of public works. The Free-Soil Party was not competitive nationally, but it won enough votes in New York to allow the Whig Party candidate, Zachary Taylor, to win the state's electoral votes and the presidency. A number of Free-Soilers were elected to Congress in 1848, but the Compromise of 1850 diminished the need for the party, at least for many of the Barnburners, who rejoined the Democratic Party. The Free-Soilers nominated John Hale for the presidency in 1852, but before the 1856 presidential election, the Free-Soil Party was absorbed into the fledgling Republican Party.

Fugitive Slave Laws

Federal acts enacted in 1793 and 1850 that required states to return escaped slaves. Laws like these existed during the colonial period and applied to all indentured servants. As slavery was abolished in the Northern states, the 1793 law was only minimally enforced. As abolitionist sentiment grew, noncompliance was manifest in the Underground Railroad. Many Northern states passed laws prohibiting state authorities from helping to capture fugitive slaves or to house them in state jails. The Compromise of 1850 included, as a concession to the South, a more stringent fugitive slave law. Under terms of the 1850 law, all citizens were required to help federal authorities enforce the policy. The law also established substantial penalties for assisting slaves to escape. When a fugitive slave was caught, he or she was taken before a federal court or commissioner, who would order the slave returned to his or her master. The 1850 law was so severe that it fueled the abolitionist movement. The law also prompted enactment of new personal liberty laws designed to nullify the 1850 statute. The actions of Northern states to render the fugitive slave laws ineffective were used by Southern states as a justification for secession. Both the 1793 and 1850 Fugitive Slave Acts were repealed by Congress on June 28, 1864.

Grant, Ulysses S. (1822–1885)

Grant was a Union general and the eighteenth president of the United States. He was born in Point Pleasant, Ohio, on April 27, 1822. In 1839, Grant was appointed to West Point. He graduated in June 1843 and was assigned to the Fourth Infantry. His unit was assigned to General Zachary Taylor, who was assembling an army to force Mexico into accepting U.S. annexation of Texas. Grant served with distinction during the Mexican War and remained in the army until 1854. He feared that a Republican victory in 1860 threatened the Union and supported Stephen Douglas. He moved to Galena, Illinois, but reentered the military when the Civil War began. His leadership skills were evident immediately, and he was promoted to colonel of the Twenty-first Illinois Volunteer Infantry in June 1860, and to brigadier general two months later. President Abraham Lincoln elevated him to head of Union armies in 1863. Grant's offensive against General Robert E. Lee's Army of Northern Virginia ultimately concluded the war—Grant's forces surrounded Lee's troops, and the Confederate general had no choice but to surrender.

Grant was a national hero by the end of the war, and following the assassination of Lincoln, Grant became a virtual certainty for the Republican presidential nomination in 1868. Grant disapproved of Andrew Johnson's administration of Reconstruction and frequent outbreaks of violence in the South, and he supported the Reconstruction program of the Radical Republicans. He reluctantly took the position of secretary of war when Johnson removed Edwin M. Stanton in August 1867. When the Senate refused to concur in Stanton's ouster under provisions of the Tenure of Office Act, Grant relinquished the office to Stanton. Grant was easily elected president in November 1868, but his lack of governmental experience was quickly evident.

The Fifteenth Amendment banning voting discrimination was ratified during Grant's first term. It was followed by several pieces of aggressive civil rights legislation from Congress—the Civil Rights Act of 1870 and three Enforcement Laws. Grant's Justice Department used these statutes to take on the Ku Klux Klan. As in 1868, Grant received overwhelming support from black voters and was easily reelected in 1872. Grant's second term was plagued by continued violence in the South in response to the punitive Reconstruction policies. When the Democrats gained control of the House of Representatives in 1874, it was the beginning of the end of Reconstruction. Although he was tempted, Grant did not seek reelection in 1876. Grant spent the next two years traveling the world with his family. He was urged to make another presidential run in 1880 and allowed his named to be placed before the nominating convention. He eventually lost on the thirty-sixth ballot. Grant settled in New York, pursued various business ventures, and wrote critically acclaimed articles about his Civil War experiences. While writing his memoirs, he developed throat cancer. He died on July 23, 1885, barely winning his battle to complete his manuscript before his death.

Grant had four of his eight Supreme Court nominees confirmed by the Senate. Grant was not fully aware of the political implications of selecting justices and deferred to the judgment of his first attorney general, Ebenezer Rockwood Hoar. Hoar and Grant's other advisers made clear the need to "pack the Court with Republican loyalists." As a result, Grant resolved that a "safe Republican record" was an indispensable requirement for any nominee. His first nominee was Hoar himself. Henry Abraham described Hoar as "superbly qualified," but the Senate disagreed (Abraham 1999, 96). Hoar's support of civil service cut into senators' patronage appointments, and he had opposed the impeachment of Andrew Johnson. Before the Senate could vote on Hoar, Justice Robert C. Grier resigned. The Senate urged Grant to nominate Lincoln's secretary of war, Edwin M. Stanton. Grant quickly agreed in hopes he could save the Hoar nomination. Stanton was approved by a vote of 46–11 the day after he was nominated, but the Hoar nomination was rejected by a 24–33 vote. Four days after his confirmation, Stanton died.

After the Senate vote on Hoar, Grant nominated William Strong of Pennsylvania and Joseph P. Bradley of New Jersey. Strong, who Grant had preferred over Stanton, was a distinguished state jurist who had been considered by Lincoln as a replacement for Chief Justice Taney in 1864. Strong was confirmed easily over token opposition from Southerners, who felt someone from their region should have been selected. Things "did not go as smoothly for Bradley, who was certainly Grant's most highly qualified nominee." He came under "heavy fire from Eastern hard-money interests who quite correctly regarded him as dedicated to a soft-money economic philosophy" (Abraham 1999, 96). He was confirmed nonetheless by a 46–9 vote.

When Justice Samuel Nelson resigned in November of 1872, Grant named New Yorker Ward Hunt to replace him. Hunt had been elected to the New York Supreme Court as a Democrat and seemed to be "an ideal candidate." He was confirmed 53–11. The following May, Chief Justice Salmon P. Chase died. Grant, now in his second term, turned the process of his last appointment into something of a "comic opera," offering the chief justiceship to no fewer than seven individuals (Abraham 1999, 97–98). He knew two sitting justices—Miller and Bradley—were interested in being promoted, but he ruled them out. He offered the post to Senator Roscoe Conkling of New York, his close friend and political supporter, but Conkling declined. He turned to his attorney general, George H. Williams of Oregon. The nomination of Williams, who was "honest but only marginally qualified," quickly stalled out and was withdrawn at Williams's request. Grant then submitted the name of his good friend, 74-year-old Caleb Cushing. Qualified but too old in the opinion of many, he had made political enemies with his "chameleonic career—he had been a Whig, a Tyler Whig, a Democrat, a Johnson Constitutional Conservative, and was now a Republican." Grant withdrew the Cushing nomination and then offered the chief justiceship to Wisconsin Senator Timothy P. Howe, Indiana Senator Oliver P. Morton, and Secretary of State Hamilton Fish. None of these candidates were formally nominated, however. Recognizing that the "time for experimenting and game-playing" was over, he yielded to "continuing clamor from the Midwest" and settled on a noncontroversial Ohioan, Morrison Remick Waite. Possibly fearful of whom he might come up with next, the Senate confirmed Waite 63–0 two days after he was nominated, but more than eight months after Chase's death (Abraham 1999, 97–98).

Hoar, Ebenezer Rockwood (1816–1895)

Hoar was a judge and attorney general. Born in Concord, Massachusetts, on February 21, 1816, he graduated third in his class from Harvard in 1835. He read law at Harvard and was admitted to the Massachusetts Bar in 1839. Hoar began a law practice in Concord and got involved with politics during the presidential campaign of William Henry Harrison. Hoar opposed slavery and in 1845 helped organize opposition to the admission of Texas to the Union as a slave state. The following year, Hoar was elected to the Massachusetts state senate, where he voiced objections to the Mexican War. Finding neither candidate acceptable, Hoar did not vote in the 1848 presidential election. He became judge of common pleas court in 1849. He considered the federal fugitive slave laws outrageous and conducted a grand jury inquiry into the return of a runaway slave by Massachusetts authorities. Hoar found the new Republican Party and its stance on slavery appealing and gave his wholehearted support to the party's 1856 nominee, John Charles Fremont.

In 1859 Hoar withdrew from politics and became a justice on the Massachusetts Supreme Court, where he served for ten years. In March 1869, Hoar was named attorney general by President Ulysses S. Grant and provided Grant effective legal and political counsel thereafter. Hoar was particularly valuable in assisting Grant with judicial appointments. Congress increased the Supreme Court's size to nine in 1869 and created a number of new lower federal court judgeships. When Hoar himself was nominated for the Supreme Court, the Senate refused to confirm him. Hoar remained in the cabinet for several months following his failed Supreme Court nomination but returned to private law practice in late June 1870. He supported Grant's candidacy for a second term in 1872 and was elected to Congress the same year. Rather than seek a second term in the House, Hoar sought election to the Senate, but the legislature chose someone else. He unsuccessfully attempted to regain his U.S. House seat in 1876, resumed his law practice, and engaged in other activities, such as serving as president of the Boston Bar Association. Hoar died in Boston on January 31, 1895.

Homestead Act

A federal statute passed in May 1862. It provided that any person who was the head of a family, and either a citizen or an alien who intended to become a citizen, could obtain title to public land if the recipient lived on the land for at least five years. The sponsors of this legislation wanted these lands settled, but they also wanted to increase the value of the land. In the sponsors' view, those who turned unoccupied land into productive farms earned title to the property. The Republican Party pledged to support homestead legislation in its 1860 platform, a pledge that aided party candidates, particularly in the Midwest. When Southern states seceded from the Union in 1861, enactment of homestead legislation was virtually guaranteed. The Homestead Act attracted thousands of settlers and by 1900 had provided farmland to half a million families. The homestead program was not altogether successful, however. Congress granted much of the best public land to the railroad or to the states for use as land-grant colleges. In addition, many who tried to develop homesteads found farming conditions unsuitable. In the early 1870s, Congress modified the original act to make larger tracts of land available, but the changes mostly benefited land speculators and those wanting access to the natural resources of the West. In the end, less than 20 percent of the land made available under the Homestead Act and its amendments was actually settled by homesteaders. After 1900, most of the homesteading under the program occurred in Alaska. The homestead program was formally terminated by Congress in 1986.

Jackson, Andrew (1767–1845)

Jackson was a military hero and the seventh president of the United States. He was born in South Carolina on March 15, 1767. When the War of Independence began, Jackson quit school and joined the army. In 1784 Jackson moved to Salisbury, North Carolina, to study law and was admitted to the North Carolina Bar three years later. He moved to Nashville, Tennessee, and served as public prosecutor for seven years. He married the daughter of one of Tennessee's leading families and was well suited to enter the political arena. He was elected to the U.S. House when Tennessee was admitted to the Union in 1796 and was elected to the U.S. Senate the following year. His record in Congress was undistinguished, and he resigned the Senate to serve on the Tennessee Supreme Court. Jackson was elected to the position of major general in the Tennessee militia in 1802.

When the War of 1812 began, Jackson and his militia defeated the Creek Indians. As a result of his military success, Jackson was commissioned as a major general in the U.S. Army. After the engagement with the Creeks, Jackson's forces won a decisive victory over the British, and Jackson rose to national prominence. His victory over the Seminole Indians in Spanish Florida led to the purchase of Florida from Spain. Jackson was named governor of the new territory when the acquisition treaty was ratified. His tenure was a success, but he left the governorship in late 1821 and returned to Tennessee. Despite his political inexperience, he was considered by many to be a viable presidential prospect. Elected to the Senate in 1823, Jackson was a candidate in a four-way contest for the presidency in 1824. Jackson won a plurality of the popular vote but less than a majority of electoral votes. The election was resolved by the House when Henry Clay threw his support to John Quincy Adams. Jackson resigned his Senate seat and returned to Tennessee to regroup for another presidential bid in 1828. Together with Martin Van Buren and John C. Calhoun, he restablished the Democratic Party. As its standard-bearer, Jackson won the presidency in 1828 and again in 1832. During Jackson's presidency, the country underwent significant social and political change. The franchise was extended, and the "common man" gained greater access to public office. The period became known as the age of Jacksonian Democracy.

When Jackson took office, he opened government employment to all males. He believed that government positions were not the exclusive domain of the upper class and that governmental institutions would function more democratically if greater numbers of citizens served in them. Among other items, his agenda consisted of bringing an end to the Second National Bank and paying off the national debt. Jackson was an assertive president who did not back away from conflicts with Congress; indeed, he used the veto more often than his six predecessors combined. He also consolidated control of the Democratic Party. Jackson was an unwavering nationalist, and although John C. Calhoun had been a political ally earlier, Jackson categorically rejected Calhoun's theory of nullification and secession. Jackson's campaign for reelection in 1832 revolved around his veto of the bill to extend the Second National Bank of the United States. In 1832 Jackson easily defeated Henry Clay, sponsor the national bank extension. When Jackson's designated successor, Martin Van Buren, was elected in 1836, Jackson retired to his Tennessee home, the Hermitage. From Tennessee, Jackson continued to influence national politics until his death on June 8, 1845.

Jackson placed six justices on the Court. One was Roger Brooke Taney, who served as chief justice from 1835 to 1864. Taney was replaced by Salmon P. Chase. Two of the remaining five Jackson appointees, James Wayne and John Catron, sat on the Court long enough to serve with Chase. Jackson's criteria for Supreme Court candidacy differed some from those of his predecessors. He considered geography and public service, but valued political loyalty above all. Five years passed between Jackson's first two nominations, John McLean and Henry Baldwin, and his last four—Wayne, Taney, Philip Barbour, and Catron. The last four nominees reflected "even more of a commitment to party principles than did his first two selections." All four of the later nominees "evinced a close adherence to the Jacksonian creed and had rendered many services to Jackson." Wayne was a former judge of the Supreme Court of Georgia and a Southern Unionist. By selecting Wayne, Jackson kept the judicial circuit's "representation" intact and "placated the Whigs, who feared designation of an avowed states' righter from the South" (Abraham 1999, 74). The last nominee was Catron, who was nominated on Jackson's last day in office. Catron was a fellow Tennessean who did not receive Senate approval until after Jackson had left the White House. Jackson's successor, Martin Van Buren, let Jackson's selection stand even though he could have offered another name. The Court slot for which Catron was nominated came to Jackson as a result of a last-minute congressional action that raised the number of associate justices from six to eight. The two additional positions were "earmarked" for two newly created circuits in the West and Southwest. Catron, Jackson's choice for the Western circuit, won Senate approval readily. Catron was a longtime personal and political friend of Jackson, a "respected member of Nashville's ruling elite," and a strong ally in the struggle against the forces of nullification (Abraham 1999, 76–77).

Jefferson, Thomas (1743–1826)

Jefferson was a philosopher, author of the Declaration of Independence, and the third president of the United States. Jefferson was born on April 13, 1743, in Shadwell, Virginia. His father died when Jefferson was fourteen and left him a large estate with slaves. Jefferson studied at the College of William and Mary, read law, and was admitted to the bar in 1767. Jefferson's successful law practice was interrupted by the independence movement, and he never returned to his legal career, turning instead to politics. He was elected to the Virginia House of Burgesses in 1769, where he served seven years. In June 1775 Jefferson took a seat in the Second Continental Congress at Philadelphia. A year later, Jefferson served on a five-man committee to draft a declaration of independence. He returned to Virginia and its House of Delegates in the fall of 1776.

Jefferson was a slaveholder, but favored at least to some extent gradual emancipation. Partly through his efforts, Virginia was the first state to stop slave trading. On June 1, 1779, Jefferson was elected governor of Virginia, followed by a brief tenure in Congress. While in Congress, he authored the ordinance that served as the blueprint for organizing territories west of the original thirteen states. He led a commission charged with negotiating commercial agreements with European states and several months later replaced Benjamin Franklin as minister to France. While in France, Jefferson openly supported the French Revolution. He returned to the United States in late 1789 fully expecting to return to Paris. Instead, he was asked by President George Washington to become the secretary of state. He ran for the presidency in 1796 but lost to John Adams. Under the constitutional arrangement in place at the time, he became Adams's vice president. He viewed enactment of the Alien and Sedition Laws in 1798 as a Federalist attempt to repress his Republican Party. Jefferson urged the states to oppose these enactments and drafted the Kentucky Resolutions of 1798, which advocated the remedy of nullification. In 1800 Jefferson defeated Adams for the presidency.

Conflict with the Federalist judiciary was a major dimension of Jefferson's first term. The opening battle was fought over the Judiciary Act of 1801. This law, enacted as the Federalists were losing control of the White House and Congress, created a new federal court and many new judgeships. It was a transparent Federalist attempt to load as many partisans into the courts as possible to hold the Jeffersonians in check until the party could reestablish itself with the electorate. The Jeffersonians countered with the Repeal Act of 1802, which effectively rescinded the Judiciary Act. Jefferson put three justices on the Supreme Court—William Johnson, Thomas Todd, and Brockholst Livingston—but was unable to change the direction of the Court under John Marshall. Jefferson's major accomplishment in his first term was the Louisiana Purchase from France, which propelled him to easy reelection in 1804. After Jefferson left the presidency, he became increasingly concerned about the country's future and the possibility of it dividing along sectional lines. Until his death on July 4, 1826, he continued to argue the virtues of states' rights politics.

Johnson, Andrew (1808–1875)

Johnson was the seventeenth president of the United States. He was born in Raleigh, North Carolina, on December 29, 1808. After apprenticing as a tailor, Johnson moved to Greenville, Tennessee, where he established a successful business. He used his public speaking skills to win election as alderman in 1829. He served in village government for eight years, including two years as mayor before his election to the Tennessee legislature in 1835. He lost his seat in 1837 but regained it in 1839. By then, Johnson had become a Jacksonian Democrat and gained election to the state senate in 1841. Two years later, Johnson was elected to the U.S. House, where he remained for ten years. His advocacy of homestead legislation separated him from the more conservative members of the Democratic Party, including President James K. Polk. His policy priorities also alienated him from Southerners such as Jefferson Davis.

Johnson was an unwavering defender of slavery, but he was not trusted by many Southern leaders. Johnson's populism kept him at odds with many Democrats and Whigs, which eventually cost him his seat in Congress. Although he was opposed by some in his own party, Johnson was elected governor in 1853 and was reelected two years later. In 1857 Johnson was sent to the U.S. Senate, where he secured passage of homestead legislation. The Democratic Party was badly split in 1860. Johnson supported the proslavery faction's ticket, headed by John C. Breckenridge. Although he defended slavery, Johnson was also a Unionist. After the election of Abraham Lincoln, he had to flee to the North because he believed secession was treasonous. Johnson was the only member of the Senate from a seceding state who remained loyal to the Union. When Nashville fell to Union troops in early March 1862, Lincoln appointed Johnson military governor of Tennessee. A little more than a year later, he had changed his views about slavery, which estranged him from many Southern Unionists.

Lincoln chose Johnson as his running mate in 1864 in an effort to win the votes of so-called War Democrats. He was elected vice president in November 1864 and succeeded Lincoln as president on April 15, 1865, following Lincoln's assassination. Johnson tried to maintain continuity by keeping Lincoln's cabinet. He encountered difficulty, however, on the issue of Reconstruction. He believed that the Confederate states were still members of the Union. As a result, he favored a relatively lenient approach to Reconstruction. He offered amnesty to all former insurgents willing to pledge loyalty to the Union and proposed restoring seceded states upon ratification of the Thirteenth Amendment and the repeal of secession ordinances. Johnson refused to require extending suffrage to freedmen. There was a resurgence of conservative dominance in the South. The restored states enacted Black Codes that came close to reestablishing prewar conditions. Johnson's plan for restoring seceded states was insufficient for the Radical Republicans in Congress. The Radicals set up a Joint Committee of Reconstruction in response. Johnson then vetoed the Freedman's Bureau Bill and the Civil Rights Act, which deepened the split. Congress upheld the Freedman's Bureau veto, but the veto of the Civil Rights Act was overridden. Johnson did not agree with the content of the Fourteenth Amendment, but because it was passed as a resolution for a constitutional amendment, he could not veto. Instead, he worked to prevent ratification of the amendment by the states.

The midterm election of 1866 was essentially a test of Johnson's popular support, and he failed the test. The election strengthened the Radical Republicans, which, in turn, led to restrictions on Johnson's powers and more stringent Reconstruction measures. The following March, the Republicans enacted the Tenure of Office Act, requiring Senate approval any time a presidential appointee was dismissed. They also passed a Reconstruction measure imposing military rule on Southern states and requiring black suffrage and ratification of the Fourteenth Amendment as conditions for readmission. Johnson's vetoes of these initiatives were all overridden. A movement to impeach Johnson followed. Johnson dismissed his secretary of war, Edwin M. Stanton, for collaborating with the Radical Republicans and named Ulysses S. Grant interim secretary without seeking Senate approval of his dismissal of Stanton. An initial impeachment resolution was defeated, but when Johnson refused a Senate order to reinstate Stanton, the House approved eleven articles of impeachment for violation of the Tenure of Office Act and his failure to enforce the Reconstruction Acts.

The impeachment trial had Thaddeus Stevens, Benjamin F. Butler, and John A. Bingham acting as managers, while Johnson's defense team consisted of former justice Benjamin R. Curtis, future secretary of state, William M. Evarts, and Henry Stanbery, the former attorney general. Johnson was acquitted of all impeachment articles, but by only a single vote. The impeachment effort failed not only because the case against Johnson was weak, but also because his would-be successor, Senate president pro tem Benjamin F. Wade, was highly unpopular. Although Johnson survived the impeachment trial, he had little power for the remainder of his term. The Democrats chose not to renominate him in 1868. As he left office, Johnson pardoned the surviving members of the Lincoln assassination conspiracy, including Dr. Samuel A. Mudd. Anxious to vindicate himself, Johnson unsuccessfully attempted to win Tennessee's Senate seat in 1870 and its House seat in 1872. In 1875, he returned to the Senate, but died shortly thereafter.

Kansas-Nebraska Act of 1854

The collapse of the Compromise of 1850, which had produced a temporary truce in the conflict over slavery in the territories, began in 1853 with the Gadsden Purchase. The purchase enabled the United States to acquire some 30,000 square miles from Mexico to enable the building of a Southern transcontinental railroad. Slavery in Kansas and Nebraska was controversial in itself, but it was part of a larger sectional controversy about the extension of slavery into the territories. Before 1854, several attempts had been made to organize Kansas into a single territory west of Missouri. These attempts were defeated by proslavery forces in Congress because under the terms of the Missouri Compromise of 1820, Kansas would be a free territory. Illinois Senator Stephen A. Douglas, chair of the Senate Committee on Territories, wanted Chicago to be the eastern end of the transcontinental railroad. He proposed two new territories—Kansas and Nebraska. To win Southern support for the proposal, he included the concept of popular sovereignty, which would allow residents of the territories to determine for themselves whether to permit slavery or not. Southerners protested that "since the Missouri Compromise prevented them from bringing slaves into the [new territory], the territorial legislatures would organize and vote on slavery before slaveholders had a chance to establish themselves." Douglas then added an amendment repealing the slavery provisions of the Missouri Compromise. With the aid of President Franklin Pierce, Douglas pushed the measure through Congress behind nearly unanimous Southern support (Urofsky and Finkelman 2002, 384–385). Passage of the Kansas-Nebraska Act reignited the sectional controversy that had been temporarily quieted by the Compromise of 1850 and led opponents of the Kansas-Nebraska Act to form the Republican Party.

Ku Klux Klan (Third Enforcement) Act of 1871

The Ku Klux Klan Act of April 20, 1871, known as the Third Enforcement Act, was designed to stop private violence against blacks after the Civil War. This act prohibited conspiracies to "deprive persons of their civil rights." In *United States v. Harris* (1883), the Waite Court significantly weakened the act when it held that state action, and not action of private individuals, came within the reach of the Fourteenth Amendment. Blacks had to endure inhumane treatment because of the Waite Court's conclusion that the Ku Klux Klan Act was invalid on the ground that protection of blacks from private conspiracies was a function of state government and not the federal government (Davis and Graham 1995, 19).

Adopted in response to President Grant's request for action to stem Southern violence directed at blacks, the statute represented the most far-reaching assertion of federal legislative power to enforce civil rights in the Reconstruction era. As initially drafted, the bill proposed to punish violations of civil rights resulting from specific crimes of murder, assault, arson, etc., as carried out by individuals. Moderate and conservative Republicans thought the bill extended federal power too far into local affairs, and they modified it to "punish only the general crime of denying equal protection of the law and privileges and immunities of citizens." References to specific crimes were dropped. The act was directed at individuals on the theory that "failure of the states to punish private violence against blacks was a form of state action justifying congressional legislation" (Kelly, Harbison, and Belz 1991, 348).

Lee, Robert E. (1807–1870)

Lee was a Confederate military leader born in Westmoreland County, Virginia, on January 19, 1807. Three years later, the family moved to Alexandria, Virginia. He finished his secondary education in 1823 and then went to West Point, where he graduated second in his class in 1829. He served in the Corps of Engineers and was assigned to a number of projects before taking a more lengthy assignment in St. Louis. Despite an excellent record with the corps, Lee knew that he could truly distinguish himself on the battlefield. His opportunity for combat came in the Mexican War. After the war, Lee was named superintendent of West Point, a post he held until March 31, 1855. While at West Point, Secretary of War Jefferson Davis wanted to upgrade the force in the territory acquired from Mexico and dispatched the new Second Cavalry, with Lee serving as a lieutenant colonel. After returning to Virginia, Lee was sent to Harper's Ferry to put down the John Brown rebellion. He was commissioned full colonel and commander of the First Cavalry soon after the first Southern states had seceded. At that point, his Southern loyalty prevailed. He opposed secession as well as slavery, but he could not go to war against his native Virginia. He resigned from the U.S. Army and accepted command of the Virginia military the next day. In addition to his command responsibilities, he became the chief military adviser to the Confederate president, Jefferson Davis. Lee's record during the war was mixed. His forces suffered defeats and heavy casualties at the outset of the war, but his defense of Richmond revitalized his reputation. Eventually, Lee's troops were surrounded at Appomattox Courthouse in Virginia and surrendered to General Ulysses S. Grant of the Union Army. Under surrender terms, Lee and most of his men became prisoners of war but were paroled soon thereafter. After the war, Lee served as president of Washington College until his death on October 12, 1870.

Lincoln, Abraham (1809–1865)

Lincoln was the sixteenth president of the United States. He was born in Hardin County, Kentucky, on February 12, 1809. In 1816, Lincoln's family moved to Indiana. In 1830, Lincoln's father sold the Indiana farm and the family moved to central Illinois. After working on the farm and hiring out as a rail-splitter, Lincoln settled in New Salem, Illinois. During his six years there, he developed a passion for politics and announced his candidacy for the state legislature. Although he lost in 1832, he won decisively in 1834. Lincoln was a Whig at the time and an admirer of Henry Clay. John T. Stuart, a Springfield lawyer and Whig leader, pushed Lincoln to study law and prepared him for the state bar examination. Once Lincoln passed the bar, he moved to Springfield and became Stuart's partner. Lincoln won three more terms in the legislature and became Whig floor leader.

Lincoln left the legislature after his fourth term and returned to his law practice, but even a successful practice was unfulfilling. His wish to run for Congress was frustrated by the large number of Whigs also wishing to run for the safe seat. Lincoln's turn to run came in 1846, and he won easily. He served only one term, during which Congress was occupied with the Mexican War. Lincoln supported the Wilmot Proviso, which prohibited slavery in all territory acquired from Mexico. Lincoln's war stance proved a problem when he campaigned for Zachary Taylor, the Whig presidential nominee, in 1848. He resumed his law practice somewhat disillusioned with politics.

The controversial Kansas-Nebraska Act, pushed through Congress by Senator Stephen A. Douglas of Illinois, prompted Lincoln's return to the political arean. The act revoked the prohibition against slavery in the Northern portion of the Louisiana Territory, greatly exacerbating the division between free and slave states and pushing Lincoln into taking a public stand against slavery. Lincoln returned to the state legislature. When that body considered the election of a U.S. senator, Lincoln resigned to become the Whig candidate. To prevent the election of a proslavery candidate, Lincoln then threw his support to Lyman Trumbull, who was elected on the tenth ballot. Two years later, Lincoln helped found the Republican Party in Illinois. He received some support for vice president at the nominating convention but was not selected for the national ticket. When Douglas came up for reelection in 1858, the Republicans chose Lincoln to oppose him. Lincoln and Douglas met in seven three-hour debates held throughout the state. Douglas charged that Lincoln's position was too extreme and would inevitably lead to the secession of slave states. The Democrats won a majority of seats in the state legislature and reelected Douglas; but Lincoln's prospects for a national candidacy were greatly enhanced by his performance in the debates and his speaking tour in the East. Lincoln's supporters in Illinois initially advanced a "favorite son" candidacy on his behalf for president, but at the Republican nominating convention he became a bona fide contender for the party's presidential nomination. The leading competitor for the nomination was New York Senator William H. Seward. The convention delegates were convinced that Lincoln offered the better chance of winning the election, and he was nominated. The four-candidate race that followed reflected the deep sectional divisions in the country. Lincoln won every free state, which gave him a majority of electoral votes even though he won less than 40 percent of the national popular vote. He had virtually no support in the slave states, seven of which seceded before Lincoln took office.

Lincoln assured both Unionists and Southern moderates that he would mount a direct attack on slavery, but only to prohibit slavery in territories. Secession by the slave states began notwithstanding Lincoln's assurances, and the firing on Fort Sumter commenced the Civil War shortly thereafter, on April 12, 1861. A week later Lincoln ordered a naval blockade of Confederate ports, and the war escalated. Lincoln may have been willing at one time to accept less than the total abolition of slavery, but once the war began, Lincoln would accept nothing short of total surrender of the Confederacy. Lincoln fully exercised his authority as commander in chief and actively managed the war. Initially, the Union was unsuccessful on the battlefield. In March 1864, Lincoln promoted Ulysses S. Grant to general in chief of all Union armies, and from that point on, Union prospects for victory improved greatly. Confederate forces surrendered to Grant at Appomattox Courthouse, Virginia, on April 9, 1865.

Internal security was a problem inseparable from the prosecution of the war. Those with allegiance to the Confederacy resided in the North as well as the South. Confederate sympathizers in the North, who were known as "Copperheads," posed serious danger to the Union war effort, in Lincoln's view. Soon after the war began, Lincoln gradually suspended the writ of habeas corpus until the suspension was nationwide. At least 15,000 civilians were arrested and detained, mostly in border states. Military courts also tried civilians, on Lincoln's orders. The Chase Court struck down these actions in *Ex parte Milligan* (1866), but only after the war had been concluded. Further, Lincoln took decisive steps regarding slavery. The president had decided by 1862 to free the slaves, but he did not want to issue an emancipation decree prematurely. Instead, he waited until January 1, 1863, to issue his Emancipation Proclamation. Once the Proclamation was delivered, the war to preserve the Union formally became a war of liberation as well.

When it became evident that the Confederacy would be defeated, Lincoln faced the issue of reconstructing the Union. He saw the Reconstruction process as executive in nature, a logical extension of his commander in chief authority. In December of 1863, Lincoln issued a Proclamation of Amnesty and Reconstruction, which offered pardons to Confederates willing to take an oath of allegiance to the United States. Lincoln agreed to recognize governments in any former Confederate state where 10 percent of those voting in the 1860 presidential election took the oath of allegiance. Congress, however, had its own ideas about Reconstruction. Congressional leaders saw Reconstruction as a legislative rather than an executive matter and presented Lincoln with a much more punitive plan—the Wade-Davis Reconstruction bill. Lincoln pocket vetoed Wade-Davis, but the conflict persisted through the election in November 1864. Lincoln used his second inaugural address to extend an olive branch to congressional Republicans. Lincoln and Congress did not reach any resolution on Reconstruction, however, because on April 14, Lincoln was shot by John Wilkes Booth, and he died the next day.

Lincoln had five chances to appoint Supreme Court justices, three of which came within two months of his inauguration. One vacancy, caused by the death of Peter V. Daniel, carried over from the Buchanan administration, and the other two were created by the death of Justice John McLean and the resignation of Justice John A. Campbell. The war dominated all aspects of Lincoln's presidency, thus the "effect a proposed Court member might have on the conduct of the war was of paramount importance to him." Although all other considerations were secondary, he "regarded as desirable geographic suitability, political loyalty, and payment of political debt," and he assigned "lesser importance to judicial background" (Abraham 1999, 87).

Noah H. Swayne was Lincoln's first nominee and filled the vacancy created by McLean's death. Swayne's "anti-slavery convictions, his loyalty to the Union, and his solidly conservative Republicanism rendered him eminently acceptable on political grounds." His Southern heritage was "certain to count in his favor in the border states." In addition, Swayne was an ideal candidate because of "ties with the financial and business community," whose support was "crucial to the Northern war effort" (Abraham 1999, 86–88). Lincoln's second appointment was "intimately linked with the politics of judicial redistricting then alive on Capitol Hill." As new states were admitted into the Union, the existing judicial circuits had become "increasingly large and unwieldy." As more territories became part of the United States, Congress readjusted circuit boundaries. The boundaries determined who was a viable candidate for the Daniel seat. Lincoln turned to Samuel Freeman Miller of Iowa, the leading attorney west of the Mississippi River. Miller had left the South because of his "opposition to slavery, and he was a loyal Republican with impeccable political and professional credentials." He was also from the "right geographic region" (Abraham 1999, 88). With the new circuit covered and the Southern circuits "contracted," Lincoln could fill Campbell's seat free of geographical considerations. Lincoln selected someone from his own state by choosing David Davis. Lincoln and Davis had been close personal and political friends for many years. Davis was instrumental in Lincoln's U.S. Senate campaign in 1858 and in securing the presidential nomination for Lincoln in 1860. Davis was "politically wise and shrewd, a loyal Republican, and a philosophical Lincolnian—anti-slavery and pro-Union to the core" (Abraham 1999, 89).

Congress created a Tenth Circuit consisting of California and Oregon in March 1863. The increase in the number of justices from nine to ten "suited Lincoln's purposes admirably—his fourth appointee would bring at least some security to the prospects of a favorable judicial stance in the enormously significant Civil War litigation now on the Court's docket." It was expected that Lincoln would select someone from the new circuit who was "familiar with its needs and problems, but also someone who could be counted on strongly and vocally to back the cause of the Union." Lincoln found just such a man in the Democrat Stephen J. Field, "easily the most distinguished jurist in the Pacific states." Field was a Buchanan Democrat in 1860, but Lincoln correctly read Field's "real politics to be akin to his own" (Abraham 1999, 90). On October 12, 1864, Chief Justice Roger Taney died. The leading contender from the outset was Salmon Portland Chase of Ohio. Although Lincoln "neither trusted nor liked Chase," Lincoln understood that Chase had "superior strength, leadership and ability to unify disparate groups within the party," and was unquestionably "dedicat[ed] to the Union cause." After delaying the nomination for two months, Lincoln "concluded that in the interest of national unity and security the nod would have to go to Chase" (Abraham 1999, 91).

Marshall, John (1755–1835)

John Marshall was the first long-term chief justice and probably had a greater impact in shaping the Constitution than any other member of the Supreme Court. Marshall was born in Germantown, Virginia, on September 24, 1755. He was tutored by two local clergymen and his father, but his education was interrupted by the Revolutionary War. He left the service in 1781 and developed a successful practice in Virginia. In 1782, Marshall was elected to the first of two consecutive terms in the Virginia House of Delegates. After service on a state court, Marshall returned to the House of Delegates, where he was instrumental in the ratification of the Virginia Constitution. Marshall had several opportunities to join the administration of President George Washington, but he declined. In 1799, Marshall won a term to the U.S. House and joined the Adams administration the following year as secretary of state. In late 1800, Chief Justice Oliver Ellsworth resigned. Adams sought out John Jay, who had served a brief time as chief justice in the early 1790s, but Jay chose not to serve. Others were suggested to Adams, but he nominated Marshall. The Senate confirmed Marshall a week later, and he began a tenure that lasted more than 34 years. Over that period, Marshall authored several hundred opinions for the Court, many of which dealt with fundamental issues of national powers, contracts, and federalism. Marshall died in 1835 and was replaced by Roger B. Taney.

There were several dominant themes in Marshall's jurisprudence. First, he had a deep appreciation for separation of powers and had a clear sense how judicial power fit into that balance. He sought to elevate the Court's role in this respect, most notably through his opinion in *Marbury v. Madison* (1803), in which the Court first invoked the principle of judicial review. Second, he fully subscribed to the notion of federal legislative and judicial supremacy, a theme that ran through most of his landmark opinions. Before getting to the supremacy issue in *McCulloch v. Maryland* (1819), for example, Marshall first considered whether Congress had authority to establish a national bank. He ruled that Congress possessed powers implied from those enumerated. When coupled with the "necessary and proper" clause, Congress possessed the choice of any and all means so long as the end was legitimate. In addition, he advocated broad and adaptive interpretations of these powers when reviewing challenges to their exercise. Although federal and state authority are each supreme within their separate spheres, the federal government must prevail where there are conflicts. This supremacy concept was also extended to judicial power. In order to provide compatibility and uniformity of interpretation of federal law, Marshall asserted that the Supreme Court must be able to review state court decisions. Third, Marshall established a broad federal power attaching to interstate commercial activities. In *Gibbons v. Ogden* (1824), Marshall nullified a state steamboat monopoly and essentially freed interstate commerce from state actions that might create impediments to the free flow of commerce. In addition, he defined commerce as encompassing virtually all commercial activity, creating a broad affirmative power at the federal level. Finally, as an economic conservative, Marshall was interested in the government providing protection for private property. Marshall fully utilized the contract clause to this end. The clause prohibits states from impairment of contract obligations, and Marshall effectively used it to thwart state initiatives that asserted regulatory authority over property.

Milligan, Lambdin (1812–1899)

Milligan was an attorney and defendant in the landmark Chase Court ruling *Ex parte Milligan* (1866). He was born in Belmont County, Ohio, on March 24, 1812. He left home in his late teens and worked as a farmhand and schoolteacher for several years before choosing law over medicine as a career. In 1835, Milligan passed the bar exam and began a successful practice. He became involved with the local Democratic Party and was an outspoken states' rights Jeffersonian. Opposed to the Civil War from the outset, he led the antiwar faction in Indiana and chaired the local party convention committee that drafted resolutions viciously critical of the Lincoln administration. In May 1863, Milligan represented state Senator Alexander Davis, who was arrested for antiwar utterances and tried before a military commission in Ohio. Milligan unsuccessfully argued that the military court had no jurisdiction over a civilian. Milligan was suggested as a possible Democratic nominee for governor of Indiana in 1864 but fell short of getting the nomination. In October 1864, Milligan was arrested and charged with conspiracy against the government of the United States. He was tried and convicted, along with three others, by a military commission. A death sentence was then imposed. His counsel filed a writ of habeas corpus in a federal court, and his execution was stayed. In 1866 the Chase Court ruled in *Ex parte Milligan* that a military commission could not try a civilian defendant if the civilian courts were operating, and Milligan's conviction was set aside. He was released after eighteen months of imprisonment and resumed his law practice in Huntington, Indiana. He retired from practice at the age of 85 and died on December 21, 1899.

Missouri Compromise of 1820

A measure passed by Congress to end the first of a series of crises concerning the extension of slavery to the territories. By 1818, the Missouri Territory had sufficient population to qualify for statehood. Most of those residing in the territory had migrated from the South, and once it was admitted to the Union, most thought Missouri would be a slave state. An amendment was added to the statehood legislation providing for a ban on the importation of slaves into the territory and calling for the eventual emancipation of slaves born in Missouri. After lengthy and bitter debate, the amendment cleared the House, but was defeated in the Senate. Early in 1820, legislation to admit Maine to the Union was adopted by the House. At the time, the number of free states equaled the number of slave states. It was decided that this equilibrium would be maintained by dealing with statehood for Maine and Missouri simultaneously, admitting one as a free state and the other as a slave state. More importantly, there was language that took up the issue of slavery for the entirety of the territory coming from the Louisiana Purchase. Slavery would be forbidden throughout the Louisiana Purchase territory north of a line at 36 degrees 30 minutes. The antislavery position was that Congress had authority to govern the territories as it wished and to establish restrictions as it saw fit. In their view, any restrictions would continue after statehood was achieved. Southerners, on the other hand, argued that Congress could prohibit slavery in a territory, but such a restriction would end at statehood. This resolution of the issue of slavery in the territories as contained in the Missouri Compromise remained in effect until rescinded by the Kansas-Nebraska Act of 1854. The Taney Court ruled in *Dred Scott v. Sandford* (1857), however, that Congress could not restrict slavery in the territories.

Morrill Land Grant Act

A land-grant college is an agricultural and mechanical college or university established by the Morrill Act of 1862. Republican Representative Justin S. Morrill of Vermont had long advocated the idea of distributing federal lands to the states for the benefit of higher education. A land-grant proposal was adopted by Congress in the late 1850s but was vetoed by President James Buchanan. On December 16, 1861, Morrill once again introduced a proposal to grant public lands to states to establish colleges for the benefit of agriculture and the mechanical arts. The act provided for the granting of public land—more than 10 million acres nationally—by the federal government to the states to be used for teaching agriculture, engineering, and home economics at the college level. The Morrill Act did not preclude the teaching of other subjects at land-grant institutions but assigned priority status to agricultural and mechanical programming. Many of the largest public universities and agricultural colleges in the United States came about as a result of the land-grant program.

Pierce, Franklin (1804–1869)

Pierce was the fourteenth president of the United States. He was born in Hillsborough, New Hampshire, on November 23, 1804. After graduating from Bowdoin College in

1824, Pierce read law and was admitted to the bar in 1827. Two years later, he was elected as a Democrat to the New Hampshire General Court, where he served two years as speaker. He was elected to the U.S. House in 1833 and served two terms before his elevation to the Senate in 1836. Pierce resigned from the Senate in 1842 and returned to New Hampshire to practice law. Pierce volunteered for service in the Mexican War and eventually advanced to the rank of brigadier general. He returned to New Hampshire after the war and resumed both his legal career and his involvement with the Democratic Party. He supported the Compromise of 1850, including its controversial Fugitive Slave Law. Pierce was not actively seeking the national political stage, but when the 1852 Democratic convention deadlocked, Pierce was nominated on the forty-eighth ballot. In the general election, Pierce ran against the Whig nominee, General Winfield Scott, and the Free-Soil Party nominee, John Hale. An acrimonious campaign ended with Pierce as the winner. Pierce attempted to reduce the rampant political divisions of the period by selecting cabinet members from all sections of the country, but he refused to include anyone from Stephen Douglas's faction of the Democratic Party. Despite being a Northerner, Pierce's presidential performance resembled that of a proslavery Southerner—one of his closest advisers was Jefferson Davis, who would later become president of the Confederacy.

The two most significant events during Pierce's single term as president were the Gadsden Purchase and the Kansas-Nebraska Act. The Gadsden Treaty enabled the United States to acquire land from Mexico that would become the Southern portions of New Mexico and Arizona. The purchase provided the land connection to California for a Southern railroad route. The Kansas-Nebraska Act of 1854 was far more controversial and damaging to both Pierce and the Democrats. The act nullified the provisions of the Missouri Compromise and greatly exacerbated sectional differences over slavery. It also led to the defeat of the Democrats in the midterm elections as well as the formation of the Republican Party. By 1856, Pierce had lost virtually all of his political support, and his own party denied him renomination for president. Pierce considered Lincoln's election in 1860 a repudiation of his presidency, and he was openly critical of Lincoln's performance, particularly of the Emancipation Proclamation. Pierce's last years were spent in New Hampshire, and he died in Concord on October 8, 1869.

Pierce had only one opportunity to nominate someone for the Supreme Court, and he chose John Archibald Campbell. The forty-one-year-old Alabaman was "respected nationwide" as an expert in both civil and common law. A strong advocate of states' rights, Campbell nonetheless "opposed secession and favored improving the lot of slaves." Campbell served on the Court but in 1861, despite his opposition to both the war and secession, felt "duty bound" to resign and join the Confederate cause (Abraham 1999, 84).

Polk, James Knox (1795–1849)

James Polk was the eleventh president of the United States. He was born in Mecklenburg County, North Carolina, on November 2, 1795. He graduated first in his class from the University of North Carolina and studied law in Nashville, Tennessee, under Felix Grundy, a locally prominent lawyer and political figure. With Grundy's support, Polk was elected clerk of the state senate. Polk began a law practice in 1920 but continued his political career, serving in the state legislature from 1823 to 1825. Supporters of Andrew Jackson propelled Polk to the U.S. House of Representatives in 1825, where he opposed the nationalistic policies of President John Quincy Adams. Polk was reelected to the House in 1827 and supported the Andrew Jackson administration in opposing the so-called American System advocated by Henry Clay. Polk supported the Force Bill, which was designed to counteract South Carolina's nullification statute. He became Speaker of the House in 1835 and had to use all of his parliamentary skills to preside over a bitterly divided Congress. When the Whigs threatened to wrest control from the Jacksonians in Tennessee, Polk left the House and was elected governor in both 1837 and 1839. He had hoped to gain the Democratic vice presidential nomination in 1840 but did not. He failed to win reelection as governor in 1841 and lost again in 1843.

The leading Democratic presidential candidate in 1844 was Martin Van Buren, who succeeded Jackson as president but was defeated in 1840. Van Buren was expected to square off with Henry Clay in the general election. The pivotal issue was the annexation of the Texas Republic. The underlying question was how annexation of Texas, where slavery was permitted, would affect geographic balance on slavery. When the Democrats met at their convention, Van Buren was unable to gather sufficient delegate support for the nomination, and Polk emerged as the compromise nominee on the ninth ballot. Polk won less than half of the popular vote but was able to secure a majority of electoral votes. Since he was not a national figure, he endeavored to build a political base. He committed himself to four goals: acquire California, resolve the Oregon boundary dispute, settle the question of Texas, and reduce tariffs. He succeeded in acquiring California, but in doing so he compounded the national problem of slavery in the territories. To make matters worse, when Polk sought to purchase territory from Mexico, Representative David Wilmot introduced a highly polarizing provision that slavery should never exist in any territory acquired from Mexico. The measure, known as the Wilmot Proviso, was not adopted in the Senate and further splintered the Democratic Party. Polk also was responsible for actions that directly led to the war with Mexico. Despite the fact the United States prevailed in Mexico, it was an unpopular conflict, known by many as "Polk's war." The hero of the Mexican War, General Zachary Taylor, became the Whig presidential candidate and defeated Polk in

1848, who returned to Nashville after leaving the White House. He died two months later on June 15, 1849.

Polk's three Supreme Court's nominees were mediocre. Polk made his selections based on party loyalty, political compatibility, and geographical suitability. He made his first nomination after six months in office. To fill the vacancy left by the deceased Henry Baldwin, he nominated James Buchanan, but Buchanan turned him down. In the meantime, Justice Joseph Story announced his resignation for the end of the term, although he died before the term ended. Polk's choice for the Story seat was Levi Woodbury, a U.S. senator from New Hampshire. Woodbury was a loyal Democrat but conservative enough to swing some Whig voters. He had served as governor of New Hampshire and in the U.S. Senate as well as in the administrations of Jackson and Van Buren. He also had judicial experience. Confirmation of Woodbury was inevitable, and Polk put him on the Court with a recess appointment. He was later confirmed unanimously by the Senate (Abraham 1999, 80–81). Meanwhile, Polk turned to George W. Woodward of Pennsylvania for the Baldwin vacancy. Although a proven Democrat, Woodward had "acquired a reputation as an extreme nativist and was staunchly opposed by several Democratic senators." Woodward was rejected in the Senate by a vote of 20–29 in late January 1846. The exasperated Polk let six months elapse before again asking Buchanan to take the job. He first accepted but then turned the job down for the third time two months later. Next the president selected Robert Cooper Grier of Pennsylvania, judge of the Allegheny County (Pittsburgh) District Court. It was now August 1846, and the Baldwin seat had been vacant for more than two years. Grier was a "conservative Democrat and a cautious constitutionalist who was generally acceptable to all factions of the party." The Senate responded by confirming Grier the day after receiving the nomination (Abraham 1999, 81–82).

Reconstruction

The process of restoring the seceded Southern states to the Union is referred to as Reconstruction. It began even before the Civil War ended and lasted until the last Republican governments were overthrown in 1877. Congress and the president engaged in an acrimonious dispute over which branch had primary responsibility for defining the terms of readmission. Abraham Lincoln and then Andrew Johnson maintained that the Southern states had not legally left the Union, and that the executive power to pardon gave the president the constitutional right to set the terms of readmission. Congress, on the other hand, believed that Reconstruction was a legislative matter. Some Republicans, known as the Radicals, argued that the Confederate states had reverted to the status of territories when they seceded, and that Congress possessed constitutional control over territories. Thaddeus Stephens of Pennsylvania, leader of the House Radicals, went even further, claiming that the seceded states must be treated as "conquered provinces." Much of the rancor on the issue stemmed from fundamental disagreements over what was to become of the slaves freed by the war. Southern whites were already distressed by having to relinquish slaves and could not be expected to tolerate racial equality. The Radical Republicans demanded political and social equality for freedmen. Between these two positions were the moderate Republicans, who also held the balance of power. President Andrew Johnson's approach was far too lenient for the moderates, who were pushed in the direction of the Radicals.

As early as December 1863, Lincoln had issued his Proclamation of Amnesty and Reconstruction, in which he proposed to pardon anyone who would agree to emancipation and would take an oath of future loyalty to the Union. With the war still raging, Lincoln's proposal was designed to minimize obstacles for Southerners who wanted to put secession behind them and move on. Concerned about the leniency of Lincoln's plan, Congress passed the Wade-Davis Act, which was substantially more punitive. The act provided that when 50 percent of those voting in 1860 would swear to future loyalty, they could select delegates to a constitutional convention. The Radicals attempted to extend suffrage to freed male slaves without success, but Wade-Davis moved in that direction. In January 1865, with Lincoln's strong support, Congress agreed to send to the states the Thirteenth Amendment abolishing slavery.

It was apparent that President Andrew Johnson, who succeeded to the presidency on Lincoln's assassination, saw Reconstruction as an executive responsibility and thought that restoration of Southern states should be quick and lenient. Johnson required ratification of the Thirteenth Amendment but was otherwise willing to let the South decide what to do about former slaves. Initially hopeful that the Thirteenth Amendment would be enough to secure basic civil rights for blacks in the South, congressional Republicans were extremely troubled with the Southern response to Reconstruction. Most Southern legislatures enacted Black Codes that severely restricted the liberties of the former slaves. When the Congress reconvened in late 1865, the Republicans refused to seat representatives from states with governments organized under Johnson's plan, and formed a joint committee to develop further legislation. Radicals such as Thaddeus Stevens and the moderates attempted to persuade Johnson to change his policy. Illinois Senator Lyman Trumbull, a moderate, offered proposals designed to modify the Johnson approach by extending the Freedman's Bureau and by introducing the Civil Rights Act of 1866. Johnson vetoed both proposals. Johnson's response to these proposals antagonized even the moderate Republicans, who led the successful efforts to override his Civil Rights Act veto. Johnson was damaged further by the race riots in Memphis and in New Orleans in 1866. The Joint Committee on Reconstruction then proposed the Fourteenth Amendment, and the Republicans delivered the required two-thirds majority to send the amendment to the states. When Republican-controlled Tennessee ratified, it was readmitted. The remaining former Confederate states, acting on Johnson's advice, rejected the amendment.

In late summer Johnson attempted to forge a coalition of conservative Republicans and Democrats to appeal to the public. The effort was an unmitigated failure—the elections increased the anti-Johnson majorities in both houses.

Congress took full control of the Reconstruction process in December 1866. Radicals such as Thaddeus Stevens pushed for more severe requirements, including long-term disenfranchisement plus confiscation and redistribution of Southern land to the former slaves. Congress passed the First Reconstruction Act over Johnson's veto on March 2, 1867. Supplemented by subsequent legislation, the act was the final congressional plan for restoring the ten remaining former Confederate states to the Union. The act divided the ten states into five military districts, each under the command of a Union general. The Second Reconstruction Act authorized the military commanders of the districts to register all adult males as voters who would elect delegates to constitutional conventions. Each piece of Reconstruction legislation that emerged from Congress was passed over Johnson vetoes. Eventually, Congress limited his authority over Reconstruction and passed the Tenure of Office Act, requiring Senate approval whenever Johnson attempted to remove appointed officials, including his own cabinet members.

When Congress recessed, Johnson removed the Radical secretary of war, Edwin Stanton. In early 1868 when the Senate refused to approve Stanton's removal, the House adopted eleven articles of impeachment against Johnson, most centering on his failure to comply with the Tenure of Office Act and his failure to effectively enforce Congress's Reconstruction plan. On May 16, 1868, Johnson was acquitted by the margin of one vote on the final article, an omnibus summary of the charges. Acquittal on two other articles followed soon thereafter and ended the drive for impeachment of Johnson.

Congress then moved to facilitate black suffrage through the Fifteenth Amendment. When the last four ex-Confederate states were readmitted in 1869 and 1870, it was on the condition of ratifying the Fifteenth Amendment. In the South, the newly enfranchised black voters provided electoral support for the Republican governments that replaced those created under Johnson. From the outset, however, the new Republican regimes faced intimidation from organizations such as the Ku Klux Klan. Responding to appeals for protection from Southern Republicans, Congress passed three enforcement acts in 1870 and 1871. The first two prohibited the use of fraud and intimidation to limit voting and gave federal courts jurisdiction over violations. In addition, they established federal supervisors for registration and congressional elections. The third law, known as the Ku Klux Klan Act, empowered the president to use the military to respond to groups conspiring to deprive citizens of political rights. Eventually, Congress and President Grant lost their resolve and took less action to protect governments in the Southern states from those seeking to institute their own versions of home rule.

Republican Party

Founded in 1854, the Republican Party was the party of Northern opposition to slavery and its spread into the territories. Neither of the two major parties had embraced abolition by 1840, and a number of abolitionists organized the Liberty Party as a means of advancing the antislavery cause. By the end of the decade, the Liberty Party and other antislavery groups had focused almost exclusively on the issue of slavery in the territories. By 1848, most of those opposed to slavery in the territories, including the Liberty Party, created the Free-Soil Party. Although the Free-Soil Party existed only briefly, it heightened the visibility of the slavery issue. During the same period, the Democratic Party split into several factions, and the Whig Party disappeared altogether. The Republican Party was formed during this period of political turmoil. The specific catalyst was the Kansas-Nebraska Act of 1854. The act provided popular sovereignty, allowing residents of the Kansas and Nebraska territories to determine whether slavery would be allowed in either or both territories. Under terms of the Missouri Compromise of 1850, both territories would have been free, but the Kansas-Nebraska Act set aside that compromise. Once the Kansas-Nebraska Act proposal became law, those opposed to it held a series of meetings and established the Republican Party.

The Republican Party's first presidential candidate was John C. Fremont, who won more than 30 percent of the popular vote in 1856. Although the election was won by the Democrat, James Buchanan, the Republicans were in position to take advantage of the opportunity provided by the badly divided Democratic Party in 1860. The two largest Democratic factions each nominated a candidate in 1860, and the Republican candidate, Abraham Lincoln, won the White House even though his support was largely confined to the Northern states. From that point on, the Republican Party has remained one of the two major parties in the U.S. party system. Eleven states seceded from the Union after Lincoln's election, and the Civil War followed. In addition to abolishing slavery, the Republicans advocated higher tariffs, a transcontinental railroad, homestead legislation, and a national banking system. Lincoln was reelected in 1864 with running mate Andrew Johnson, a Democrat, which would prove problematic when Lincoln was assassinated in 1865.

Following the war, Republicans were severely divided about Reconstruction. The Radical Republicans insisted on conditions for the readmission of the former Confederate states: ratification of the Thirteenth and Fourteenth Amendments and the extension of full legal and political rights to male former slaves. The Reconstruction Acts adopted by Congress gave the Republicans in 1867 full control of the Southern states. During the presidency of Republican Ulysses S. Grant, which began in 1868, the party remained divided. It was able to unify itself sufficiently to hold onto the White House in 1872, 1876, 1880, and 1888. Beginning with the presidential election of 1896, the Republicans established themselves as the majority party and have remained one of the two broad-based major parties in the United States.

Seward, William Henry (1801–1872)

Seward was governor of New York, a U.S. senator, and secretary of state. He was born in Orange County, New York, on May 16, 1801. He interrupted his studies to teach in rural Georgia before graduating from Union College in 1820. He completed his legal training and moved to Auburn in upstate New York to start a law practice. Initially a Jeffersonian Republican, Seward switched to the Anti-Masonic Party in 1829. The party switch put Seward together with Thurlow Weed, a newspaper publisher. Weed orchestrated Seward's successful state senate bid in 1830. Seward then joined the Whigs. Weed assisted Seward in winning the Whig nomination for governor in 1834. Seward lost the election to Democrat William Marcy, but four years later, he defeated Marcy for the first of his two terms as governor.

Seward was a leader of the antislavery movement. He convinced the state legislature to require jury trials in fugitive slave cases, and he would not extradite persons alleged to have aided fugitives. When the Whigs took control of the New York legislature in 1849, Weed organized Seward's election to the U.S. Senate. Seward began his Senate service with a speech arguing that settlement of the West could not happen on the back of slave labor. It was a speech that raised red flags for most Whigs, including President Zachary Taylor. The Whig Party fell victim to the sectional politics of the period and was well on its way to extinction. The antislavery faction of the party was able to prevent the renomination of President Millard Fillmore, who had succeeded to the presidency upon Taylor's death in 1850. Blocking Fillmore's renomination, however, further weakened the proslavery faction. Seward opposed the Kansas-Nebraska Act of 1854 and challenged antislavery forces to settle the territories in sufficient numbers to keep slavery from being adopted. Soon thereafter, the Republican Party was formed as the political vehicle for the antislavery movement.

Many Whigs such as Seward and Weed joined the new Republican Party in late 1855. As a leader in the antislavery movement, Seward was an immediate Republican presidential prospect in 1856. Weed was doubtful that any Republican nominee could win in 1856, however, and he counseled Seward to bide his time. Seward followed Weed's advice while remaining in the public eye. Seward was considered a genuine abolitionist, but some Republicans thought he was driven by presidential ambition. When the Republicans gathered for their nominating convention in Chicago in June of 1860, Abraham Lincoln's organizers were able to successfully exploit the misgivings some had about Seward and capture the nomination. Although he was denied the nomination, Seward campaigned for Lincoln, and when Lincoln organized his cabinet, Seward was chosen as secretary of state. With the Civil War already under way,

Seward's first significant task was to keep Great Britain and France from providing the Confederacy with any kind of aid. Seward performed effectively in his cabinet role and soon was among Lincoln's inner circle of advisers. He did not see emancipation of slaves as an objective of the war but understood Lincoln's need to recruit blacks into the Union Army.

At war's end, Seward supported Lincoln's restrained Reconstruction policy and favored rapid readmission of Confederate states to the Union. He supported ratification of the Thirteenth Amendment, which abolished slavery, but was reluctant to go further. On April 14, 1865, the same night John Wilkes Booth assassinated Lincoln, Seward and his son were both seriously wounded as part of the assassination conspiracy. He recovered from the attack, and remained in the cabinet until the end of Johnson's term. Although Seward traveled extensively during his retirement, health problems ended his travels, and he died at his home in Auburn, New York, on October 10, 1872.

Sherman, William Tecumseh (1820–1891)

Sherman was a soldier during the Civil War. He was born in Lancaster, Ohio, on February 8, 1820. He received an appointment to West Point and served a variety of military assignments after graduation, mostly in the South. When the Mexican War broke out in 1846, Sherman received orders to go to California, where he served until 1850. Over the next three years, Sherman served in St. Louis and New Orleans. In 1853, Sherman accepted an offer to manage a bank in San Francisco. He remained in California for four years before accepting a position with a bank in New York City. Difficult economic times led Sherman to join his brothers-in-law's law practice and real estate business in Kansas. When the business venture failed, Sherman became superintendent of the Louisiana Military Seminary. The secession of Louisiana from the Union led Sherman to move to St. Louis and assume the presidency of a street railway company.

In May 1861, Sherman returned to the military as commander of the Third Brigade of the First Division, which was preparing to invade Virginia. President Abraham Lincoln later transferred him to Missouri, but he was so disheartened by Union prospects in the Civil War that he developed severe depression. His mental health improved considerably when he was sent to join Ulysses S. Grant and realized the Union cause was not lost. When the Union took control of Memphis in June of 1862, Sherman became its military governor. When Grant took charge of all Union forces in March of 1864, Sherman was named commander of the Military Division of Mississippi. Sherman believed in psychological warfare, insisting that "war is hell," and that the South could be intimidated into ending the war sooner if it became convinced of the total destruction that would be inflicted by Union forces. Although Lincoln and Grant had misgivings, Sherman implemented the strategy and marched through Georgia to the Atlantic Ocean. His judgment proved correct, and many Confederate soldiers lay down their arms and surrendered. Grant became president in 1869, at which point Sherman succeeded him as commanding general. He held the position until his retirement in 1884. Sherman died in New York City on February 14, 1891.

Stanton, Edwin McMasters (1814–1869)

Stanton was U.S. attorney general and secretary of war. He was born in Steubenville, Ohio, on December 19, 1814. He began study at Kenyon College in 1831 but dropped out for financial reasons. He returned to Steubenville, studied law, and entered a partnership in Cadiz, Ohio, in 1836. The following year, Stanton formed a partnership with Judge Benjamin Tappan, a family friend. Tappan was an antislavery Democrat who influenced Stanton's political development. Stanton was elected prosecuting attorney of Harrison County, managed Tappan's successful campaign for the U.S. Senate, and served as recorder of the Ohio Supreme Court in Columbus. Stanton had long held objections to slavery but chose to keep his beliefs separate from his public political positions. He supported the James Polk administration during the Mexican War, despite his serious concern about the expansion of slavery as a result. In 1847, Stanton moved to Pittsburgh, where he remained until 1856. During this period, he was recognized for his work in representing the state of Pennsylvania in cases heard by the U.S. Supreme Court. While in Pittsburgh, Stanton developed a friendship with Jeremiah Black, a justice on the Pennsylvania Supreme Court who became attorney general in the administration of James Buchanan. Black retained Stanton as special counsel in a California land title case. Stanton remained in Washington where he continued to work with Black.

Sectional politics seriously divided the Democratic Party in 1860, and Stanton supported John Breckinridge, the presidential candidate nominated by the Southern faction of the party. Near the end of the Buchanan administration, Black was shifted to the State Department, and Stanton was appointed to replace Black as attorney general. In the waning months of Buchanan's term, he worked diligently to maintain the Union. After Abraham Lincoln was inaugurated in March of 1861, Stanton occasionally served as legal counsel to Secretary of War Simon Cameron. During this period, he also began to distance himself from the conservative Democrats on the issue of slavery. Early in January 1862, charges of corruption forced Cameron to resign as secretary of war, and Lincoln named Stanton as Cameron's replacement. Stanton's selection was engineered by Secretary of State William Seward and Treasury Secretary Salmon P. Chase. Stanton proved himself an excellent choice by his skillful management of the war. As secretary of war, Stanton was responsible for internal security. The Lincoln administration suspended habeas corpus and arrested large numbers of people as security threats. Congress passed the Enrollment Act in March of 1863, which created the equivalent of a national police force. Stanton used the act to maintain internal security as well as enforce the draft law. Following the end of the war in April of 1865, Stanton remained in the War Department and supervised the demobilization of the Union armies.

Stanton favored a moderate approach to Reconstruction and attempted to soften President Andrew Johnson's opposition to congressional Reconstruction. Differences between Johnson and Stanton grew, however. In March of 1867, Congress approved the Tenure of Office Act, which required Senate approval for the removal of appointed officials. The act was designed, at least in part, to protect Stanton from dismissal. He supported the First and Second Reconstruction Acts, which established military-supervised governments in the former Confederate states. By mid-1867, Stanton had abandoned the compromise approach in favor of joining the Radical Reconstruction position. He and Grant drafted the Third Reconstruction Act, which removed the army supervising Reconstruction governments in the South from presidential control. Johnson had resisted dismissing Stanton, but after Stanton's role in crafting the Third Reconstruction Act, Johnson demanded Stanton's resignation. When Stanton refused to resign, Johnson ordered his suspension. Ironically, Johnson named Grant as Stanton's replacement. In January 1868, the Senate ordered Stanton reinstated under terms of the Tenure of Office Act. When Johnson refused, the House voted eleven impeachment articles against Johnson, based largely on his refusal to reinstate Stanton. When the Senate failed to convict Johnson of the impeachment charges, Stanton resigned as war secretary on May 26, 1868. Stanton returned to private life exhausted and in poor health. Within a year, he was disabled. Yet, President Grant nominated him to fill a vacancy on the U.S. Supreme Court. But Stanton died in Washington on December 24, 1869, before he could even take the oath of office.

Stevens, Thaddeus (1792–1868)

Stevens was a congressman during the Civil War and Reconstruction periods. He was born in Danville, Vermont, on April 4, 1792. After graduating from Dartmouth College in 1814, Stevens taught in York, Pennsylvania, while reading law with a local attorney. After passing the bar, Stevens moved to Gettysburg and established himself as one of the leading attorneys in the community. He also began his political career and was elected to five terms on the Gettysburg Council. In the late 1820s, Stevens affiliated himself with the Anti-Masonic Party and was elected to four nonconsecutive terms in the Pennsylvania House. In the period he was out of the assembly, Stevens was a delegate to the state constitutional convention. He objected so strenuously to efforts to withhold voting rights from black males that he refused to sign the new constitution. In 1842, Stevens relocated in Lancaster to resume the practice of law and recoup his losses. The dissolution of the Anti-Masons left Stevens looking for another party affiliation. He found a temporary home with the Whigs, although many party members were more conservative than Stevens. A failed attempt to land a cabinet post in the short-lived administration of President William Henry Harrison placed him further from the party's leadership. He and others were able to take control of the local party, however, and Stevens was elected to Congress as a Whig.

In Congress, Stevens steadfastly opposed slavery and wanted to prevent the extension of slavery in the territories. He was an outspoken critic of the Compromise of 1850, believing that the federal government had no authority to regulate in the territories. His separation from the Whigs was underscored by his defiance of the Fugitive Slave Act, passed in 1850. He represented fugitive slaves and frequently violated the Fugitive Slave Law by assisting runaway slaves to avoid capture. As a consequence of these activities, the Whigs refused to renominate him to Congress. At this point, Stevens participated in the establishment of the Pennsylvania Republican Party. As a Republican, he was returned to Congress in 1858, and he began working his way up the congressional leadership ladder. In 1860 he became chair of the powerful Ways and Means Committee and later became House majority leader.

Stevens was not close to Abraham Lincoln on a personal level, but he provided critical congressional support to the administration's war policies, such as enactment of a military draft law and suspension of habeas corpus. Stevens lost patience with Lincoln's cautious, piecemeal approach in dealing with the slavery issue, but nonetheless campaigned on the president's behalf in 1864. Even before the end of the war, the issue of reconstructing the Union generated a number of different options. Stevens was among those offering the so-called "radical" version of Reconstruction. After a period in which Stevens was both majority leader and a leading Radical Reconstructionist, he opted to focus on leadership of congressional Republicans and moderated his position on Reconstruction. The Military Reconstruction Act of 1867 reflected Stevens's more moderate approach—the law was a restrained measure that Radical Reconstructionists reluctantly accepted. He led the efforts to override Andrew Johnson's veto of the Freedman's Bureau and Civil Rights Act of 1866 and subsequently engineered passage of the Fourteenth Amendment. Stevens was in such poor health during the impeachment trial of Andrew Johnson that his role was limited, even though he was designated one of the prosecution managers. It was his "omnibus" impeachment article that came within one vote of conviction. Stevens died at his Washington, D.C., home on August 11, 1868, less than two months after Johnson's acquittal.

Taney, Roger Brooke (1777–1864)

Roger Taney was born in Calvert County, Maryland, in 1777 to an established Maryland family. At the time of his birth, the family was part of the landed aristocracy, and owned a large tobacco plantation. He enrolled at Dickinson College at the age of fifteen and graduated at the top of his class in 1795. Taney was admitted to the bar in

1799, after a lengthy apprenticeship. Immediately thereafter, Taney was elected to the Maryland legislature as a Federalist. Defeated in his bid for reelection, Taney moved to Frederick, Maryland, where he developed a successful private practice. He remained active with the Federalist Party, although he did not always subscribe to mainstream party doctrine.

In 1816, Taney was elected to a single term in the state senate. He briefly returned to his Frederick practice and then relocated in Baltimore, where he established himself as a leading attorney and underwent a political relocation. The Federalist Party had deteriorated to insignificance, and Taney was drawn to the Jacksonian Democrats. He supported Jackson in the election of 1824 and chaired the Jackson organization in Maryland in 1828. Between the Jackson campaigns, Taney had been chosen state attorney general. He left the attorney generalship in 1831 to take the position of attorney general in the Jackson cabinet. Taney served two years as Jackson's attorney general and political adviser. He was instrumental in the formulation of Jackson's rationale for vetoing the legislation that would have rechartered the National Bank. When Jackson's treasury secretary became undependable in implementing administration policy decisions, Jackson dismissed him and replaced him with Taney. After Taney removed deposits from the bank, supporters of the bank refused to confirm Taney as treasury secretary. Jackson then nominated Taney to replace Justice Gabriel Duvall on the Supreme Court, but the Senate review was indefinitely postponed. Upon the death of Chief Justice John Marshall in late 1835, Jackson proposed Taney's name to replace Marshall. He was confirmed three months later by a 29–15 vote and served as chief justice for twenty-eight years, until his death in 1864.

Taney was a states' rightist, and many felt that his appointment would bring about the complete reversal of the pronational decisions of the Marshall Court. Although the jurisprudence of the Taney Court differed from Marshall's in a number of important respects, the Taney Court generally worked within the framework of Marshall Court doctrine rather than rejecting it. Although Taney personally preferred to assign a broad array of matters to the exclusive control of the states, as chief justice he chose to resolve many of these matters on the basis of concurrent power or the principle of dual sovereignty. This approach was evident in commerce power jurisprudence. In Taney's view, while states could not regulate foreign commerce, a state could exercise its police power on behalf of public health and safety once items arrived inside the state. The property rights differences between Marshall and Taney were reflected in the contract case of *Charles River Bridge Company v. Warren Bridge Company* (1837). There Taney held that a public contract must be interpreted literally and narrowly, and that no state interest may be contracted away implicitly. This decision did not reverse the Marshall Court's Contract Clause ruling in *Trustees of Dartmouth College v. Woodward* (1819) but weakened its effectiveness as a means of insulating private property from state regulation.

Dred Scott v. Sandford (1857) represents the Taney Court's misguided attempt to resolve the slavery issue. Although each member of the Court offered a separate opinion, Taney's opinion is generally regarded as the Court's statement in the case. He was drawn into broadening the scope of the decision unnecessarily and offered remarks about the status of blacks that unfortunately escalated an already volatile situation. While discussion of Taney is incomplete without treatment of *Dred Scott*, the case and its injurious consequences should not tarnish Taney's achievements as chief justice. Taney believed in dual sovereignty, and that view governed all else. It was because he believed that power could be shared by federal and state governments that he sought to preserve some of Marshall's nationalism by tempering it with state authority.

Taylor, Zachary (1784–1850)

Taylor was a military hero and the twelfth president of the United States. He was born in Orange County, Virginia, on November 24, 1784. In 1807 Taylor joined the army and quickly rose to the rank of captain, distinguishing himself in campaigns against various Native American tribes. He spent more than twenty years commanding military forts in the West. In 1841 Taylor became commander of the Second Military Department at Fort Smith, Arkansas. Taylor was a Whig, even though he had no history of political activity during his years in the military. He became a national hero as a result of his performance in the Mexican War. After victory in the Battle of Monterrey, Taylor made an agreement with the Mexicans not to press further militarily for several weeks. He was criticized by President James K. Polk for making such an agreement, which led Taylor to conclude that Polk and General Winfield Scott were conspiring against him. Correctly anticipating that Taylor might be a presidential candidate, Polk selected Scott for a pivotal invasion at Veracruz, leaving Taylor with insufficient forces to effectively engage the Mexicans. Nonetheless, Taylor won an important victory at Buena Vista. Soon thereafter, a group of Whig congressmen set in motion a plan to draft Taylor to run for president.

In 1848 the Whigs nominated Taylor, despite political inexperience and his ownership of a large number of slaves. The 1848 presidential election had three candidates of consequence—Taylor, the Democrat Lewis Cass, and the Free-Soil Party candidate, former president Martin Van Buren. Taylor obtained a majority of electoral votes but secured only a plurality of popular votes. Taylor's main objective was to reduce sectional conflict, which he pursued by selecting cabinet members from all parts of the country. The Democrats wanted to divide the Whigs before the 1852 election and were highly critical of Taylor for his failure to support the Compromise of 1850. Taylor opposed Henry Clay's so-called Omnibus Bill, preferring his own plan instead. Clay's bill was defeated, but before Congress could take further action, Taylor died. After his death, the Clay bill was broken into component pieces, which were passed individually.

Thirteenth Amendment

One of the three amendments added to the Constitution after the Civil War. The Thirteenth Amendment provides that "neither slavery or involuntary servitude, except as a punishment for crime whereof the party shall have been duly convicted, shall exist within the United States, or any place subject to their jurisdiction." The amendment was proposed on January 31, 1865, declared ratified on December 6, 1865, and took effect twelve days later. The amendment gave legal effect to the Emancipation Proclamation of 1863. In addition, it fundamentally altered the federal-state relationship in that it conferred on the federal government authority over a policy area that previously resided in the states' domain. A state could no longer permit slavery through the exercise of its own authority. The amendment does not preclude military conscription, criminal sentences involving hard labor, or other similar requirements of involuntary service. The amendment was designed to apply to black persons in the particular context of the Emancipation Proclamation. Section 2 of the amendment empowered Congress to "enforce this article by appropriate legislation."

The Thirteenth Amendment gave Congress authority to legislate against racial discrimination and the denial of civil rights. Such power was crucial to the power to outlaw slavery. Consistent with this view, Congress passed the Civil Rights Act of 1866, which clarified the citizenship status of freed slaves and protected certain rights, such as entering into contracts and holding or conveying real property. Early Supreme Court construction of the amendment defined slavery very narrowly, however, and placed private discrimination outside the amendment's reach.

Trumbull, Lyman (1813–1896)

Trumbull was a politician and jurist born in Colchester, Connecticut, on October 12, 1813. Trumbull taught school and studied law in Greenville, Georgia, and was admitted to the bar in 1836. The following year, he established an office in Bellville, Illinois, and became one of the area's better trial lawyers. He was elected as a Democrat to the state legislature in 1840 but resigned in 1841 to become Illinois secretary of state. After a failed congressional bid in 1846, he vowed not to seek legislative office again. Two years later, however, he was elected to fill out a term as justice of the Illinois Supreme Court and in 1852 won a full nine-year term on the court. The Kansas-Nebraska Act of 1854 drew Trumbull into the legislative arena. The act outraged him and also split the Democrats in Illinois. Trumbull led the so-called "anti-Nebraska faction" and defeated a "pro-Nebraska" Democrat for a seat in the U.S. House. The following year, the Illinois legislature sent Trumbull to the U.S. Senate.

The transition from anti-Nebraska Democrat to the new antislavery Republican Party in 1857 was a logical step for Trumbull. He opposed the Kansas constitution submitted on behalf of the proslavery residents and strongly urged that Congress should resolve all matters regarding slavery in the territories, notwithstanding resident input. Trumbull supported the Lincoln war policy, although he was disturbed by the shortcuts taken with civil liberties. Trumbull was one of those in Washington who argued that emancipation of all slaves should be an explicit objective of the war. He sponsored the resolution sending the Thirteenth Amendment to the states for ratification. As for Reconstruction, Trumbull initially favored the moderate approach set out by Lincoln. He was chair of the Senate Judiciary Committee and used that position to take charge of the Senate's Reconstruction efforts in 1866. He authored legislation to extend the Freedman's Bureau and supported the Civil Rights Act of 1866. When Johnson vetoed these measures, Trumbull and other moderate Republicans joined the Radicals.

Trumbull strongly backed the Fourteenth Amendment, the Military Reconstruction Acts of 1867, and the Fifteenth Amendment. He could not bring himself to vote for Johnson's impeachment but voted for the resolution against Johnson's removal of Secretary of War Edwin Stanton in February of 1868. When Ulysses S. Grant replaced Johnson, Trumbull backed away from the Radical Reconstruction policy and opposed the Ku Klux Klan (Third Enforcement) Act of 1871. Trumbull wanted to challenge Grant for president in 1872 but failed to garner sufficient support to make a serious run. He left the Senate in 1873 on the expiration of his third term and resumed his law practice in Chicago. He served as Samuel Tilden's counsel in the disputed election of 1876, was defeated as the Democratic gubernatorial candidate in 1880, and gravitated to the Populists by the 1890s. He died in Chicago on June 25, 1896.

Tyler, John (1790–1862)

Tyler was the tenth president of the United States. He was born in Charles City County, Virginia, on March 29, 1790. He graduated from the College of William and Mary in 1807 and, after reading law with his father, was admitted to the bar. Tyler's political career began in 1811 when he was elected to the Virginia legislature. He served until 1815, when he was elevated to the executive council of the commonwealth. Tyler was elected to the U.S. House of Representatives in 1816, where he served three terms before he declined renomination because of poor health. Tyler returned to the state legislature, and in 1825 the assembly selected him to be governor of Virginia. During his early political career, Tyler was a proponent of states' rights and the political agenda of the so-called Old Republicans. In 1827 Tyler was elected to the U.S. Senate, where he led the opposition to the protective tariff. He supported Andrew Jackson in 1828, albeit reluctantly, and usually supported the administration's initiatives. He supported Jackson again in 1832 but opposed Jackson's removal of government deposits from the Bank of the United States.

During Jackson's second term, Tyler increasingly acted with the Whigs and was considered a strong candidate for the U.S. Senate. In 1840, Tyler was selected by the Whigs to run as the vice presidential candidate with William Henry Harrison. The ticket was elected, and when Harrison died thirty days after his inauguration, Tyler became president. Initially, Tyler and the Whig leadership in Congress believed they could work together. When Tyler vetoed measures designed to replace the Bank of the United States, however, most Whigs, including his cabinet, deserted him. Indeed, congressional Whigs not only abandoned him but considered impeachment. Tyler was forced to cobble together an administration of Democrats and the few Whigs who would still support him. His former party nominated Henry Clay for president in 1844, and the Democrat James K. Polk won the election. Tyler returned to Virginia and became a Democrat.

Although his political future was limited, Tyler spoke regularly on issues of the day. He thought congressional initiatives such as the Wilmot Proviso constituted indefensible interference into the business of those living in the territories—particularly those who wanted to own slaves. He approved of the Compromise of 1850 and the Kansas-Nebraska Act of 1854. He applauded the Supreme Court's ruling in the *Dred Scott* decision, feeling that it vindicated his position on congressional authority to regulate slavery in the territories. He later supported Democrat James Buchanan's Kansas policy and urged Congress to accept the constitution of the proslavery group in Kansas. Tyler was elected as a delegate to the Virginia convention, which was considering the issue of secession, among others. He voted for secession, but the resolution to secede was defeated. On April 17, 1861, the convention delegates reversed themselves and voted for Virginia to secede. Tyler was elected to the Confederate House of Representatives in the state's first election after secession. Tyler died in Richmond on January 18, 1862, before he could take office.

John Tyler succeeded to the presidency a month after William Henry Harrison was inaugurated. Tyler lacked a personal political base and was in constant conflict with Henry Clay and his Whig followers. Tyler is rated by many historians as an ineffective president, a judgment that is consistent with his record in nominating Supreme Court justices—he had five nominations rejected. Between December 1843 and April 1844, Justices Smith Thompson and Henry Baldwin died. Tyler made a total of six nominations in trying to replace these two justices. Tyler's first choice for the Thompson seat was John C. Spencer, a New York lawyer and a Whig who had held two cabinet posts in the Tyler administration. He was a political enemy of Henry Clay, and he was rejected by the Senate by a 21–26 vote. Tyler next selected Chancellor Reuben H. Walworth of New York. Before the Senate could vote on the Walworth nomination, Justice Baldwin died. Tyler wanted to nominate James Buchanan for the Baldwin seat, but Buchanan declined. Tyler then chose a distinguished Philadelphia lawyer, Judge Edward King. It was now June and the Whig senators, thinking they had victory in their grasp in the forthcoming presidential election, moved to "postpone" both the Walworth and the King nominations. Angry and frustrated, Tyler renominated King. The Senate would not act on the nominations, however, and the president withdrew both nominations in January 1845 (Abraham 1999, 79). Tyler was about to be replaced by Democrat James K. Polk, who had won the election over Henry Clay. Having broken with the Whigs, Tyler decided to take another crack at the Supreme Court vacancies. He selected Samuel Nelson, a longtime justice and chief justice of the Supreme Court of New York. Nelson was Tyler's first successful nomination; within ten days, and "with only scattered Whig opposition, Nelson won confirmation to the seat that had been vacant for fourteen months." Tyler nominated John Meredith Read for the still-vacant Baldwin seat. Read was a "well-known Philadelphia lawyer with supporters in both the Whig and Democratic camps." But "it was now mid-February, and a weary Senate adjourned without acting on the nomination, thus handing Tyler his fifth failure" (Abraham 1999, 80).

Underground Railroad

The Underground Railroad enabled many slaves to escape from the South. The Railroad was not a railroad, but a series of routes through which fugitive slaves could find assistance in their flight north using a loose network of trails, ships, wagons, and other modes of travel. The railroad metaphor was used to symbolize the connecting of people and forces to provide safe passage to those fleeing slavery. The key element was the people known as "conductors," who facilitated the escape of slaves. There is some evidence that the Railroad was created in the late eighteenth century, but the number of runaways using it increased as the Civil War moved closer. Much of the assistance given to fugitive slaves was provided by Quaker abolitionists, although non-Quakers taking the risk of violating fugitive slave laws by aiding runaways felt a deep moral if not religious obligation to do so. Runaways or "passengers" usually traveled in small numbers and were typically assisted by the conductors when travel conditions were safe. Some of the conductors would travel into the South and assist in the initial escape, while others would provide assistance as fugitive slaves passed through their areas.

Van Buren, Martin (1782–1862)

Van Buren was the eighth president of the United States. He was born in Kinderhook, New York, on December 5, 1782, and was introduced to politics in the late 1790s when he was apprenticed to lawyer Francis Silvester. Van Buren resisted the Federalists all around him and chose to become a Republican instead. After moving to New York City, Van Buren was active in the Aaron Burr faction of the party. He returned to Kinderhook in 1803 to start a law practice and gradually affiliated with the Clinton-

Livingston faction. With his law practice off to a successful start, he became county surrogate in 1808. In 1812, he was elected to the state senate and appeared to move away from the "regular" Republicans. Although DeWitt Clinton and Van Buren became bitter rivals, Van Buren reestablished himself as a regular Republican. In 1815 he was named New York attorney general, followed by reelection to the state senate in 1816 (he served in both offices simultaneously). Clinton was elected governor in 1817 and within two years had replaced Van Buren as attorney general.

Deeply affected by the death of his wife and his descending political fortunes, Van Buren struggled to recover his equilibrium. He organized a group known as the Bucktails to counter the Clinton faction. Clinton was re-elected governor in 1820, but Van Buren's Bucktails captured the state legislature and he was elected to the U.S. Senate. Two years later, the Bucktails ousted Clinton and won the governor's office. Once in Washington, Van Buren caught presidential fever. He steadfastly clung to his Jeffersonian states' rights beliefs but realized that the way he and his party could win the presidency was to grab onto the rising star, Andrew Jackson. Van Buren traveled extensively in the South on Jackson's behalf and organized the congressional party to counter John Quincy Adams's administration. By 1828 Van Buren had helped several diverse groups coalesce, and together they put Jackson in the White House. Meanwhile, Van Buren was elected governor of New York, but he resigned shortly thereafter to become Jackson's secretary of state.

A conflict developed between Van Buren and Vice President John C. Calhoun over which of the two would follow Jackson as president. Before the end of his first term, Jackson settled the issue in Van Buren's favor. By the spring of 1831 the acrimony was intense enough that Jackson reorganized his cabinet and sent Van Buren to England. His tenure abroad was brief, and he returned to become Jackson's running mate in 1832. Although he was now the vice president, Van Buren's influence with Jackson and within the party had diminished, and his status was further threatened by South Carolina's nullification of federal tariff acts. However, Van Buren regained the prominence he had enjoyed earlier. While presiding over the Senate, Van Buren effectively held off the opposing Whig Party, whose leaders included former Jackson ally Calhoun, Henry Clay, and Daniel Webster.

Van Buren was able to defeat the Whigs in 1836, despite running poorly in the South. He tried to follow the policy path started by Jackson. One of those policies involved forcible relocation of Indian tribes. The campaign against the Seminoles went badly, though, and lasted through much of Van Buren's term. More damaging was the economic panic, which many blamed on the Jackson-Van Buren administration's monetary policies. The economic woes worsened and ultimately cost Van Buren reelection in 1840. After losing the White House to William Henry Harrison, Van Buren returned to Kinderhook, but beginning in 1842, he traveled extensively in hopes of securing the presidential nomination in 1844. His opposition to the annexation of

Texas damaged him in the South and West and cost him his front-runner status. The convention deadlocked, and Van Buren withdrew in favor of James K. Polk.

In 1848, Van Buren made one more presidential run, but this time as the somewhat reluctant nominee of the new antislavery Free-Soil Party. He garnered only 10 percent of the popular vote in the election, which was won by Zachary Taylor and the Whigs. After the election, Van Buren returned to the Democratic Party thinking it was the best chance of saving the Union. He remained with that party, even though the Democratic candidate in 1852, Franklin Pierce, had a decidedly pro-Southern look. Although very troubled by the Kansas-Nebraska Act of 1854, he supported the Democratic Party's nominee, James Buchanan, in 1856. Parting company with many antislavery men, he endorsed the Compromise of 1850 and supported pro-Southern Democrat Franklin Pierce in 1852. Although disturbed by the Kansas-Nebraska Act two years later, he continued to back the Democratic Party. The Democrats then suffered a fatal division before the election of 1860. Van Buren was distressed not only by the split, but also by his inability to bring the party closer together. He died at Lindenwald, his home in Kinderhook, New York, on July 24, 1862.

The Court in place during Van Buren's presidential term was relatively young, and he had two chances to nominate a justice. The first came when Jackson nominee William Smith refused to serve. Van Buren selected Alabama Senator John McKinley to replace Smith. McKinley was an experienced lawyer who had impeccable political credentials and also came from the right geographic region. Although he had been a Democrat only a short time, McKinley had demonstrated sufficient commitment to Jacksonian views. During the nullification battle, which came from his native South, McKinley was an unwavering supporter of the Union. These factors alone would have been "more than adequate rationale for confirmation," but McKinley also had been one of Van Buren's "key managers during the presidential campaign of 1836 and was personally responsible for capturing Alabama's electoral votes" (Abraham 1999, 78).

On February 24, 1841, Justice Philip Barbour died after serving less than five years on the Court. Van Burens's choice was Peter V. Daniel, another Jacksonian, and a "Van Buren loyalist." Daniel was serving in his fifth year as a U.S. district judge in Virginia when Van Buren chose him. A member of the "ruling Democratic elite," he was a "stormy petrel in the law, life, and politics of his day and generation." Daniel had served his state government as both a member of the lower house and as lieutenant governor. He had supported Jackson from the campaign of 1824, and "during the Bank and nullification controversies he had stood with, and spoken for, the president." When Van Buren was nominated, Daniel's support did not diminish. Indeed, Daniel became one of Van Buren's closest political advisers. Before Daniel was confirmed by the Senate, he and Van Buren had some "anxious moments." Van Buren was a lame duck, having lost the 1840 election to Whig William Henry Harrison. He "rushed Daniel's name to the Senate even before there was time to bury Barbour." The victorious Whigs "launched a series of tactical maneuvers" to prevent the nomination from reaching the Senate floor, but because of their "defective strategy, absenteeism, and crossed signals," the Whigs were ultimately outmaneuvered by the Democrats. With many Whigs absent and barely a quorum present, Daniel was confirmed by a 22–5 vote (Abraham 1999, 78–79).

Wade, Benjamin (1800–1878)

Wade was a U.S. senator born in Feeding Hills, Massachusetts, on October 27, 1800. Wade moved with his family to Andover, Ohio, in 1821, where he supported himself as a farmer and teacher. He worked for a time on the Erie Canal before returning to Ohio to study law and was admitted to the bar in 1828. An active Whig, Wade was elected prosecuting attorney of Ashtabula County in 1836 and state senator the following year. His opposition to slavery was his undoing in his bid for reelection in 1839, although he regained the seat in 1841. He served only one additional term before returning to his law practice and was elected to a state judgeship in 1847. Wade denounced the Fugitive Slave Law, which led to his election to the U.S. Senate in 1851, where he served eighteen years. He entered the Senate with Charles Sumner and other abolitionists and developed a reputation as a radical on the slavery issue. Wade strongly opposed the Kansas-Nebraska Act of 1854 and joined others in founding the Ohio Republican Party. His leadership of the antislavery senators resulted in his consideration for the presidency in 1860, but the nomination went to Abraham Lincoln instead. As the Civil War progressed, Wade came to represent the most outspoken and radical faction of Senate Republicans. Wade is best known for his radical position on slavery and Reconstruction, but he also played a prominent role in the passage of both the Homestead Act and the Morrill Land Grant Act.

The issue of what to do with the Confederate states after the war brought about a fundamental split between Wade and Lincoln. Wade was convinced that only the Congress had authority to restore seceded states. It was Wade's view that those states had reverted to territorial status, which made them the exclusive domain of the legislative branch. Wade joined with Representative Henry Winter Davis of Maryland in 1864 to introduce the Wade-Davis Bill, which required a majority of the electorate in each seceded state to initiate a new government. The bill also had loyalty oath provisions and formally abolished slavery in the states of the former Confederacy. Lincoln pocket vetoed the measure, which made Wade so irate that he and others accused Lincoln of playing reelection politics with the Reconstruction issue. The disagreement Wade and others had with Lincoln's much more lenient Reconstruction policy led them to keep senators elected under Lincoln's plan from taking their seats.

The situation worsened when Andrew Johnson became president. Wade opposed Johnson at virtually every turn while supporting the Freedmen's Bureau, the

Civil Rights Act of 1866, and black suffrage. Wade strongly favored adoption of the Fourteenth Amendment and considered its ratification a necessary condition for the readmission of seceded states. Wade was selected president pro tem of the Senate in 1867, but despite Wade's new leadership position, he suffered political reversals when the Democrats captured the state legislature and chose to replace him. He remained in the Senate long enough to weigh in on the side of Andrew Johnson's impeachment. When the impeachment effort failed, Wade's political life ended. He returned to Jefferson, Ohio, and practiced law until his death on March 2, 1878.

Wade-Davis Act of 1864

In early 1864, Republicans began considering what role, if any, Congress should play in Reconstruction. In December of 1863, Lincoln issued a Proclamation of Amnesty and Reconstruction. He proposed to pardon anyone who would take an oath of future loyalty to the Union and agree to emancipation. The Radical Republicans in Congress believed Lincoln's approach to amnesty and Reconstruction was far too lenient. Furthermore, Lincoln's action was based on his presidential war powers, which many in Congress believed were insufficient to allow executive Reconstruction.

The first congressional action on Reconstruction was the Wade-Davis Act. Although the Republicans had just renominated Lincoln, the Wade-Davis Act essentially repudiated his Reconstruction program. The act called for the president to nominate, with Senate approval, a provisional civilian governor for each Confederate state to replace the military governors Lincoln had appointed without Senate confirmation. This governor would direct civil affairs in the state and oversee the creation of a new state government. Federal marshals would enroll all white male citizens, and once a majority swore future loyalty to the Union, the governor would oversee the election of delegates to a convention, which in turn would draft a new state constitution. (Lincoln's plan required only 10 percent of the electorate to take the loyalty oath as a precondition for assembling a constitutional convention.) A republican government, according to Wade-Davis, required all voters and elected officials to have been civilians during the rebellion, not to have held the rank of colonel or above in the Confederate Army, or held a position in the Confederate government beyond the clerical level. Another condition was that slavery had to be abolished. The new state constitution would be submitted to eligible voters, and upon majority approval, the governor would send it to the president. After he had obtained congressional assent, the president could then proclaim the state rejoined to the Union.

The Wade-Davis Act provided a "more coherent policy than did the president's." Lincoln sought "speed in returning the rebellious states to the Union and relied on the democratic process to reform internal policies." Congress wanted a "more orderly procedure" based on statutory authority that required substantive domestic changes before a state could return. In addition, Congress wanted to "ensure some protections for the freedman." Although it was not a perfect plan, Wade-Davis provided far more guidelines than Lincoln's plan and "might have prevented the debacle under Andrew Johnson." Lincoln, however, pocket vetoed Wade-Davis (Urofsky and Finkelman 2002, 433–435).

Waite, Morrison Remick (1816–1888)

Waite was born into a prominent New England family in Lyme, Connecticut, in 1816. His father was chief justice of the Connecticut Supreme Court. He earned his undergraduate degree from Yale, graduating in 1837. The following year, Waite moved to Ohio, settling in Maumee City. There he studied law with a leading local attorney. He was admitted to the bar in 1839 and established a practice in Maumee City, where he stayed until moving to nearby Toledo in 1850. He built a very successful practice there specializing in railroad law. In 1846, he unsuccessfully ran for Congress as a Whig. Three years later, he won a seat in the state legislature but served only a single term. In 1862, Waite ran again for Congress, this time as a Republican. The following year, Waite declined appointment to the Ohio Supreme Court, choosing instead to serve as an adviser to the Ohio governor. In 1871, Waite was named to the delegation representing the U.S. compensation claims against Great Britain at the Geneva Arbitration. Waite's performance during these proceedings contributed to a substantial judgment for the United States and brought him national recognition. Waite returned to the United States and was elected to the Ohio Constitutional Convention, where he presided over the convention proceedings.

Early in 1873, Chief Justice Salmon P. Chase died, creating a vacancy on the Supreme Court. President Ulysses S. Grant's first three choices either declined or withdrew, fearing rejection by the Senate. Waite did not seek appointment to the Court, but he had substantial support from both inside and outside government. Recognizing the volume of support for Waite, Grant yielded to political pressure and nominated him. He was confirmed unanimously. During his fourteen years as chief justice, he tended to the responsibilities of the office conscientiously, and undertook much more of the actual work of the Court than did his predecessor. He died in 1888 and was replaced as chief justice by Melville W. Fuller.

Waite joined a Court that had been deeply involved in Lincoln's nationalistic policies during the Civil War and Reconstruction. Waite was successful in redirecting the Court's attention away from the political limelight. Because Waite had no prior judicial experience and was the product of Grant's ill-administered selection process, he was viewed with some suspicion by his colleagues when he began his tenure. Nonetheless, he became an effective leader of his Court. The jurisprudence of the Waite Court was essentially established the year before his appointment, in the *Slaughterhouse Cases*

(1873) decision. There the Court refused to use the Due Process Clause of the Fourteenth Amendment as the basis for federal intervention against a state property regulation. This decision reflected two major themes of the Waite Court—deference to state regulatory initiatives and restrictive interpretation of the post–Civil War amendments.

Representative of this first theme is *Munn v. Illinois* (1877), perhaps Waite's best remembered opinion. In *Munn*, the Court upheld a state regulation on warehouse operations, including the rates that could be charged. Waite said that when private property has been used in a manner to make it of public consequence, the property owner "grants to the public an interest in that use," and he must "submit to be controlled by the public for the common good." The state-power theme of *Munn* carried over to several important Contract Clause opinions from Waite. Notwithstanding some acknowledged property protections, it was Waite's view that the public interest may override property and contract interests. In *Stone v. Mississippi* (1880), the Court upheld a state constitutional provision that negated a previously granted lottery charter. Waite said that the Contract Clause could not extend to governmental rights. No legislatively granted charter could "bargain away the police power of the state." Items subject to the police power, such as public health and morals, require supervision that is "continuing" in nature. These concerns are to be dealt with as the "special exigencies of the moment may require"; thus a state cannot be bound by the Contract Clause in a way that precludes appropriate response.

The other side of the states' rights theme was the narrow interpretation of the postwar amendments and the negative consequences of this on the civil rights of blacks. Illustrative is *United States v. Cruikshank* (1874), a decision that severely narrowed the impact of the Fifteenth Amendment on black voting rights. Waite said that the amendment did not directly grant black suffrage. Rather, it had only precluded race from being the reason for denial of suffrage and dictated that the right to vote was still a state matter. In similar fashion, the Court voided the Civil Rights Act of 1875 in the *Civil Rights Cases* (1883) and established "state action" as the threshold condition for federal "corrective" legislation.

Whig Party

The Whig Party had its roots in the Henry Clay–John Quincy Adams faction of the old Jeffersonian Party, the National Republicans. It was formed largely to oppose Andrew Jackson. The party took its name from those who opposed the English monarchy in the seventeenth century. The center of the party's platform came from Henry Clay's so-called American System, which urged extension of the national bank, government subsidies for public works or internal improvement projects, and protective tariffs. Clay's unsuccessful challenge of Andrew Jackson in the 1832 presidential election stressed the bank issue, since Jackson had vetoed its extension. The party broadened its base considerably when John C. Calhoun and his followers broke rank with Jackson.

The Calhoun group brought its commitment to states' rights into the party. Calhoun's faction favored state nullification of federal laws. There were other Southerners who, like Calhoun, favored states' rights but did not support nullification. They, too, joined the Whigs. This coalition brought the Whigs electoral success in 1840, when William Henry Harrison won the presidency. But the coalition was as fragile as Harrison, who died less than a month after taking office. His successor, John Tyler, vetoed several measures supported by the Whigs and was unceremoniously tossed out of the party. Although the Whigs would win the presidency again in 1848 with Zachary Taylor heading the ticket, the policy priorities of the American System were no longer politically viable. President Millard Fillmore, who succeeded to the presidency upon Taylor's death, supported the efforts of Clay, Daniel Webster, and other Whigs to secure passage of the Compromise of 1850. The compromise temporarily eased sectional tensions, but the Whigs could not capitalize on its enactment. Rather, the sectional conflict defined by the issue of slavery took center stage. The Whigs nominated General Winfield Scott in 1852, but he was beaten decisively in the general election and the party never recovered. By 1856, most Northern Whigs had migrated to the Free-Soil Party and on to the Republican Party. The Whig nominating convention in 1856 endorsed the candidacy of Fillmore, who was now the candidate of the American or Know-Nothing Party. The Democrats won in 1856, but with Abraham Lincoln's election in 1860, the Republican Party established itself as the second major party in the U.S. party system; the Whig Party collapsed and was never heard from again.

Wilmot Proviso

In the early part of the Mexican War, Representative David Wilmot, a Pennsylvania Democrat, offered an amendment to a military appropriation bill which stated that "as an express and fundamental condition to the acquisition of any territory from the Republic of Mexico by the United States, neither slavery nor involuntary servitude shall ever exist in any part of the territory, except for crime, whereof the party shall first be duly convicted." The familiar language had been part of the Northwest Ordinance, but now it "exploded as a bombshell, setting off a political and constitutional crisis." Within a short time, every free-state legislature but one had directed its congressional delegation to support the Wilmot Proviso. Northern Democrats rallied behind it. The proviso allowed Northern Democrats to support the war while avoiding the accusation in the next election that they had helped expand slavery. However, the proviso split the party. Southern interests killed it in the Senate, but the damage had already been done. For the first time, the antislavery movement had a focal point that attracted militant abolitionists, mainstream politicians, and a wide cross section of the Northern population (Urofsky and Finkelman 2002, 376).

References and Further Reading

Abraham, Henry J. 1999. *Justices, Presidents, and Senators: A History of the U.S. Supreme Court Appointments from Washington to Clinton.* Rev. ed. Lanham, MD: Rowman and Littlefield.

Castel, Albert. 1979. *The Presidency of Andrew Johnson.* Lawrence: University Press of Kansas.

Davis, Abraham L., and Barbara Luck Graham. 1995. *The Supreme Court, Race, and Civil Liberties.* Thousand Oaks, CA: Sage.

Hyman, Harold M., and William M. Wiecek. 1982. *Equal Justice under Law: Constitutional Development, 1835–1875.* New York: Harper and Row.

Kelly, Alfred H., Winfred A. Harbison, and Herman Belz. 1991. *The American Constitution: Its Origins and Developments.* New York: W. W. Norton.

Mantell, Martin E. 1973. *Johnson, Grant, and the Politics of Reconstruction.* New York: Columbia University Press.

Paludan, Philip Shaw. 1994. *The Presidency of Abraham Lincoln.* Lawrence: University Press of Kansas.

Urofsky, Melvin I., and Paul Finkelman. 2002. *A March of Liberty: A Constitutional History of the United States*, Vol. 1: *From the Founding to 1890.* New York: Oxford University Press.

Appendix: Documents

First Inaugural Address, President Abraham Lincoln (excerpts) (1861)

Apprehension seems to exist among the people of the Southern States that by the accession of a Republican administration their property and their peace and personal security are to be endangered. There has never been any reasonable cause for such apprehension. Indeed, the most ample evidence to the contrary has all the while existed and been open to their inspection. It is found in nearly all the published speeches of him who now addresses you. I do but quote from one of those speeches when I declare that "I have no purpose, directly or indirectly, to interfere with the institution of slavery where it exists. I believe I have no lawful right to do so, and I have no inclination to do so." Those who nominated and elected me did so with full knowledge that I had made this and many similar declarations, and had never recanted them. And, more than this, they placed in the platform for my acceptance, and as a law to themselves and to me, the clear and emphatic resolution which I now read:

> Resolved: that the maintenance inviolate of the rights of the States, and especially the right of each State to order and control its own domestic institutions according to its own judgment exclusively, is essential to that balance of power on which the perfection and endurance of our political fabric depend, and we denounce the lawless invasion by armed force of the soil of any State or Territory, no matter under what pretext, as among the gravest of crimes.

I now reiterate these sentiments; and, in doing so, I only press upon the public attention the most conclusive evidence of which the case is susceptible, that the property, peace, and security of no section are to be in any wise endangered by the now incoming administration. I add, too, that all the protection which, consistently with the Constitution and the laws, can be given, will be cheerfully given to all the States when lawfully demanded, for whatever cause—as cheerfully to one section as to another. . . .

It is seventy-two years since the first inauguration of a President under our national Constitution. During that period fifteen different and greatly distinguished citizens have, in succession, administered the executive branch of the government. They have conducted it through many perils, and generally with great success. Yet, with all this scope of precedent, I now enter upon the same task for the brief Constitutional term of four years under great and peculiar difficulty. A disruption of the Federal Union, heretofore only menaced, is now formidably attempted.

I hold that, in contemplation of universal law and of the Constitution, the Union of these States is perpetual. Perpetuity is implied, if not expressed, in the fundamental law of all national governments. It is safe to assert that no government proper ever had a provision in its organic law for its own termination. Continue to execute all the express provisions of our National Constitution, and the Union will endure forever—it being impossible to destroy it except by some action not provided for in the instrument itself.

Again, if the United States be not a government proper, but an association of States in the nature of contract merely, can it, as a contract, be peaceably unmade by less than all the parties who made it? One party to a contract may violate it—break it, so to speak; but does it not require all to lawfully rescind it?

Descending from these general principles, we find the proposition that in legal contemplation the Union is perpetual confirmed by the history of the Union itself. The Union is much older than the Constitution. It was formed, in fact, by the Articles of Association in 1774. It was matured and continued by the Declaration of Independence in 1776. It was further matured, and the faith of all the then thirteen States expressly plighted and engaged that it should be perpetual, by the Articles of Confederation in 1778. And, finally, in 1787 one of the declared objects for ordaining and establishing the Constitution was "TO FORM A MORE PERFECT UNION."

It follows from these views that no State upon its own mere motion can lawfully get out of the Union; that Resolves and Ordinances to that effect are legally void; and that acts of violence, within any State or States, against the authority of the United States, are insurrectionary or revolutionary, according to circumstances.

I therefore consider that, in view of the Constitution and the laws, the Union is unbroken; and to the extent of my ability I shall take care, as the Constitution itself expressly enjoins upon me, that the laws of the Union be faithfully executed in all the States. Doing this I deem to be only a simple duty on my part; and I shall perform it so far as practicable, unless my rightful masters, the American people, shall withhold the requisite means, or in some authoritative manner direct the contrary. I trust this will not be regarded as a menace, but only as the declared purpose of the Union that it WILL Constitutionally defend and maintain itself.

In doing this there needs to be no bloodshed or violence; and there shall be none, unless it be forced upon the national authority. The power confided to me will be used to hold, occupy, and possess the property and places belonging to the government, and to collect the duties and imposts; but beyond what may be necessary for these objects, there will be no invasion, no using of force against or among the people anywhere. Where hostility to the United States, in any interior locality, shall be so great and universal as to prevent competent resident citizens from holding the Federal offices, there will be no attempt to force obnoxious strangers among the people for that object. While the strict legal right may exist in the government to enforce the exercise of these offices, the attempt to do so would be so irritating, and so nearly impracticable withal, that I deem it better to forego for the time the uses of such offices.

The mails, unless repelled, will continue to be furnished in all parts of the Union. So far as possible, the people everywhere shall have that sense of perfect security which is most favorable to calm thought and reflection. The course here indicated will be followed unless current events and experience shall show a modification or change to be proper, and in every case and exigency my best discretion will be exercised according to circumstances actually existing, and with a view and a hope of a peaceful solution of the national troubles and the restoration of fraternal sympathies and affections.

That there are persons in one section or another who seek to destroy the Union at all events, and are glad of any pretext to do it, I will neither affirm nor deny; but if there be such, I need address no word to them. To those, however, who really love the Union may I not speak?

Before entering upon so grave a matter as the destruction of our national fabric, with all its benefits, its memories, and its hopes, would it not be wise to ascertain precisely why we do it? Will you hazard so desperate a step while there is any possibility that any portion of the ills you fly from have no real existence? Will you, while the certain ills you fly to are greater than all the real ones you fly from—will you risk the commission of so fearful a mistake?

All profess to be content in the Union if all Constitutional rights can be maintained. Is it true, then, that any right, plainly written in the Constitution, has been denied? I think not. Happily the human mind is so constituted that no party can reach to the audacity of doing this. Think, if you can, of a single instance in which a plainly written provision of the Constitution has ever been denied. If by the mere force of numbers a majority should deprive a minority of any clearly written Constitutional right, it might, in a moral point of view, justify revolution—certainly would if such a right were a vital one. But such is not our case. All the vital rights of minorities and of individuals are so plainly assured to them by affirmations and negations, guaranties and prohibitions, in the Constitution, that controversies never arise concerning them. But no organic law can ever be framed with a provision specifically applicable to every question which may occur in practical administration. No foresight can anticipate, nor any document of reasonable length contain, express provisions for all possible questions. Shall fugitives from labor be surrendered by national or State authority? The Constitution does not expressly say. May Congress prohibit slavery in the Territories? The Constitution does not expressly say. MUST Congress protect slavery in the Territories? The Constitution does not expressly say.

From questions of this class spring all our constitutional controversies, and we divide upon them into majorities and minorities. If the minority will not acquiesce, the majority must, or the government must cease. There is no other alternative; for continuing the government is acquiescence on one side or the other.

If a minority in such case will secede rather than acquiesce, they make a precedent which in turn will divide and ruin them; for a minority of their own will secede from them whenever a majority refuses to be controlled by such minority. For instance, why may not any portion of a new confederacy a year or two hence arbitrarily secede again, precisely as portions of the present Union now claim to secede from it? All who cherish disunion sentiments are now being educated to the exact temper of doing this. . . .

Plainly, the central idea of secession is the essence of anarchy. A majority held in restraint by constitutional checks and limitations, and always changing easily with deliberate changes of popular opinions and sentiments, is the only true sovereign of a free people. Whoever rejects it does, of necessity, fly to anarchy or to despotism. Unanimity is impossible; the rule of a minority, as a permanent arrangement, is wholly inadmissible; so that, rejecting the majority principle, anarchy or despotism in some form is all that is left.

I do not forget the position, assumed by some, that Constitutional questions are to be decided by the Supreme Court; nor do I deny that such decisions must be binding, in any case, upon the parties to a suit, as to the object of that suit, while they are also entitled to very high respect and consideration in all parallel cases by all other departments of the government. And while it is obviously possible that such decision may be erroneous in any given case, still the evil effect following it, being limited to that particular case, with the chance that it may be overruled and never become a precedent for other cases, can better be borne than could the evils of a different practice. At the same time, the candid citizen must confess that if the policy of the government, upon vital questions affecting the whole people, is to be irrevocably fixed by decisions of the Supreme Court, the instant they are made, in ordinary litigation between parties in personal actions, the people will have ceased to be their own rulers, having to that extent practically resigned their government into the hands of that eminent tribunal. Nor is there in this view any assault upon the court or the judges. It is a duty from which they may not shrink to decide cases properly brought before them, and it is no fault of theirs if others seek to turn their decisions to political purposes. One section of our country believes slavery is RIGHT, and ought to be extended, while the other believes it is WRONG, and ought not to be extended. This is the only substantial dispute. The fugitive-slave clause of the Constitution, and the law for the suppression of the foreign slave-trade, are each as well enforced, perhaps, as any law can ever be in a community where the moral sense of the people imperfectly supports the law itself. The great body of the people abide by the dry legal obligation in both cases, and a few break over in each. This, I think, cannot be perfectly cured; and it would be worse in both cases AFTER the separation of the sections than BEFORE. The foreign slave-trade, now imperfectly suppressed, would be ultimately revived, without restriction, in one section, while fugitive slaves, now only partially surrendered, would not be surrendered at all by the other.

Physically speaking, we cannot separate. We cannot remove our respective sections from each other, nor build an impassable wall between them. A husband and wife may be divorced, and go out of the presence and beyond the reach of each other; but the different parts of our country cannot do this. They cannot but remain face to face, and intercourse, either amicable or hostile, must continue between them. Is it possible, then, to make that intercourse more advantageous or more satisfactory after separation than before? Can aliens make treaties easier than friends can make laws? Can treaties be more faithfully enforced between aliens than laws can among friends? Suppose you go to war, you cannot fight always; and when, after much loss on both sides, and no gain on either, you cease fighting, the identical old questions as to terms of intercourse are again upon you. . . .

My countrymen, one and all, think calmly and WELL upon this whole subject. Nothing valuable can be lost by taking time. If there be an object to HURRY any of you in hot haste to a step which you would never take DELIBERATELY, that object will be frustrated by taking time; but no good object can be frustrated by it. Such of you as are now dissatisfied, still have the old Constitution unimpaired, and, on the sensitive point, the laws of your own framing under it; while the new administration will have no immediate power, if it would, to change either. If it were admitted that you who are dissatisfied hold the right side in the dispute, there still is no single good reason for precipitate action. Intelligence, patriotism, Christianity, and a firm reliance on him who has never yet forsaken this favored land, are still competent to adjust in the best way all our present difficulty.

In YOUR hands, my dissatisfied fellow-countrymen, and not in MINE, is the momentous issue of civil war. The government will not assail YOU. You can have no conflict without being yourselves the aggressors. YOU have no oath registered in heaven to destroy the government, while I shall have the most solemn one to "preserve, protect, and defend it."

I am loathe to close. We are not enemies, but friends. We must not be enemies. Though passion may have strained, it must not break our bonds of affection. The mystic chords of memory, stretching from every battlefield and patriot grave to every living heart and hearthstone all over this broad land, will yet swell the chorus of the Union when again touched, as surely they will be, by the better angels of our nature.

Inaugural Address to the Confederacy, Jefferson Davis (1861)

Gentlemen of the Congress of the Confederate States of America, Friends and Fellow-Citizens:

Called to the difficult and responsible station of Chief Executive of the Provisional Government which you have instituted, I approach the discharge of the duties assigned to me with an humble distrust of my abilities, but with a sustaining confidence in the wisdom of those who are to guide and aid me in the administration of public affairs, and an abiding faith in the virtue and patriotism of the people.

Looking forward to the speedy establishment of a permanent government to take the place of this, and which, by its greater moral and physical power, will be better able to combat with the many difficulties which arise from the conflicting interests of separate nations, I enter upon the duties of the office, to which I have been chosen, with the hope that the beginning of our career, as a Confederacy, may not be obstructed by hostile opposition to our enjoyment of the separate existence and independence which we have asserted, and, with the blessing of Providence, intend to maintain. Our present condition, achieved in a manner unprecedented in the history of nations, illustrates the American idea that governments rest upon the consent of the governed, and that it is the right of the people to alter or abolish governments whenever they become destructive of the ends for which they were established.

The declared purpose of the compact of union from which we have withdrawn, was "to establish justice, insure domestic tranquility, provide for the common defense, promote the general welfare;" and when in the judgment of the sovereign States now composing this Confederacy, it had been perverted from the purposes for which it was ordained, and had ceased to answer the ends for which it was established, a peaceful appeal to the ballot-box, declared that so far as they were concerned, the government created by that compact should cease to exist. In this they merely asserted a right which the Declaration of Independence of 1776 had defined to be inalienable. Of the time and occasion for its exercise, they as sovereigns, were the final judges, each for itself. The impartial and enlightened verdict of mankind will vindicate the rectitude of our conduct, and he, who knows the hearts of men, will judge of the sincerity with which we labored to preserve the government of our fathers in it spirit. The right solemnly proclaimed at the birth of the States and which has been affirmed and re-affirmed in the bills of rights of States subsequently admitted into the Union of 1789, undeniably recognizes in the people the power to resume the authority delegated for the purposes of government. Thus the sovereign States, here represented, proceeded to form this Confederacy, and it is by abuse of language that their act has been denominated a revolution. They formed a new alliance, but within each State its government has remained, and the rights of person and property have not been disturbed. The agent, through whom they communicated with foreign nations, is changed; but this does not necessarily interrupt their international relations.

Sustained by the consciousness that the transition from the former Union to the present Confederacy has not proceeded from a disregard on our part of just obligations, or any failure to perform any constitutional duty; moved by no interest or passion to invade the rights of others; anxious to cultivate peace and commerce with all nations, if we may not hope to avoid war, we may at least expect that posterity will acquit us of having needlessly engaged in it. Doubly justified by the absence of wrong on our part, and by wanton aggression on the part of others, there can be no cause to doubt that the courage and patriotism of the people of the Confederate States will be found equal to any measures of defense which honor and security may require.

An agricultural people, whose chief interest is the export of a commodity required in every manufacturing country, our true policy is peace and the freest trade which our necessities will permit. It is alike our interest, and that of all those to whom we would sell and from whom we would buy, that there should be fewest practicable restrictions upon the interchange of commodities. There can be but little rivalry between ours and any manufacturing or navigating community, such as the northeastern States of the American Union. It must follow, therefore, that a mutual interest would invite good will and kind offices. If, however, passion or the lust of dominion should cloud the judgment or inflame the ambition of those States, we must prepare to meet the emergency, and to maintain, by the final arbitrament of the sword, the position which we have assumed among the nations of the earth. We have entered upon the career of independence, and it must be inflexibly pursued. Through many years of controversy with our late associates, the Northern States, we have vainly endeavored to secure tranquility, and to obtain respect for the rights to which we are entitled. As a necessity, not a choice, we have resorted to the remedy of separation; and henceforth our energies must be directed to the conduct of our own affairs, and the perpetuity of the Confederacy which we have formed. If a just perception of mutual interest shall permit us peaceably to pursue our separate political career, my most earnest desire will have been fulfilled; but if this be denied to us, and the integrity of our territory and jurisdiction be assailed, it will but remain for us, with firm resolve, to appeal to arms and invoke the blessings of Providence on a just cause.

As a consequence of our new condition, and with a view to meet anticipated wants, it will be necessary to provide for the speedy and efficient organization of branches of the Executive Department, having special charge of foreign intercourse, finance, military affairs, and the postal service.

For purposes of defense, the Confederate States may, under ordinary circumstances, rely mainly upon the militia; but it is deemed advisable, in the present condition of affairs, that there should be a well-instructed and disciplined army, more numerous than would usually be required on a peace establishment. I also suggest that, for the protection of our harbors and commerce on the high seas, a navy adapted to those objects will be required. These necessities have doubtless engaged the attention of Congress.

With a constitution differing only from that of our fathers, in so far as it is explanatory of their well-known intent, freed from the sectional conflicts which have interfered with the pursuit of the general welfare, it is not unreasonable to expect that States from which we have recently parted, may seek to unite their fortunes with ours under the government which we have instituted. For this your constitution makes adequate provision; but beyond this, if I mistake not, the judgment and will of the people, a re-union with the States from which we have separated is neither practicable nor desirable. To increase the power, develop the resources, and promote the happiness of the Confederacy, it is requisite that there should be so much homogeneity that the welfare of every portion shall be the aim of the whole. Where this does not exist, antagonisms are engendered which must and should result in separation.

Actuated solely by the desire to preserve our own rights and promote our own welfare, the separation of the Confederate States has been marked by no aggression upon others, and followed by no domestic convulsion. Our industrial pursuits have received no check; the cultivation of our fields has progressed as heretofore; and even should we be involved in war, there would be no considerable diminution in the production of the staples which have constituted our exports, and in which the commercial world has an interest scarcely less than our own. This common interest of the producer and consumer can only be interrupted by an exterior force, which should obstruct its transmission to foreign markets—a course of conduct which would be as unjust towards us as it would be detrimental to manufacturing and commercial interests abroad. Should reason guide the action of the government from which we have separated, a policy so detrimental to the civilized world, the Northern States included, could not be dictated by even the strongest desire to inflict injury upon us; but if otherwise, a terrible responsibility will rest upon it, and the suffering of millions will bear testimony to the folly and wickedness of our aggressors. In the meantime, there will remain to us, besides the ordinary means before suggested, the well-known resources for retaliation upon the commerce of the enemy.

Experience in public stations, of subordinate grades to this which your kindness has conferred, has taught me that care, and toil, and disappointment, are the price of official elevation. You will see many errors to forgive, many deficiencies to tolerate, but you shall not find in me either a want of zeal or fidelity to the cause that is to me highest in hope and of most enduring affection. Your generosity has bestowed upon me an undeserved distinction—one which I never sought nor desired. Upon the continuance of that sentiment, and upon your wisdom and patriotism, I rely to direct and support me in the performance of the duty required at my hands.

We have changed the constituent parts but not the system of our government. The constitution formed by our fathers is that of these Confederates States, in their exposition of it; and, in the judicial construction it has received, we have a light that reveals its true meaning.

Thus instructed as to the just interpretation of the instrument, and ever remembering that all offices are but trusts held for the people, and that delegated powers are to be strictly construed, I will hope by due diligence in the performance of my duties, though I may disappoint your expectations, yet to retain, when retiring, something of the good will and confidence which welcomed my entrance into office.

It is joyous, in the midst of perilous times, to look around upon a people united in heart, where one purpose of high resolve animates and actuates the whole—where the sacrifices to be made are not weighed in the balance against honor, and right, and liberty, and equality. Obstacles may retard—they cannot long prevent—the progress of a movement sanctified by its justice, and sustained by a virtuous people. Reverently let us invoke the God of our fathers to guide and protect us in our efforts to perpetuate the principles which, by his blessing, they were able to vindicate, establish, and transmit to their posterity, and with a continuance of his favor, ever gratefully acknowledged, we may hopefully look forward to success, to peace, and to prosperity.

Confederate Constitution (1861)

Preamble

We, the people of the Confederate States, each State acting in its sovereign and independent character, in order to form a permanent federal government, establish justice, insure domestic tranquillity, and secure the blessings of liberty to ourselves and our posterity invoking the favor and guidance of Almighty God do ordain and establish this Constitution for the Confederate States of America.

Article I

Section I. All legislative powers herein delegated shall be vested in a Congress of the Confederate States, which shall consist of a Senate and House of Representatives.

Sec. 2. (I) The House of Representatives shall be composed of members chosen every second year by the people of the several States; and the electors in each State shall be citizens of the Confederate States, and have the qualifications requisite for electors of the most numerous branch of the State Legislature; but no person of foreign birth, not a citizen of the Confederate States, shall be allowed to vote for any officer, civil or political, State or Federal.

(2) No person shall be a Representative who shall not have attained the age of twenty-five years, and be a citizen of the Confederate States, and who shall not when elected, be an inhabitant of that State in which he shall be chosen.

(3) Representatives and direct taxes shall be apportioned among the several States, which may be included within this Confederacy, according to their respective numbers, which shall be determined by adding to the whole number of free persons, including those bound to service for a term of years, and excluding Indians not taxed, three-fifths of all slaves. The actual enumeration shall be made within three years after the first meeting of the Congress of the Confederate States, and within every subsequent term of ten years, in such manner as they shall by law direct. The number of Representatives shall not exceed one for every fifty thousand, but each State shall have at least one Representative; and until such enumeration shall be made, the State of South Carolina shall be entitled to choose six; the State of Georgia ten; the State of Alabama nine; the State of Florida two; the State of Mississippi seven; the State of Louisiana six; and the State of Texas six.

(4) When vacancies happen in the representation from any State the executive authority thereof shall issue writs of election to fill such vacancies.

(5) The House of Representatives shall choose their Speaker and other officers; and shall have the sole power of impeachment; except that any judicial or other Federal officer, resident and acting solely within the limits of any State, may be impeached by a vote of two-thirds of both branches of the Legislature thereof.

Sec. 3. (I) The Senate of the Confederate States shall be composed of two Senators from each State, chosen for six years by the Legislature thereof, at the regular session next immediately preceding the commencement of the term of service; and each Senator shall have one vote.

(2) Immediately after they shall be assembled, in consequence of the first election, they shall be divided as equally as may be into three classes. The seats of the Senators of the first class shall be vacated at the expiration of the second year; of the second class at the expiration of the fourth year; and of the third class at the expiration of the sixth year; so that one-third may be chosen every second year; and if vacancies happen by resignation, or other wise, during the recess of the Legislature of any State, the Executive thereof may make temporary appointments until the next meeting of the Legislature, which shall then fill such vacancies.

(3) No person shall be a Senator who shall not have attained the age of thirty years, and be a citizen of the Confederate States; and who shall not, then elected, be an inhabitant of the State for which he shall be chosen.

(4) The Vice President of the Confederate States shall be president of the Senate, but shall have no vote unless they be equally divided.

(5) The Senate shall choose their other officers; and also a president pro tempore in the absence of the Vice President, or when he shall exercise the office of President of the Confederate States.

(6) The Senate shall have the sole power to try all impeachments. When sitting for that purpose, they shall be on oath or affirmation. When the President of the Confederate States is tried, the Chief Justice shall preside; and no person shall be convicted without the concurrence of two-thirds of the members present.

(7) Judgment in cases of impeachment shall not extend further than to removal from office, and disqualification to hold any office of honor, trust, or profit under the Confederate States; but the party convicted shall, nevertheless, be liable and subject to indictment, trial, judgment, and punishment according to law.

Sec. 4. (I) The times, places, and manner of holding elections for Senators and Representatives shall be prescribed in each State by the Legislature thereof, subject to the provisions of this Constitution; but the Congress may, at any time, by law, make or alter such regulations, except as to the times and places of choosing Senators.

(2) The Congress shall assemble at least once in every year; and such meeting shall be on the first Monday in December, unless they shall, by law, appoint a different day.

Sec. 5. (I) Each House shall be the judge of the elections, returns, and qualifications of its own members, and a majority of each shall constitute a quorum to do business; but a smaller number may adjourn from day to day, and may be authorized to compel the attendance of absent members, in such manner and under such penalties as each House may provide.

(2) Each House may determine the rules of its proceedings, punish its members for disorderly behavior, and, with the concurrence of two-thirds of the whole number, expel a member.

(3) Each House shall keep a journal of its proceedings, and from time to time publish the same, excepting such parts as may in their judgment require secrecy; and the yeas and nays of the members of either House, on any question, shall, at the desire of one-fifth of those present, be entered on the journal.

(4) Neither House, during the session of Congress, shall, without the consent of the other, adjourn for more than three days, nor to any other place than that in which the two Houses shall be sitting.

Sec. 6. (I) The Senators and Representatives shall receive a compensation for their services, to be ascertained by law, and paid out of the Treasury of the Confederate States. They shall, in all cases, except treason, felony, and breach of the peace, be privileged from arrest during their attendance at the session of their respective Houses, and in going to and returning from the same; and for any speech or debate in either House, they shall not be questioned in any other place. No Senator or Representative shall, during the time for which he was elected, be appointed to any civil office under the authority of the Confederate States, which shall have been created, or the emoluments whereof shall have been increased during such time; and no person holding any office under the Confederate States shall be a member of either House during his continuance in office. But Congress may, by law, grant to the principal officer in each of the Executive Departments a seat upon the floor of either House, with the privilege of discussing any measures appertaining to his department.

Sec. 7. (I) All bills for raising revenue shall originate in the House of Representatives; but the Senate may propose or concur with amendments, as on other bills.

(2) Every bill which shall have passed both Houses, shall, before it becomes a law, be presented to the President of the Confederate States; if he approve, he shall sign it; but if not, he shall return it, with his objections, to that House in which it shall have originated, who shall enter the objections at large on their journal, and proceed to reconsider it. If, after such reconsideration, two-thirds of that House shall agree to pass the bill, it shall be sent, together with the objections, to the other House, by which it shall likewise be reconsidered, and if approved by two-thirds of that House, it shall become a law. But in all such cases, the votes of both Houses shall be determined by yeas and nays, and the names of the persons voting for and against the bill shall be entered on the journal of each House respectively. If any bill shall not be returned by the President within ten days (Sundays excepted) after it shall have been presented to him, the same shall be a law, in like manner as if he had signed it, unless the Congress, by their adjournment, prevent its return; in which case it shall not be a law. The President may approve any appropriation and disapprove any other appropriation in the same bill. In such case he shall, in signing the bill, designate the appropriations disapproved; and shall return a copy of such appropriations, with his objections, to the House in which the bill shall have originated; and the same proceedings shall then be had as in case of other bills disapproved by the President.

(3) Every order, resolution, or vote, to which the concurrence of both Houses may be necessary (except on a question of adjournment) shall be presented to the President of the Confederate States; and before the same shall take effect, shall be approved by him; or, being disapproved by him, shall be repassed by two-thirds of both Houses, according to the rules and limitations prescribed in case of a bill.

Sec. 8. The Congress shall have power—

(I) To lay and collect taxes, duties, imposts, and excises for revenue, necessary to pay the debts, provide for the common defense, and carry on the Government of the Confederate States; but no bounties shall be granted from the Treasury; nor shall any duties or taxes on importations from foreign nations be laid to promote or foster any branch of industry; and all duties, imposts, and excises shall be uniform throughout the Confederate States.

(2) To borrow money on the credit of the Confederate States.

(3) To regulate commerce with foreign nations, and among the several States, and with the Indian tribes; but neither this, nor any other clause contained in the Constitution, shall ever be construed to delegate the power to Congress to appropriate money for any internal improvement intended to facilitate commerce; except for the purpose of furnishing lights, beacons, and buoys, and other aids to navigation upon the coasts, and the improvement of harbors and the removing of obstructions in river navigation; in all which cases such duties shall be laid on the navigation facilitated thereby as may be necessary to pay the costs and expenses thereof.

(4) To establish uniform laws of naturalization, and uniform laws on the subject of bankruptcies, throughout the Confederate States; but no law of Congress shall discharge any debt contracted before the passage of the same.

(5) To coin money, regulate the value thereof, and of foreign coin, and fix the standard of weights and measures.

(6) To provide for the punishment of counterfeiting the securities and current coin of the Confederate States.

(7) To establish post offices and post routes; but the expenses of the Post Office Department, after the Ist day of March in the year of our Lord eighteen hundred and sixty-three, shall be paid out of its own revenues.

(8) To promote the progress of science and useful arts, by securing for limited times to authors and inventors the exclusive right to their respective writings and discoveries.

(9) To constitute tribunals inferior to the Supreme Court.

(10) To define and punish piracies and felonies committed on the high seas, and offenses against the law of nations.

(11) To declare war, grant letters of marque and reprisal, and make rules concerning captures on land and water.

(12) To raise and support armies; but no appropriation of money to that use shall be for a longer term than two years.

(13) To provide and maintain a navy.

(14) To make rules for the government and regulation of the land and naval forces.

(15) To provide for calling forth the militia to execute the laws of the Confederate States, suppress insurrections, and repel invasions.

(16) To provide for organizing, arming, and disciplining the militia, and for governing such part of them as may be employed in the service of the Confederate States; reserving to the States, respectively, the appointment of the officers, and the authority of training the militia according to the discipline prescribed by Congress.

(17) To exercise exclusive legislation, in all cases whatsoever, over such district (not exceeding ten miles square) as may, by cession of one or more States and the

acceptance of Congress, become the seat of the Government of the Confederate States; and to exercise like authority over all places purchased by the consent of the Legislature of the State in which the same shall be, for the erection of forts, magazines, arsenals, dockyards, and other needful buildings; and

(18) To make all laws which shall be necessary and proper for carrying into execution the foregoing powers, and all other powers vested by this Constitution in the Government of the Confederate States, or in any department or officer thereof.

Sec. 9. (I) The importation of negroes of the African race from any foreign country other than the slaveholding States or Territories of the United States of America, is hereby forbidden; and Congress is required to pass such laws as shall effectually prevent the same.

(2) Congress shall also have power to prohibit the introduction of slaves from any State not a member of, or Territory not belonging to, this Confederacy.

(3) The privilege of the writ of habeas corpus shall not be suspended, unless when in cases of rebellion or invasion the public safety may require it.

(4) No bill of attainder, ex post facto law, or law denying or impairing the right of property in negro slaves shall be passed.

(5) No capitation or other direct tax shall be laid, unless in proportion to the census or enumeration hereinbefore directed to be taken.

(6) No tax or duty shall be laid on articles exported from any State, except by a vote of two-thirds of both Houses.

(7) No preference shall be given by any regulation of commerce or revenue to the ports of one State over those of another.

(8) No money shall be drawn from the Treasury, but in consequence of appropriations made by law; and a regular statement and account of the receipts and expenditures of all public money shall be published from time to time.

(9) Congress shall appropriate no money from the Treasury except by a vote of two-thirds of both Houses, taken by yeas and nays, unless it be asked and estimated for by some one of the heads of departments and submitted to Congress by the President; or for the purpose of paying its own expenses and contingencies; or for the payment of claims against the Confederate States, the justice of which shall have been judicially declared by a tribunal for the investigation of claims against the Government, which it is hereby made the duty of Congress to establish.

(10) All bills appropriating money shall specify in Federal currency the exact amount of each appropriation and the purposes for which it is made; and Congress shall grant no extra compensation to any public contractor, officer, agent, or servant, after such contract shall have been made or such service rendered.

(11) No title of nobility shall be granted by the Confederate States; and no person holding any office of profit or trust under them shall, without the consent of the

Congress, accept of any present, emolument, office, or title of any kind whatever, from any king, prince, or foreign state.

(12) Congress shall make no law respecting an establishment of religion, or prohibiting the free exercise thereof; or abridging the freedom of speech, or of the press; or the right of the people peaceably to assemble and petition the Government for a redress of grievances.

(13) A well-regulated militia being necessary to the security of a free State, the right of the people to keep and bear arms shall not be infringed.

(14) No soldier shall, in time of peace, be quartered in any house without the consent of the owner; nor in time of war, but in a manner to be prescribed by law.

(15) The right of the people to be secure in their persons, houses, papers, and effects, against unreasonable searches and seizures, shall not be violated; and no warrants shall issue but upon probable cause, supported by oath or affirmation, and particularly describing the place to be searched and the persons or things to be seized.

(16) No person shall be held to answer for a capital or otherwise infamous crime, unless on a presentment or indictment of a grand jury, except in cases arising in the land or naval forces, or in the militia, when in actual service in time of war or public danger; nor shall any person be subject for the same offense to be twice put in jeopardy of life or limb; nor be compelled, in any criminal case, to be a witness against himself; nor be deprived of life, liberty, or property without due process of law; nor shall private property be taken for public use, without just compensation.

(17) In all criminal prosecutions the accused shall enjoy the right to a speedy and public trial, by an impartial jury of the State and district wherein the crime shall have been committed, which district shall have been previously ascertained by law, and to be informed of the nature and cause of the accusation; to be confronted with the witnesses against him; to have compulsory process for obtaining witnesses in his favor; and to have the assistance of counsel for his defense.

(18) In suits at common law, where the value in controversy shall exceed twenty dollars, the right of trial by jury shall be preserved; and no fact so tried by a jury shall be otherwise reexamined in any court of the Confederacy, than according to the rules of common law.

(19) Excessive bail shall not be required, nor excessive fines imposed, nor cruel and unusual punishments inflicted.

(20) Every law, or resolution having the force of law, shall relate to but one subject, and that shall be expressed in the title.

Sec. 10. (I) No State shall enter into any treaty, alliance, or confederation; grant letters of marque and reprisal; coin money; make anything but gold and silver coin a tender in payment of debts; pass any bill of attainder, or ex post facto law, or law impairing the obligation of contracts; or grant any title of nobility.

(2) No State shall, without the consent of the Congress, lay any imposts or duties on imports or exports, except what may be absolutely necessary for executing its inspection laws; and the net produce of all duties and imposts, laid by any State on imports, or exports, shall be for the use of the Treasury of the Confederate States; and all such laws shall be subject to the revision and control of Congress.

(3) No State shall, without the consent of Congress, lay any duty on tonnage, except on seagoing vessels, for the improvement of its rivers and harbors navigated by the said vessels; but such duties shall not conflict with any treaties of the Confederate States with foreign nations; and any surplus revenue thus derived shall, after making such improvement, be paid into the common treasury. Nor shall any State keep troops or ships of war in time of peace, enter into any agreement or compact with another State, or with a foreign power, or engage in war, unless actually invaded, or in such imminent danger as will not admit of delay. But when any river divides or flows through two or more States they may enter into compacts with each other to improve the navigation thereof.

Article II

Section I. (I) The executive power shall be vested in a President of the Confederate States of America. He and the Vice President shall hold their offices for the term of six years; but the President shall not be reeligible. The President and Vice President shall be elected as follows:

(2) Each State shall appoint, in such manner as the Legislature thereof may direct, a number of electors equal to the whole number of Senators and Representatives to which the State may be entitled in the Congress; but no Senator or Representative or person holding an office of trust or profit under the Confederate States shall be appointed an elector.

(3) The electors shall meet in their respective States and vote by ballot for President and Vice President, one of whom, at least, shall not be an inhabitant of the same State with themselves; they shall name in their ballots the person voted for as President, and in distinct ballots the person voted for as Vice President, and they shall make distinct lists of all persons voted for as President, and of all persons voted for as Vice President, and of the number of votes for each, which lists they shall sign and certify, and transmit, sealed, to the seat of the Government of the Confederate States, directed to the President of the Senate; the President of the Senate shall, in the presence of the Senate and House of Representatives, open all the certificates, and the votes shall then be counted; the person having the greatest number of votes for President shall be the President, if such number be a majority of the whole number of electors appointed; and if no person have such majority, then from the persons having the highest numbers, not exceeding three, on the list of those voted for as President, the House of Representatives shall choose immediately, by ballot, the President. But in choosing the

President the votes shall be taken by States, the representation from each State having one vote; a quorum for this purpose shall consist of a member or members from two-thirds of the States, and a majority of all the States shall be necessary to a choice. And if the House of Representatives shall not choose a President, whenever the right of choice shall devolve upon them, before the 4th day of March next following, then the Vice President shall act as President, as in case of the death, or other constitutional disability of the President.

(4) The person having the greatest number of votes as Vice President shall be the Vice President, if such number be a majority of the whole number of electors appointed; and if no person have a majority, then, from the two highest numbers on the list, the Senate shall choose the Vice President; a quorum for the purpose shall consist of two-thirds of the whole number of Senators, and a majority of the whole number shall be necessary to a choice.

(5) But no person constitutionally ineligible to the office of President shall be eligible to that of Vice President of the Confederate States.

(6) The Congress may determine the time of choosing the electors, and the day on which they shall give their votes; which day shall be the same throughout the Confederate States.

(7) No person except a natural-born citizen of the Confederate States, or a citizen thereof at the time of the adoption of this Constitution, or a citizen thereof born in the United States prior to the 20th of December, 1860, shall be eligible to the office of President; neither shall any person be eligible to that office who shall not have attained the age of thirty-five years, and been fourteen years a resident within the limits of the Confederate States, as they may exist at the time of his election.

(8) In case of the removal of the President from office, or of his death, resignation, or inability to discharge the powers and duties of said office, the same shall devolve on the Vice President; and the Congress may, by law, provide for the case of removal, death, resignation, or inability, both of the President and Vice President, declaring what officer shall then act as President; and such officer shall act accordingly until the disability be removed or a President shall be elected.

(9) The President shall, at stated times, receive for his services a compensation, which shall neither be increased nor diminished during the period for which he shall have been elected; and he shall not receive within that period any other emolument from the Confederate States, or any of them.

(10) Before he enters on the execution of his office he shall take the following oath or affirmation. . . .

Sec. 2. (I) The President shall be Commander-in-Chief of the Army and Navy of the Confederate States, and of the militia of the several States, when called into the actual service of the Confederate States; he may require the opinion, in writing, of the principal officer in each of the Executive Departments, upon any subject relating to the duties of their respective offices; and he shall have power to grant reprieves and pardons for offenses against the Confederate States, except in cases of impeachment.

(2) He shall have power, by and with the advice and consent of the Senate, to make treaties; provided two-thirds of the Senators present concur; and he shall nominate, and by and with the advice and consent of the Senate shall appoint, ambassadors, other public ministers and consuls, judges of the Supreme Court, and all other officers of the Confederate States whose appointments are not herein otherwise provided for, and which shall be established by law; but the Congress may, by law, vest the appointment of such inferior officers, as they think proper, in the President alone, in the courts of law, or in the heads of departments.

(3) The principal officer in each of the Executive Departments, and all persons connected with the diplomatic service, may be removed from office at the pleasure of the President. All other civil officers of the Executive Departments may be removed at any time by the President, or other appointing power, when their services are unnecessary, or for dishonesty, incapacity, inefficiency, misconduct, or neglect of duty; and when so removed, the removal shall be reported to the Senate, together with the reasons therefor.

(4) The President shall have power to fill all vacancies that may happen during the recess of the Senate, by granting commissions which shall expire at the end of their next session; but no person rejected by the Senate shall be reappointed to the same office during their ensuing recess.

Sec. 3. (I) The President shall, from time to time, give to the Congress information of the state of the Confederacy, and recommend to their consideration such measures as he shall judge necessary and expedient; he may, on extraordinary occasions, convene both Houses, or either of them; and in case of disagreement between them, with respect to the time of adjournment, he may adjourn them to such time as he shall think proper; he shall receive ambassadors and other public ministers; he shall take care that the laws be faithfully executed, and shall commission all the officers of the Confederate States.

Sec. 4. (I) The President, Vice President, and all civil officers of the Confederate States, shall be removed from office on impeachment for and conviction of treason, bribery, or other high crimes and misdemeanors.

Article III

Section I. (I) The judicial power of the Confederate States shall be vested in one Supreme Court, and in such inferior courts as the Congress may, from time to time, ordain and establish. The judges, both of the Supreme and inferior courts, shall hold their offices during good behavior, and shall, at stated times, receive for their services a compensation which shall not be diminished during their continuance in office.

Sec. 2. (I) The judicial power shall extend to all cases arising under this Constitution, the laws of the Confederate States, and treaties made, or which shall be made, under their authority; to all cases affecting ambassadors, other public ministers and consuls; to all cases of admiralty and maritime jurisdiction; to controversies to which the Confederate States shall be a party; to controversies between two or more States; between a State and citizens of another State, where the State is plaintiff; between citizens claiming lands under grants of different States; and between a State or the citizens thereof, and foreign states, citizens, or subjects; but no State shall be sued by a citizen or subject of any foreign state.

(2) In all cases affecting ambassadors, other public ministers and consuls, and those in which a State shall be a party, the Supreme Court shall have original jurisdiction. In all the other cases before mentioned, the Supreme Court shall have appellate jurisdiction both as to law and fact, with such exceptions and under such regulations as the Congress shall make.

(3) The trial of all crimes, except in cases of impeachment, shall be by jury, and such trial shall be held in the State where the said crimes shall have been committed; but when not committed within any State, the trial shall be at such place or places as the Congress may by law have directed.

Sec. 3. (I) Treason against the Confederate States shall consist only in levying war against them, or in adhering to their enemies, giving them aid and comfort. No person shall be convicted of treason unless on the testimony of two witnesses to the same overt act, or on confession in open court.

(2) The Congress shall have power to declare the punishment of treason; but no attainder of treason shall work corruption of blood, or forfeiture, except during the life of the person attainted.

Article IV

Section I. (I) Full faith and credit shall be given in each State to the public acts, records, and judicial proceedings of every other State; and the Congress may, by general laws, prescribe the manner in which such acts, records, and proceedings shall be proved, and the effect thereof.

Sec. 2. (I) The citizens of each State shall be entitled to all the privileges and immunities of citizens in the several States; and shall have the right of transit and sojourn in any State of this Confederacy, with their slaves and other property; and the right of property in said slaves shall not be thereby impaired.

(2) A person charged in any State with treason, felony, or other crime against the laws of such State, who shall flee from justice, and be found in another State, shall, on demand of the executive authority of the State from which he fled, be delivered up, to be removed to the State having jurisdiction of the crime.

(3) No slave or other person held to service or labor in any State or Territory of the Confederate States, under the laws thereof, escaping or lawfully carried into

another, shall, in consequence of any law or regulation therein, be discharged from such service or labor; but shall be delivered up on claim of the party to whom such slave belongs, or to whom such service or labor may be due.

Sec. 3. (I) Other States may be admitted into this Confederacy by a vote of two-thirds of the whole House of Representatives and two-thirds of the Senate, the Senate voting by States; but no new State shall be formed or erected within the jurisdiction of any other State, nor any State be formed by the junction of two or more States, or parts of States, without the consent of the Legislatures of the States concerned, as well as of the Congress.

(2) The Congress shall have power to dispose of and make all needful rules and regulations concerning the property of the Confederate States, including the lands thereof.

(3) The Confederate States may acquire new territory; and Congress shall have power to legislate and provide governments for the inhabitants of all territory belonging to the Confederate States, lying without the limits of the several Sates; and may permit them, at such times, and in such manner as it may by law provide, to form States to be admitted into the Confederacy. In all such territory the institution of negro slavery, as it now exists in the Confederate States, shall be recognized and protected be Congress and by the Territorial government; and the inhabitants of the several Confederate States and Territories shall have the right to take to such Territory any slaves lawfully held by them in any of the States or Territories of the Confederate States.

(4) The Confederate States shall guarantee to every State that now is, or hereafter may become, a member of this Confederacy, a republican form of government; and shall protect each of them against invasion; and on application of the Legislature or of the Executive when the Legislature is not in session, against domestic violence.

Article V

Section I. (I) Upon the demand of any three States, legally assembled in their several conventions, the Congress shall summon a convention of all the States, to take into consideration such amendments to the Constitution as the said States shall concur in suggesting at the time when the said demand is made; and should any of the proposed amendments to the Constitution be agreed on by the said convention, voting by States, and the same be ratified by the Legislatures of two-thirds of the several States, or by conventions in two-thirds thereof, as the one or the other mode of ratification may be proposed by the general convention, they shall thenceforward form a part of this Constitution. But no State shall, without its consent, be deprived of its equal representation in the Senate.

Article VI

I. The Government established by this Constitution is the successor of the Provisional Government of the Confederate States of America, and all the laws passed by the latter shall continue in force until the same shall be repealed or modified; and all the officers appointed by the same shall remain in office until their successors are appointed and qualified, or the offices abolished.

2. All debts contracted and engagements entered into before the adoption of this Constitution shall be as valid against the Confederate States under this Constitution, as under the Provisional Government.

3. This Constitution, and the laws of the Confederate States made in pursuance thereof, and all treaties made, or which shall be made, under the authority of the Confederate States, shall be the supreme law of the land; and the judges in every State shall be bound thereby, anything in the constitution or laws of any State to the contrary notwithstanding.

4. The Senators and Representatives before mentioned, and the members of the several State Legislatures, and all executive and judicial officers, both of the Confederate States and of the several States, shall be bound by oath or affirmation to support this Constitution; but no religious test shall ever be required as a qualification to any office or public trust under the Confederate States.

5. The enumeration, in the Constitution, of certain rights shall not be construed to deny or disparage others retained by the people of the several States.

6. The powers not delegated to the Confederate States by the Constitution, nor prohibited by it to the States, are reserved to the States, respectively, or to the people thereof.

Article VII

I. The ratification of the conventions of five States shall be sufficient for the establishment of this Constitution between the States so ratifying the same.

2. When five States shall have ratified this Constitution, in the manner before specified, the Congress under the Provisional Constitution shall prescribe the time for holding the election of President and Vice President; and for the meeting of the Electoral College; and for counting the votes, and inaugurating the President. They shall, also, prescribe the time for holding the first election of members of Congress under this Constitution, and the time for assembling the same. Until the assembling of such Congress, the Congress under the Provisional Constitution shall continue to exercise the legislative powers granted them; not extending beyond the time limited by the Constitution of the Provisional Government.

Adopted unanimously by the Congress of the Confederate States of South Carolina, Georgia, Florida, Alabama, Mississippi, Louisiana, and Texas, sitting in convention at the capitol, the city of Montgomery, Ala., on the eleventh day of March, in the year eighteen hundred and Sixty-one.

HOWELL COBB, President of the Congress.

South Carolina: R. Barnwell Rhett, C. G. Memminger, Wm. Porcher Miles, James Chesnut, Jr., R. W. Barnwell, William W. Boyce, Lawrence M. Keitt, T. J. Withers.

Georgia: Francis S. Bartow, Martin J. Crawford, Benjamin H. Hill, Thos. R. R. Cobb.

Florida: Jackson Morton, J. Patton Anderson, Jas. B. Owens.

Alabama: Richard W. Walker, Robt. H. Smith, Colin J. McRae, William P. Chilton, Stephen F. Hale, David P. Lewis, Tho. Fearn, Jno. Gill Shorter, J. L. M. Curry.

Mississippi: Alex. M. Clayton, James T. Harrison, William S. Barry, W. S. Wilson, Walker Brooke, W. P. Harris, J. A. P. Campbell.

Louisiana: Alex. de Clouet, C. M. Conrad, Duncan F. Kenner, Henry Marshall.

Texas: John Hemphill, Thomas N. Waul, John H. Reagan, Williamson S. Oldham, Louis T. Wigfall, John Gregg, William Beck Ochiltree.

Letter from President Abraham Lincoln to Horace Greeley, editor of the New York Herald Tribune *(excerpt) (1862)*

"I would save the Union. I would save it the shortest way under the Constitution. The sooner the national authority can be restored; the nearer the Union will be the Union as it was. If there be those who would not save the Union, unless they could at the same time save slavery, I do not agree with them. If there be those who would not save the Union unless they could at the same time destroy slavery, I do not agree with them. My paramount object in this struggle is to save the Union, and is not either to save or destroy slavery. If I could save the Union without freeing any slave, I would do it; and if I could save it by freeing all the slaves, I would do it; and if I could save it by freeing some and leaving others alone I would also do that. . . . I have here stated my purpose according to my view of official duty; and I intend no modification of my oft-expressed personal wish that all men everywhere could be free."

Emancipation Proclamation, President Abraham Lincoln (1862)

Whereas on the 22nd day of September, A.D. 1862, a proclamation was issued by the President of the United States, containing, among other things, the following, to wit:

"That on the 1st day of January, A.D. 1863, all persons held as slaves within any State or designated part of a State the people whereof shall then be in rebellion against the United States shall be then, thenceforward, and forever free; and the executive government of the United States, including the military and naval authority thereof, will recognize and maintain the freedom of such persons and will do no act or acts to repress such persons, or any of them, in any efforts they may make for their actual freedom.

"That the executive will on the 1st day of January aforesaid, by proclamation, designate the States and parts of States, if any, in which the people thereof, respectively, shall then be in rebellion against the United States; and the fact that any State or the people thereof shall on that day be in good faith represented in the Congress of the United States by members chosen thereto at elections wherein a majority of the qualified voters of such States shall have participated shall, in the absence of strong countervailing testimony, be deemed conclusive evidence that such State and the people thereof are not then in rebellion against the United States."

Now, therefore, I, Abraham Lincoln, President of the United States, by virtue of the power in me vested as Commander-In-Chief of the Army and Navy of the United States in time of actual armed rebellion against the authority and government of the United States, and as a fit and necessary war measure for supressing said rebellion, do, on this 1st day of January, A.D. 1863, and in accordance with my purpose so to do, publicly proclaimed for the full period of one hundred days from the first day above mentioned, order and designate as the States and parts of States wherein the people thereof, respectively, are this day in rebellion against the United States the following, to wit:

Arkansas, Texas, Louisiana (except the parishes of St. Bernard, Palquemines, Jefferson, St. John, St. Charles, St. James, Ascension, Assumption, Terrebone, Lafourche, St. Mary, St. Martin, and Orleans, including the city of New Orleans), Mississippi, Alabama, Florida, Georgia, South Carolina, North Carolina, and Virginia (except the forty-eight counties designated as West Virginia, and also the counties of Berkeley, Accomac, Morthhampton, Elizabeth City, York, Princess Anne, and Norfolk, including the cities of Norfolk and Portsmouth), and which excepted parts are for the present left precisely as if this proclamation were not issued.

And by virtue of the power and for the purpose aforesaid, I do order and declare that all persons held as slaves within said designated States and parts of States are, and henceforward shall be, free; and that the Executive Government of the United States, including the military and naval authorities thereof, will recognize and maintain the freedom of said persons.

And I hereby enjoin upon the people so declared to be free to abstain from all violence, unless in necessary self-defence; and I recommend to them that, in all case when allowed, they labor faithfully for reasonable wages.

And I further declare and make known that such persons of suitable condition will be received into the armed service of the United States to garrison forts, positions, stations, and other places, and to man vessels of all sorts in said service.

And upon this act, sincerely believed to be an act of justice, warranted by the Constitution upon military necessity, I invoke the considerate judgment of mankind and the gracious favor of Almighty God.

Proclamation of Amnesty and Reconstruction, Abraham Lincoln (1863)

Whereas, in and by the Constitution of the United States, it is provided that the President "shall have power to grant reprieves and pardons for offences against the United States, except in cases of impeachment;" and

Whereas a rebellion now exists whereby the loyal State governments of several States have for a long time been subverted, and many persons have committed and are now guilty of treason against the United States; and

Whereas, with reference to said rebellion and treason, laws have been enacted by Congress declaring forfeitures and confiscation of property and liberation of slaves, all upon terms and conditions therein stated, and also declaring that the President was thereby authorized at any time thereafter, by proclamation, to extend to persons who may have participated in the existing rebellion, in any State or part thereof, pardon and amnesty, with such exceptions and at such times and on such conditions as he may deem expedient for the public welfare; and

Whereas the congressional declaration for limited and conditional pardon accords with well-established judicial exposition of the pardoning power; and

Whereas, with reference to said rebellion, the President of the United States has issued several proclamations, with provisions in regard to the liberation of slaves; and

Whereas it is now desired by some persons heretofore engaged in said rebellion to resume their allegiance to the United States, and to reinaugurate loyal State governments within and for their respective States; therefore,

I, Abraham Lincoln, President of the United States, do proclaim, declare, and make known to all persons who have, directly or by implication, participated in the existing rebellion, except as hereinafter excepted, that a full pardon is hereby granted to them and each of them, with restoration of all rights of property, except as to slaves, and in property cases where rights of third parties shall have intervened, and upon the condition that every such person shall take and subscribe an oath, and thenceforward keep and maintain said oath inviolate; and which oath shall be registered for permanent preservation, and shall be of the tenor and effect following, to wit:

"I,————, do solemnly swear, in presence of Almighty God, that I will henceforth faithfully support, protect and defend the Constitution of the United States, and the union of the States thereunder; and that I will, in like manner, abide by and faithfully support all acts of Congress passed during the existing rebellion with reference to slaves, so long and so far as not repealed, modified or held void by Congress, or by decision of the Supreme Court; and that I will, in like manner, abide by and faithfully support all proclamations of the President made during the existing rebellion having reference to slaves, so long and so far as not modified or declared void by decision of the Supreme Court. So help me God."

The persons excepted from the benefits of the foregoing provisions are all who are, or shall have been, civil or diplomatic officers or agents of the so-called confederate government; all who have left judicial stations under the United States to aid the rebellion; all who are, or shall have been, military or naval officers of said so-called confederate government above the rank of colonel in the army, or of lieutenant in the navy; all who left seats in the United States Congress to aid the rebellion; all who resigned commissions in the army or navy of the United States, and afterwards aided the rebellion; and all who have engaged in any way in treating colored persons or white persons, in charge of such, otherwise than lawfully as prisoners of war, and which persons may have been found in the United States service, as soldiers, seamen, or in any other capacity.

And I do further proclaim, declare, and make known, that whenever, in any of the States of Arkansas, Texas, Louisiana, Mississippi, Tennessee, Alabama, Georgia, Florida, South Carolina, and North Carolina, a number of persons, not less than one-tenth in number of the votes cast in such State at the Presidential election of the year of our Lord one thousand eight hundred and sixty, each having taken the oath aforesaid and not having since violated it, and being a qualified voter by the election law of the State existing immediately before the so-called act of secession, and excluding all others, shall re-establish a State government which shall be republican, and in no wise contravening said oath, such shall be recognized as the true government of the State, and the State shall receive thereunder the benefits of the constitutional provision which declares that "The United States shall guaranty to every State in this union a republican form of government, and shall protect each of them against invasion; and, on application of the legislature, or the executive (when the legislature cannot be convened), against domestic violence."

And I do further proclaim, declare, and make known that any provision which may be adopted by such State government in relation to the freed people of such State, which shall recognize and declare their permanent freedom, provide for their education, and which may yet be consistent, as a temporary arrangement, with their present condition as a laboring, landless, and homeless class, will not be objected to by the national Executive. And it is suggested as not improper, that, in constructing a loyal State government in any State, the name of the State, the boundary, the subdivisions, the constitution, and the general code of laws, as before the rebellion, be maintained, subject only to the modifications made necessary by the conditions hereinbefore stated, and such others, if any, not contravening said conditions, and which may be deemed expedient by those framing the new State government.

To avoid misunderstanding, it may be proper to say that this proclamation, so far as it relates to State governments, has no reference to States wherein loyal State governments have all the while been maintained. And for the same reason, it may be proper to further say that whether members sent to Congress from any State shall be admitted to seats, constitutionally rests exclusively with the respective Houses, and not to any extent with the Executive. And still further, that this proclamation is intended to present the people of the States wherein the national authority has been suspended, and loyal State governments have been subverted, a mode in and by which the national authority and loyal State governments may be re-established within said States, or in any of them; and, while the mode presented is the best the Executive can suggest with his present impressions, it must not be understood that no other possible mode would be acceptable.

Given under my hand at the city, of Washington, the 8th. day of December, A.D. one thousand eight hundred and sixty-three, and of the independence of the United States of America.

Abraham Lincoln

By the President:

William H. Seward, Secretary of State

Second Inaugural Address, President Abraham Lincoln (1865)

Fellow Countrymen:

At this second appearing to take the oath of the presidential office, there is less occasion for an extended address than there was at the first. Then a statement, somewhat in detail, of a course to be pursued, seemed fitting and proper. Now, at the expiration of four years, during which public declarations have been constantly called forth on every point and phase of the great contest which still absorbs the attention, and engrosses the energies of the nation, little that is new could be presented. The progress of our arms, upon which all else chiefly depends, is as well known to the public as to myself; and it is, I trust, reasonably satisfactory and encouraging to all. With high hope for the future, no prediction in regard to it is ventured.

On the occasion corresponding to this four years ago, all thoughts were anxiously directed to an impending civil-war. All dreaded it—all sought to avert it. While the inaugeral [sic] address was being delivered from this place, devoted altogether to saving the Union without war, insurgent agents were in the city seeking to destroy it without war—seeking to dissolve the Union, and divide effects, by negotiation. Both parties deprecated war; but one of them would make war rather than let the nation survive; and the other would accept war rather than let it perish. And the war came.

One eighth of the whole population were colored slaves, not distributed generally over the Union, but localized in the Southern part of it. These slaves constituted a peculiar and powerful interest. All knew that this interest was, somehow, the cause of the war. To strengthen, perpetuate, and extend this interest was the object for which the insurgents would rend the Union, even by war; while the government claimed no right to do more than to restrict the territorial enlargement of it. Neither party expected for the war, the magnitude, or the duration, which it has already attained. Neither anticipated that the cause of the conflict might cease with, or even before, the conflict itself should cease. Each looked for an easier triumph, and a result less fundamental and astounding. Both read the same Bible, and pray to the same God; and each invokes His aid against the other. It may seem strange that any men should dare to ask a just God's assistance in wringing their bread from the sweat of other men's faces; but let us judge not that we be not judged. The prayers of both could not be answered; that of neither has been answered fully. The Almighty has His own purposes. "Woe unto the world because of offences! for it must needs be that offences come; but woe to that man by whom the offence cometh!" If we shall suppose that American Slavery is one of those offences which, in the providence of God, must needs come, but which, having continued through His appointed time, He now wills to remove, and that He gives to both North and South, this terrible war, as the woe due to those by whom the offence came, shall we discern therein any departure from those divine attributes which the believers in a Living God always ascribe to Him? Fondly do we hope—fervently do we pray—that this mighty scourge of war may speedily pass away. Yet, if God wills that it continue, until all the wealth piled by the bond-man's two hundred and fifty years of unrequited toil shall be sunk, and until every drop of blood drawn with the lash, shall be paid by another drawn with the sword, as was said three thousand years ago, so still it must be said "the judgments of the Lord, are true and righteous altogether."

With malice toward none; with charity for all; with firmness in the right, as God gives us to see the right, let us strive on to finish the work we are in; to bind up the nation's wounds; to care for him who shall have borne the battle, and for his widow, and his orphan—to do all which may achieve and cherish a just, and a lasting peace, among ourselves, and with all nations.

Thirteenth Amendment to the U.S. Constitution (1865)

Section 1. Neither slavery nor involuntary servitude, except as a punishment for crime whereof the party shall have been duly convicted, shall exist within the United States, or any place subject to their jurisdiction.

Section 2. Congress shall have power to enforce this article by appropriate legislation.

Fourteenth Amendment to the U.S. Constitution (1868)

Section 1. All persons born or naturalized in the United States, and subject to the jurisdiction thereof, are citizens of the United States and of the state wherein they reside. No state shall make or enforce any law which shall abridge the privileges or immunities of citizens of the United States; nor shall any state deprive any person of life, liberty, or property, without due process of law; nor deny to any person within its jurisdiction the equal protection of the laws.

Section 2. Representatives shall be apportioned among the several states according to their respective numbers, counting the whole number of persons in each state, excluding Indians not taxed. But when the right to vote at any election for the choice of electors for President and Vice President of the United States, Representatives in Congress, the executive and judicial officers of a state, or the members of the legislature thereof, is denied to any of the male inhabitants of such state, being twenty-one years of age, and citizens of the United States, or in any way abridged, except for participation in rebellion, or other crime, the basis of representation therein shall be reduced in the proportion which the number of such male citizens shall bear to the whole number of male citizens twenty-one years of age in such state.

Section 3. No person shall be a Senator or Representative in Congress, or elector of President and Vice President, or hold any office, civil or military, under the United States, or under any state, who, having previously taken an oath, as a member of Congress, or as an officer of the United States, or as a member of any state legislature, or as an executive or judicial officer of any state, to support the Constitution of the United States, shall have engaged in insurrection or rebellion against the same, or given aid or comfort to the enemies thereof. But Congress may by a vote of two-thirds of each House, remove such disability.

Section 4. The validity of the public debt of the United States, authorized by law, including debts incurred for payment of pensions and bounties for services in suppressing insurrection or rebellion, shall not be questioned. But neither the United States nor any state shall assume or pay any debt or obligation incurred in aid of insurrection or rebellion against the United States, or any claim for the loss or emancipation of any slave; but all such debts, obligations and claims shall be held illegal and void.

Section 5. The Congress shall have power to enforce, by appropriate legislation, the provisions of this article.

Fifteenth Amendment to the U.S. Constitution (1870)

Section 1. The right of citizens of the United States to vote shall not be denied or abridged by the United States or by any state on account of race, color, or previous condition of servitude.

Section 2. The Congress shall have power to enforce this article by appropriate legislation.

Chronology

1860 May 16 Republicans nominate Abraham Lincoln of Illinois for president and Hannibal Hamlin of Maine for vice president.

June 18 Democratic Party nominates Stephen A. Douglas for president and Herschel V. Johnson of Georgia for vice president.

November 6 Lincoln elected president.

December 20 South Carolina votes to secede from the United States.

1861 February 8 Representatives from six Southern states form provisional government of the Confederate States of America.

February 9 Jefferson Davis of Mississippi is selected as provisional president of the Confederacy.

March 2 Morrill Tariff Act increasing duties on foreign-made products is adopted by Congress.

March 11 Constitution adopted for the Confederate states.

March 14 *Kentucky v. Dennison.*

April 4 Justice John McLean dies.

April 12 Confederates fire on Fort Sumter.

April 19 Southern ports are blockaded by President Lincoln.

1861, cont. April 26 Justice John A. Campbell resigns from the Court.

August 16 Lincoln bans trade with states that have seceded.

1862 January 20 *Farni v. Tesson.*

January 21 Noah H. Swayne nominated by President Abraham Lincoln to the U.S. Supreme Court.

May 20 Lincoln signs the Homestead Act.

June 19 Congress prohibits slavery in U.S. territories.

July 2 Lincoln signs the Morrill Act, which establishes land grants for state colleges.

July 16 Samuel F. Miller nominated by President Abraham Lincoln to the U.S. Supreme Court.

December 1 David Davis nominated by President Abraham Lincoln to the U.S. Supreme Court.

December 15 *Leffingwell v. Warren.*

1863 January 1 Lincoln issues the Emancipation Proclamation.

March 3 Congress establishes a national draft to obtain manpower for service in the Union Army.

March 6 Stephen J. Field nominated by President Abraham Lincoln to the U.S. Supreme Court.

March 10 *The Prize Cases.*

July 1 Battle of Gettysburg begins—lasts three days and is the decisive battle of the Civil War.

July 13 Violent protests against the military draft begin in New York City.

November 19 Lincoln delivers the Gettysburg Address.

December 21 *Roosevelt v. Meyer.*

1864 January 11 *Gelpcke v. Dubuque.*

February 15 *Ex parte Vallandigham.*

March 9 Gen. Ulysses Grant put in overall command of Union forces.

May 4 Gen. William Sherman and his troops leave Chattanooga, Tennessee, on their march to Atlanta.

June 7 Republican Party nominates President Lincoln for reelection.

July 2 Act calling for Reconstruction of the South passes Congress.

October 12 Chief Justice Roger B. Taney dies.

November 8 Lincoln is reelected president.

December 6 Salmon P. Chase nominated for chief justice by President Abraham Lincoln.

1865 February 1 Congress proposes adoption of the Thirteenth Amendment, which prohibits slavery.

March 3 Congress creates the Freedman's Bureau.

March 4 Lincoln is inaugurated for his second term.

April 9 Confederate Gen. Robert E. Lee surrenders to Gen. Ulysses S. Grant at Appomattox Courthouse in Virginia.

April 14 President Lincoln shot while attending a play at Ford's Theater in Washington.

April 15 Lincoln dies of his wound. Vice President Andrew Johnson of Tennessee succeeds him.

May 30 Justice John Catron retires from the Court.

1865, cont. December 4 Congress creates a Joint Committee on Reconstruction.

December 18 Thirteenth Amendment prohibiting slavery is ratified.

1866 April 3 *Ex parte Milligan.*

April 9 Civil Rights Act passed by Congress providing, among other things, that all native-born persons are U.S. citizens regardless of race, and making it a federal crime to deprive another of his/her civil rights.

June 13 Congress proposes the Fourteenth Amendment.

1867 January 14 *Cummings v. Missouri* and *Ex parte Garland.*

February 18 *Insurance Co. v. Ritchie.*

March 2 First Reconstruction Act passed partitioning the former Confederate States into five military districts.

Tenure of Office Act adopted by Congress, which requires Senate approval for the removal of any federal official appointed with Senate confirmation.

March 23 Congress adopts first (of three) supplemental Reconstruction Acts.

March 30 United States purchases Alaska from Russia.

April 15 *Mississippi v. Johnson.*

May 16 *Georgia v. Stanton.*

July 5 Justice James Wayne retires from the Court.

July 19 Congress adopts second supplementary Reconstruction Act.

August 12 President Johnson suspends Secretary of War Edwin M. Stanton because of ties to the Radical Republicans.

1868 February 21 Following Stanton's reinstatement by Congress, President Johnson dismisses War Secretary Stanton without obtaining Senate consent as required by the Tenure of Office Act.

February 24 U.S. House adopts eleven articles of impeachment against President Johnson, all but two for Tenure of Office Act violations.

March 11 Third supplementary Reconstruction Act is adopted by Congress.

March 13 Senate impeachment trial of President Johnson begins. Trial is concluded in late May with acquittal on all charges.

March 16 *Crandall v. Nevada.*

May 21 Republicans nominate Gen. Ulysses S. Grant for president.

July 4 Democrats nominate Horatio Seymour of New York for president.

July 28 Fourteenth Amendment is ratified.

November 3 Ulysses S. Grant is elected president.

1869 February 27 Congress proposes the Fifteenth Amendment guaranteeing voting rights regardless of race.

March 4 Ulysses S. Grant is inaugurated as president.

April 12 *Ex parte McCardle* and *Texas v. White.*

May 10 Transcontinental railroad completed.

October 25 *Ex parte Yerger.*

November 1 *Paul v. Virginia.*

December 13 *Veazie Bank v. Fenno.*

1870 January 31 Justice Robert C. Grier retires from the Court.

February 7 William Strong and Joseph P. Bradley nominated by President Ulysses S. Grant.

Hepburn v. Griswold.

1870, cont. March 30 Fifteenth Amendment is ratified.

May 31 Ku Klux Klan Act adopted by Congress.

June 21 Justice Department created by Congress.

July 14 Congress reduces tariff rates in the Tariff Act of 1870.

July 15 Georgia readmitted to the Union—the last state to be readmitted.

December 5 Congress convenes with representatives from all the states—the first time for complete representation since 1860.

1871 February 28 Supplementary Enforcement Act adopted by Congress to facilitate enforcement of the Fifteenth Amendment.

March 3 Civil Service Reform Commission created by Congress.

April 3 *Collector v. Day.*

April 20 Ku Klux Klan Act of 1871 enables the president to use military force to enforce the Fourteenth Amendment.

May 1 *Knox v. Lee* and *Parker v. Davis.*

May 11 *Cherokee Tobacco Case.*

October 8 Chicago fire.

1872 March 1 Yellowstone Park created by Congress.

May 22 Amnesty Act adopted removing restrictions from most former Confederates.

June 5 Republicans nominate President Ulysses S. Grant for reelection.

June 6 Duties are cut by the Tariff Act.

July 9 Democrats nominate Horace Greeley of New York for president.

September 4 Reports begin of Credit Mobilier scandal.

November 5 Ulysses S. Grant reelected president.

November 28 Justice Samuel Nelson retires from the Court.

December 3 Ward Hunt nominated for Supreme Court by President Ulysses S. Grant.

1873 March 3 *Philadelphia and Reading Railroad Co. v. Pennsylvania.*

March 4 President Grant inaugurated.

April 14 *Slaughterhouse Cases.*

April 15 *Bradwell v. Illinois.*

1874 January 19 Morrison R. Waite nominated for chief justice by President Ulysses S. Grant.

November 18 Women's Christian Temperance Union organized.

1875 February 1 *Loan Association v. Topeka.*

March 1 Civil Rights Act adopted guaranteeing equal opportunity to utilize public accommodations.

March 3 Congress raises tariff rates to pre-1870 levels.

March 29 *Minor v. Happersett.*

Table of Cases

Allgeyer v. Louisiana, 165 U.S. 578 (1897)
Bradwell v. Illinois, 83 U.S. 130 (1873)
Butchers' Union Co. v. Crescent City Co., 111 U.S. 746 (1884)
Charles River Bridge Co. v. Warren Bridge Co., 36 U.S. 420 (1837)
Cherokee Tobacco Case, 78 U.S. 616 (1871)
Chicago, Milwaukee and St. Paul Railroad Co. v. Minnesota, 134 U.S. 418 (1890)
Civil Rights Cases, 109 U.S. 3 (1883)
Collector v. Day, 78 U.S. 113 (1871)
Cooley v. Board of Port Wardens, 53 U.S. 299 (1851)
Crandall v. Nevada, 73 U.S. 35 (1868)
Cummings v. Missouri, 71 U.S. 277 (1867)
Dred Scott v. Sandford, 60 U.S. 393 (1857)
Ex parte Garland, 71 U.S. 333 (1867)
Ex parte McCardle, 74 U.S. 506 (1869)
Ex parte Merryman, 17 Fed. Cas. 144 (D. Md. 1861)
Ex parte Milligan, 71 U.S. 1 (1866)
Ex parte Quirin, 317 U.S. 1 (1942)
Ex parte Vallandigham, 68 U.S. 243 (1864)
Ex parte Yerger, 75 U.S. 85 (1869)
Farni v. Tesson, 66 U.S. 309 (1862)
Gelpcke v. Dubuque, 68 U.S. 175 (1864)
Georgia v. Stanton, 73 U.S. 50 (1868)
Gibbons v. Ogden, 22 U.S. 1 (1824)
Granger Cases, see *Munn v. Illinois*
Graves v. New York, 306 U.S. 466 (1939)
Hepburn v. Griswold, 75 U.S. 603 (1870)
In re Turner, 24 Fed. Cas. 337 (D. Md. 1867)
Insurance Co. v. Ritchie, 72 U.S. 541 (1867)
Kentucky v. Dennison, 65 U.S. 66 (1861)
Knox v. Lee, 79 U.S. 457 (1871)

Leffingwell v. Warren, 68 U.S. 599 (1862)
Legal Tender Cases, see *Hepburn v. Griswold, Knox v. Lee* and *Parker v. Davis*
License Cases, 46 U.S. 504 (1847)
Loan Association v. Topeka, 87 U.S. 655 (1875)
Lochner v. New York, 198 U.S. 45 (1905)
Marbury v. Madison, 5 U.S. 137 (1803)
McCulloch v. Maryland, 17 U.S. 316 (1819)
Minor v. Happersett, 88 U.S. 163 (1875)
Mississippi v. Johnson, 71 U.S. 475 (1867)
Munn v. Illinois, 94 U.S. 113 (1877)
Parker v. Davis, 79 U.S. 457 (1871)
Passenger Cases, 48 U.S. 283 (1849)
Paul v. Virginia, 75 U.S. 168 (1869)
Philadelphia and Reading Railroad Co. v. Pennsylvania, 82 U.S. 232 (1873)
Prize Cases, 67 U.S. 635 (1863)
Roosevelt v. Meyer, 68 U.S. 512 (1863)
Slaughterhouse Cases, 83 U.S. 36 (1873)
South Carolina v. Katzenbach, 383 U.S. 301 (1966)
Stone v. Mississippi, 101 U.S. 814 (1880)
Test Oath Cases, see *Cummings v. Missouri* and *Ex parte Garland*
Texas v. White, 74 U.S. 700 (1869)
Toth v. Quarles, 350 U.S. 11 (1955)
Trustees of Dartmouth College v. Woodward, 17 U.S. 518 (1819)
United States v. Butler, 297 U.S. 1 (1936)
United States v. Cruikshank, 92 U.S. 542 (1874)
United States v. Harris, 106 U.S. 629 (1883)
United States v. Reese, 92 U.S. 214 (1875)
Veazie Bank v. Fenno, 75 U.S. 533 (1869)
Virginia v. Rives, 100 U.S. 313 (1879)

Glossary

Adversary proceeding A legal process that involves a contest between two opposing parties. Formal notice is served on the party against whom an action has been filed to allow that party an opportunity to respond. This system is generally regarded as the most effective means for the evaluation of evidence.

Advisory opinion An opinion of a court indicating how it would rule on an issue if the issue were presented in an actual case; an interpretation of law without binding effect. An advisory opinion offers a view on the legal effect of a law although no real case exists to present the legal question.

Affirm An appellate court ruling that upholds the judgment of a lower court—that the judgment of the lower court is correct and should stand.

Appeal A process by which a final judgment of a lower court ruling is reviewed by a higher court.

Appellant The party who seeks review of a lower court ruling before a higher court; the party dissatisfied with a lower court ruling who appeals the case to a superior court for review.

Appellate jurisdiction Authority of a superior court to review decisions of inferior courts. Appellate jurisdiction empowers a higher court to conduct such a review and affirm, modify, or reverse the lower court decision. Appellate jurisdiction is conveyed through constitutional or statutory mandate. Federal appellate jurisdiction is granted by Article III of the Constitution, which says that the Supreme Court possesses such jurisdiction "both as to law and fact, with such exceptions and under such regulations as the Congress shall make."

Appellee The party that prevails in a lower court and against whom an appeal of the judgment is sought; in some situation called a "respondent."

Brief A document containing arguments on a matter under consideration by a court. A brief submitted to a court by an attorney typically contains, among other things, points of law from previous rulings.

Case A general term for an action, cause, suit, or controversy, at law.

Case law Precedent created as courts resolve disputes. Case law is judge-made law resulting from ruling on a specific set of facts.

Citizenship A legal status that entitles a person to all the rights and privileges guaranteed and protected by the Constitution of the United States. All persons born in the United States or to parents who are American citizens possess American citizenship. Others may obtain citizenship through naturalization, a process established by Congress.

Civil liberties Those liberties spelled out in a bill of rights or a constitution that guarantee the protection of persons, opinion, and property from the arbitrary interference of government officials. Civil liberties create immunities from certain governmental actions that interfere with an individual's protected rights.

Civil rights Positive acts of government designed to protect persons against arbitrary and discriminatory treatment by government or individuals. Civil rights guarantees may be found in constitutions, but more frequently take the form of statutes.

Comity Legal principle that prompts a court to defer to the exercise of jurisdiction by another court. Comity is a rule of judicial courtesy rather than a firm requirement of law, and it suggests that a court that first asserts jurisdiction will not undergo interference by another court without its consent.

Commerce Clause Provision found in Article I, Section 8 of the U.S. Constitution. The clause empowers Congress to "regulate commerce with foreign nations, and among the several states, and with the Indian tribes." Since the 1930s, the commerce power has been the basis for extensive federal regulation of the economy and, to a limited extent, federal criminal law.

Common law A body of principles that derive their authority from court judgments that are grounded in common customs and usages. Common law consists of principles that do not have their origin in statute and, as such, is distinct from law created by legislative enactments.

Concurrent jurisdiction Authority that is shared by different courts and may be exercised at the same time over the same subject matter.

Concurring opinion An opinion by a judge that agrees with the decision of the majority but disagrees with the majority's rationale; has arrived at the same conclusion but for different reasons.

Conference A meeting of Supreme Court justices in which the justices conduct all business associated with deciding cases. Conferences, which are closed to all but the justices, are where the Supreme Court determines which cases will be reviewed, discusses the merits of cases after oral argument, and decides by vote which party to a case will prevail.

Constitutional court A federal court created by Congress under authority conveyed by Article III. Judges of constitutional courts serve for the duration of good behavior (life tenure) and are protected from having their salaries reduced by the legislature.

Controversy The Constitution requires that, as a precondition for adjudication by federal courts, disputes must be definite and concrete, and involve parties whose legal interests are truly adverse. This requirement is contained in Article III of the U.S. Constitution. A dispute that meets these requirements is considered a bona fide controversy or case.

Declaratory judgment A ruling of a court that clarifies rights of the parties or offers an opinion or a legal question, and is invoked when a plaintiff seeks a declaration of his or her rights. It differs from a conventional action in that no specific order is issued, nor is any relief or remedy granted.

Defendant The party who is sued in a civil action or charged in a criminal case; the party responding to a civil complaint. A defendant in a criminal case is the person(s) formally accused of criminal conduct.

Demurrer An allegation by a defendant that even if the facts alleged were true, their legal consequences are not such as to require an answer or further proceedings in the cause. Under contemporary rules of civil procedure, a motion to dismiss a case for failure to establish a claim is more commonly used to accomplish the same objective.

Dissenting opinion The opinion of a judge that disagrees with the result reached by the majority.

Diversity jurisdiction Authority conveyed by Article III of the U.S. Constitution empowering federal courts to hear civil actions involving parties from different states.

Due process Government procedures that follow principles of essential or fundamental fairness. Provisions designed to insure that laws will be reasonable both in substance and in means of implementation are contained in two clauses of the Constitution of the United States. The Fifth Amendment prohibits deprivation of "life, liberty, or property, without due process of law." It sets a limit on arbitrary and unreasonable actions by the federal government. The Fourteenth Amendment contains parallel language aimed at the states. Due process requires that actions of government occur through ordered and regularized processes.

Equity A system of remedial justice administered by certain courts empowered to order remedies based on principles and precedents developed by courts.

Exclusive power Authority that is assigned to either the national or state level of government but not exercised by both.

Executive order A regulation issued by the president, a state governor, or some other executive authority for the purpose of giving effect to a constitutional or statutory provision. An executive order has the force of law and is one means by which the executive branch implements laws.

Ex parte Latin for "only one side." Done for, in behalf of, or on the application of one party only.

Federal question An issue arising out of provisions of the U.S. Constitution, federal statutes, or treaties. A federal court has authority to hear federal questions under powers conferred by Article III of the U.S. Constitution.

Federalism A political system in which a number of sovereign political units join together forming a larger political unit that has authority to act on behalf of the whole. A federal system or federation preserves the political integrity of all the entities comprising the federation. Federal systems are regarded as "weak" if the central government has control over very few policy questions; a "strong" system is one in which the central government possesses authority over most significant policy issues. Authority that is not exclusively assigned may be shared by the two levels and exercised concurrently. The Supremacy Clause of the U.S. Constitution requires that conflicts arising from the exercise of federal and state power are resolved in favor of the central government. Powers not assigned to the national government are "reserved" for the states by the Tenth Amendment.

Grand jury A panel of twelve to twenty-three citizens who review prosecutorial evidence to determine if there are sufficient grounds to formally accuse an individual of criminal conduct. The charges a grand jury issues are contained in a document called an indictment.

Habeas corpus Latin for "we have the body." Habeas corpus was a procedure in English law designed to prevent the improper detention of prisoners. The habeas process forced jailers to bring a detained person before a judge, who would examine the justification for his or her detention. If the court found the person was being improperly held, it could order the prisoner's release by issuing a writ of habeas corpus.

Implied power Authority that is possessed by inference from provisions of a constitution or statute. The intention is not manifested by explicit and direct words; the meaning is gathered by necessary deduction. Implied power is not conveyed by explicit language, but rather by implication or necessary deduction from circumstances, general language, or the conduct of parties.

Indictment A written accusation presented by a grand jury to a court, charging that a person has done some act or omission that by law is a punishable offense.

Judgment of the court The final conclusion reached by a court—as distinguished from the legal reasoning supporting the conclusion.

Judicial activism An interventionist approach or role orientation for appellate decision making that has the appellate courts playing an affirmative policy role. Judicial activists are inclined to find more constitutional violations than those who see a more restrained role for courts; activists are more likely to invalidate legislative and executive policy initiatives. Judicial activism is seen by its critics as legislating by justices to achieve policy outcomes compatible with their own social priorities.

Judicial notice The act by which a court recognizes the existence and truth of certain facts. These facts are recognized by the court's own initiative and not offered as evidence by either party.

Judicial review The power of a court to examine the actions of the legislative and executive branches with the possibility that those actions could be declared unconstitutional. The power of judicial review was discussed extensively at the Constitutional Convention of 1787, but it was not included in the Constitution as an expressly delegated judicial function. The Supreme Court first asserted the power of judicial review in *Marbury v. Madison*, 5 U.S. 137 (1803).

Judicial self-restraint A role view of appellate court decision making that minimizes the extent to which judges apply their personal views to the legal judgments they render. Judicial self-restraint holds that courts should defer to the policy judgments made by the elected branches of government.

Jurisdiction Defines the boundaries within which a particular court may exercise judicial power; it defines the power of a court to hear and decide cases. The jurisdiction of federal courts is provided in Article III of the Constitution in the case of the Supreme Court, and in acts of Congress in the case of the lower federal courts. Federal judicial power may extend to classes of cases defined in terms of substance and party as well as to cases in law and equity stemming directly from the federal Constitution, federal statutes, treaties, or those cases falling into the admiralty and maritime category. Federal judicial power also extends to cases involving specified parties. Regardless of the substance of the case, federal jurisdiction includes actions where the federal government itself is a party, between two or more states, between a state and a citizen of another state, between citizens of different states, between a state and an alien, between a citizen of a state and an alien, where foreign ambassadors are involved. State constitutions and statutes define the jurisdiction of state courts.

Jurisprudence A legal philosophy or the science of law. A term used to refer to the course or direction of judicial rulings. Jurisprudence draws upon philosophical thought, historical and political analysis, sociological and behavioral evidence, and legal experience; it is grounded on the view that ideas about law evolve from critical thinking in a number of disciplines. Jurisprudence enables people to understand how law has ordered both social institutions and individual conduct.

Jus belli Latin for the "law of war," it applies directly to wartime. Jus belli addresses the rights and legal obligations of those nations engaged in warfare as well as the status of neutral nations.

Justiciable A matter that may be appropriate for a court to hear and decide.

Laissez-faire An economic theory that advocates the government ought not interfere with the dynamics of a free-market economy—government should stay out of economic matters. Those subscribing to the laissez-faire view reject any form of government control or regulation of the economy. The decisions of the U.S. Supreme Court from the 1890s through 1937 frequently reflected laissez-faire values.

Legislative court A court created by Congress under authority of Article I of the U.S. Constitution. Legislative courts may be assigned administrative functions in addition to or instead of judicial functions. Such courts facilitate development of some level of specialization in a court system. Judges of federal legislative courts may be granted life tenure by Congress but do not have the same level of protection as judges of Article III or constitutional courts.

Liberty of contract A laissez-fairist doctrine used to free private agreements from governmental regulation. The liberty of contract concept holds that individuals have a right to assume contractual obligations affecting their personal affairs. This includes the right of employers and employees to agree about wages, hours, and conditions of work without government interference. The concept was a central element of substantive due process, in which the courts closely examined the reasonableness of governmental regulations. The liberty of contract concept was used to strike down laws establishing minimum wages and maximum hours of work.

Litigant A party to a lawsuit.

Mandamus Latin for "we command." A writ issued by a court of superior jurisdiction to an inferior court or governmental official commanding the performance of an official act.

Martial law Military government established over a civilian population during an emergency. Under martial law, military decrees supersede civilian laws and military tribunals replace civil courts. Martial law can be invoked by the president when necessary for the security of the nation. State governors, as commanders in chief of state militias, may declare martial law during an emergency occasioned by internal disorders or natural disasters.

Moot A question presented in a lawsuit that cannot be answered by a court either because the issue has resolved itself or conditions have so changed that the court is unable to grant the requested relief.

Motion A request made to a court for a certain ruling or action.

Natural law Laws considered applicable to all persons because they are basic to human nature. Applies to all nations and people; contrasts with positive law.

Naturalization Legal procedure by which an alien is admitted to citizenship. Congress is authorized by Article I, Section 8 of the Constitution to establish uniform rules for naturalization. An individual over eighteen years of age may be naturalized after meeting certain qualifications. These include residence in the United States for five years; ability to read, write, and speak English; proof of good moral character; and approval by a judge or a federal court or a state court of record. The residence requirement is lowered for spouses of citizens and for aliens who serve in the armed services. Minors become citizens when their parents are naturalized.

Obiter dicta Latin for "A remark by the way." Dicta are statements contained in a court's opinion that are incidental to the disposition of the case. Obiter dicta often are directed to issues upon which no formal arguments have been heard, thus the positions represented in dicta are not binding on later cases.

Opinion of the court The statement of a court that expresses the reasoning or ratio decidendi upon which a decision is based. The opinion summarizes the principles of law that apply in a given case and represents the views of the majority of a court's members. Occasionally the opinion of a court may reflect the views of less than a majority of its members and is then called a plurality opinion.

Order A written command issued by a judge.

Original jurisdiction The authority of a court to hear and decide a legal question before any other court. Original jurisdiction typically is vested with trial courts rather than appellate courts, although Article III of the Constitution extends very limited original jurisdiction to the United States Supreme Court. Trial courts are assigned specific original jurisdiction defined in terms of subject matter or party.

Per curiam opinion Latin for "by the court." An unsigned written opinion issued by a court.

Petitioner A party seeking relief in court.

Plaintiff The party who brings a legal action to court for resolution or remedy.

Plurality opinion An opinion announcing a court's judgment and supporting reasoning in a case, but which is not endorsed by a majority of the justices hearing the case.

Police power Authority that empowers government to regulate private behavior in the interest of public health, safety, and general welfare. In the American constitutional system, police power resides with the state and not the federal government. The police power enables states and their respective local units of government to enact and enforce policies deemed appropriate to serve the public good. It is a comprehensive power, and substantial discretion is possessed by the states for its exercise. It is limited by various provisions of the U.S. Constitution and state constitutions, however, and must conform to the requirements of due process.

Political question An issue that is not justiciable or that is not appropriate for judicial determination. A political question is one in which the substance of an issue is primarily political or involves a matter directed toward either the legislative or executive branch by constitutional language. The political question doctrine is sometimes invoked by the Supreme Court, not because the Court is without power or jurisdiction, but because the Court adjudges the question inappropriate for judicial response. In the Court's view, to intervene or respond would be to encroach upon the functions and prerogatives of one of the other two branches of government.

Prior restraint A restriction placed on a publication before it can be published or circulated. Prior restraint typically occurs through a licensure or censorship process or by a full prohibition on publication. Censorship requirements involve a review of materials by the state for objectionable content. Prior restraint poses a greater threat to free expression than after-the-fact prosecution because government restrictions are imposed in a manner that precludes public scrutiny, and the First Amendment prohibits prior restraint in most instances. Prior restraint may be justified, however, if the publication threatens national security, incites overthrow of the government, is obscene, or interferes with the private rights of others, and is otherwise heavily suspect.

Procedural due process Fundamental fairness is the means by which governmental actions are executed. Procedural due process demands that before any deprivation of liberty or property can occur, a person must be formally notified and provided an opportunity for a fair hearing. Procedural due process must also be accorded persons accused of crimes including access to legal counsel, the ability to confront witnesses against the accused, and a trial by jury.

Quash To annul, vacate, make void, or totally do away with.

Recusal The process by which a judge is disqualified from participating in the hearing or review of a case. Disqualification may be initiated by a party (or parties) to a case or by the judge himself or herself when a judge's participation might be inappropriate because of self-interest or bias.

Remand To send a case back to an inferior court for additional action. Appellate courts send cases back to lower courts with instructions to correct specified error.

Removal jurisdiction The power to transfer a case, before trial or final hearing, from one court to another.

Republicanism (Guaranty Clause) Government by representatives chosen by the people. A republic is distinguished from a pure democracy, where the people make policy decisions themselves rather than through an elected representative. Article IV, Section 4 of the Constitution provides that the national government shall guarantee to each state a "republican form of government."

Respondent The party against whom a legal action is filed.

Reverse An appellate court decision to set aside or changing a decision of a lower court. The opposite of affirm.

Right A power or privilege to which a person is entitled. A right is legally conveyed by a constitution, statutes, or common law. A right may be absolute, such as one's right to spiritual beliefs, or it may be conditional so that the acting out of one's beliefs will not injure other members of a political community.

Ripeness A condition in which a legal dispute has evolved to the point where the issue(s) it presents can be determined by a court. Ripeness is an issue that requires a court to consider whether a case has matured or developed into a controversy worthy of adjudication.

Separation of powers The principle of dividing the powers of government among several coordinate branches to prevent excessive concentration of power. The principle of separation of powers is designed to limit abusive exercise of governmental authority by partitioning power and then assigning that power to several locations. The distribution of powers embodied in the U.S. Constitution functionally distinguishes between government and people, and between legislative, executive, and judicial branches. Although the Constitution creates three separate branches, it also assigns overlapping responsibilities that makes the branches interdependent through the operation of a system of checks and balances.

Sovereignty The supreme power of a state or independent nation free from external interference. Sovereignty is exercised by government, which has exclusive and absolute jurisdiction within its geographical boundaries.

Standing The requirement that a real dispute exists between the prospective parties in a lawsuit before it can be heard by a court. As a result, courts typically are unable to respond to hypothetical questions. If a party does not have standing to sue, the matter is not justiciable.

Stare decisis Latin for "let the decision stand." Stare decisis holds that once a principle of law is established for a particular fact situation, courts should adhere to that principle in similar cases in the future. The case in which the rule of law is established is called a precedent. Stare decisis creates and maintains stability and predictability in the law. Precedents may be modified or abandoned if circumstances require, but the expectation is that rules from previously adjudicated cases will prevail.

State action An action taken by an agency or official of government. The state action concept is used to determine whether an action complained of has its source in state authority or policy. The concept is critically important in cases presenting allegations of discrimination. The Equal Protection Clause typically cannot be applied to private acts of discrimination. Rather, it requires conduct that occurs "under color" of governmental authority.

Stay To stop, suspend, or hold in abeyance.

Substantive due process Fundamental fairness in the content or substance of government policy. Substantive due process review requires courts to examine the reasonableness of legislative enactments—that laws be fair and reasonable in substance as well as application. Substantive due process is distinguished from procedural due process.

Summary judgment A decision by a court made without a full hearing or without receiving briefs or oral arguments.

Taxing power Article I, Section 8 of the U.S. Constitution permits Congress to "lay and collect taxes, duties, imposts and excises" and to provide for the "common defense and general welfare" of the United States. The scope of federal power to tax and spend has depended, at least in part, on the Court's interpretation of the "general welfare" phrase.

Tenth Amendment Provision added to the U.S. Constitution in 1791 that retains or "reserves" for the states powers not assigned to the federal government. The Tenth Amendment has frequently been used to limit the actions of the federal government.

Vacate To void, rescind, annul, or render void.

Vested right A right that so completely applies to a person that it cannot be impaired by the act of another person. Such rights must be recognized and protected by the government.

Warrant A judicial order authorizing an arrest or search and seizure.

Writ A written order of a court commanding the recipient to perform certain specified acts.

Annotated Bibliography

Abraham, Henry J. 1999. *Justices, Presidents, and Senators: A History of the U.S. Supreme Court Appointments from Washington to Clinton.* Rev. ed. Lanham, MD: Rowman and Littlefield.

Written by a preeminent constitutional scholar, this volume provides commentary on the objectives of presidents in nominating each of the 107 Supreme Court justices selected to date. Abraham discusses every nomination, successful or not, Senate response to the nominations, and the on-bench performance of each justice.

Blight, David W. 2001. *Race and Reunion: The Civil War in American Memory.* Cambridge, MA: Belknap Press of Harvard University Press.

Blight discusses how Americans remembered the Civil War over the following fifty years and examines the interrelationship between the themes of race and reunion in U.S. society.

Castel, Albert. 1979. *The Presidency of Andrew Johnson.* Lawrence: University Press of Kansas.

One of the volumes in the University Press of Kansas series on the U.S. presidency. Castel examines the Johnson presidency from his succession to the office following Lincoln's assassination through the troubled Reconstruction period and impeachment trial. The final chapter offers an assessment of Johnson's place in history.

Cushman, Claire. 1993. *The Supreme Court Justices: Illustrated Biographies, 1789–1993.* Washington, DC: Congressional Quarterly Press.

Single-volume reference book produced by the Supreme Court Historical Society. Contains five-page essays on each Supreme Court justice that provide a glimpse into the justice's family roots, education, pre-Court career, and era.

Davis, Abraham L., and Barbara Luck Graham. 1995. *The Supreme Court, Race, and Civil Liberties.* Thousand Oaks, CA: Sage.

A comprehensive discussion of the Supreme Court's "institutional commitment" to equality. Each chapter examines an historical period with a narrative overview as well as excerpts from important Court opinions.

Fairman, Charles. 1971. *Reconstruction and Reunion, 1864–1888.* New York: Macmillan.

Detailed account of the personalities, politics, and decisions of the Chase Court. The work constitutes volume 6 of the Holmes-devised *History of the Supreme Court of the United States.*

Finkelman, Paul. 1997. *Dred Scott v. Sandford.* Boston: Bedford Books.

The volume provides a concise description of the *Dred Scott* case and contains a valuable collection of documents related to the case.

Fisher, Louis. 2003. *Nazi Saboteurs on Trial: A Military Tribunal and American Law.* Lawrence: University Press of Kansas.

An authoritative analysis of the political, legal, and administrative context of the Supreme Court's decision in *Ex parte Quirin* (1942). Fisher concludes that the secret trial before a military tribunal is flawed and should not provide the basis for a similar process to be used to try of current terrorists.

Friedman, Leon, and Fred Israel, eds. 1969. *The Justices of the United States Supreme Court, 1789–1969: Their Lives and Opinions.* 5 vols. New York: Chelsea House.

A superb five-volume set containing extended essays by Leon Friedman, Frank O. Gattell, William Gillette, Stanley Kutler, and Robert McCloskey on all of the Supreme Court justices. Each essay provides biographical background information as well as substantial discussion of the justices' jurisprudence.

Goldman, Robert M. 2001. *Reconstruction and Black Suffrage: Losing the Vote in* Reese *and* Cruikshank. Lawrence: University Press of Kansas.

Goldman argues that federal courts abandoned the objective of the Fifteenth Amendment in such cases as *Reese* and *Cruikshank* by interpreting the amendment to neither grant the right to vote nor impose on the states the obligation to protect minority voters at the polls.

Hall, Kermit. 1992. *The Oxford Companion to the Supreme Court of the United States.* New York: Oxford University Press.

Comprehensive guide to the history and current operations of the Supreme Court. The volume contains more than a thousand entries on landmark decisions of the Court, historical themes, biographical information on Court justices and others associated with the Court's history, concepts central to the meaning of U.S. constitutionalism, and important terms and phrases. See especially the entries by Michael Les Benedict: *Allgeyer v. Louisiana;* Paul Finkelman: The Prize Cases; Paul Kens: *Lochner v. New York;* Donald Nieman: *Ex Parte Milligan* and *Texas v. White;* William Wiecek: *Strauder v. West Virginia.*

Hyman, Harold M. 1997. *The Reconstruction Justice of Salmon P. Chase:* In re Turner, *and* Texas v. White. Lawrence: University Press of Kansas.

Contains discussion of Chase and his Supreme Court and circuit cases relating to Reconstruction.

Hyman, Harold M., and William M. Wiecek. 1982. *Equal Justice under Law: Constitutional Development, 1835–1875.* New York: Harper and Row.

Treats the era of constitutional history dating from the Jacksonian period through Reconstruction. The authors argue that the era was particularly critical in U.S. constitutional development because it began the shift from state to national authority.

Johnson, John W., ed. 2001. *Historic U.S. Court Cases.* 2nd ed. New York: Routledge.

Two-volume encyclopedia with over 200 entries on major U.S. court cases. Each entry is written by a leading scholar in the field of U.S. legal history. See especially John Walker Mauer, "The Test Oath Cases," and Thomas D. Morris, "Texas v. White."

Kelly, Alfred H., Winfred A. Harbison, and Herman Belz. 1991. *The American Constitution: Its Origins and Developments.* New York: W. W. Norton.

An excellent two-volume narrative on the evolution of U.S. constitutional law.

Kens, Paul. 1997. *Justice Stephen Field: Shaping Liberty from the Gold Rush to the Gilded Age.* Lawrence: University Press of Kansas.

The definitive biography of Field. Kens provides valuable insights into his differences with Chief Justice Waite and Justice Miller on the scope of the Fourteenth Amendment.

———. 1998. *Lochner v. New York: Economic Regulation on Trial.* Lawrence: University Press of Kansas.

A carefully developed discussion of the *Lochner* ruling and the legal and political context in which it was decided. Kens also examines the role of state legislatures in regulating the workplace and the role of the judiciary as monitor of the constitutional limits on state economic regulation.

Labbe, Ronald, and Jonathan Lurie. 2003. *The Slaughterhouse Cases: Regulation, Reconstruction, and the Fourteenth Amendment.* Lawrence: University Press of Kansas.

A new study providing a detailed account of the cases known as the *Slaughterhouse Cases.* The discussion focuses on the context, content, and consequences of these rulings and concludes that in terms of the traditional "police power," Justice Samuel Miller's majority opinion was correct.

Lowe, Jennifer M., ed. 1996. *The Supreme Court and the Civil War.* Washington, DC: Supreme Court Historical Society.

Valuable collection of essays on the Supreme Court and the constitutional issues arising out of the Civil War. See especially G. Edward White, "Salmon Portland Chase and the Judicial Culture of the Supreme Court in the Civil War Era."

Lurie, Jonathan. 1983. *Law and the Nation: 1865–1912.* New York: Alfred A. Knopf.

Part of a series on law and American society, the first chapter of the volume deals extensively with the history of the Fourteenth Amendment.

———. 1986. "Mr. Justice Bradley: A Reassessment." *Seton Hall Law Review* 16: 343.

Initially presented at a symposium on Supreme Court justices from New Jersey, the article reassesses the contributions of Justice Joseph Bradley and concludes that his contemporary significance is limited.

———. 1992. *Arming Military Justice: Origins of the U.S. Court of Military Appeals, 1775–1950.* Princeton: Princeton University Press.

Comprehensive examination of U.S. appellate military justice. Contains a chapter that focuses on the Supreme Court during the Civil War with extensive discussion of *Ex parte Milligan.*

Mantell, Martin E. 1973. *Johnson, Grant, and the Politics of Reconstruction.* New York: Columbia University Press.

Provides a detailed discussion of the problems Reconstruction posed for Presidents Andrew Johnson and Ulysses S. Grant and the congressional Republicans at the conclusion of the Civil War. Informative discussion of the Johnson impeachment, the financial issues associated with Reconstruction, and the political transition from Johnson to Grant.

McPherson, James. 2001. *Ordeal by Fire.* 3rd ed. New York: McGraw-Hill.

Comprehensive historical treatment of the events leading up to the Civil War (1800–1860), the war itself (1860–1865), and Reconstruction.

Novak, William J. 1996. *The People's Welfare: Law and Regulation in Nineteenth Century America.* Chapel Hill: University of North Carolina Press.

Argues that the nineteenth century was not the "golden age of American liberalism" but instead embraced a traditional view of governance and regulation.

Paludan, Phillip S. 1975. *A Covenant with Death: The Constitution, Law, and Equality in the Civil War Era.* Urbana: University of Illinois Press.

A comprehensive history of Reconstruction that asserts the roots of Reconstruction date back to the Jacksonian era; that as U.S. political leaders developed responses to the problems of the 1830s, they established a mindset that structured the ways they perceived both the Civil War and Reconstruction.

———.1988. *A People's Contest: The Union and Civil War, 1861–1865.* New York: Harper and Row.

A detailed description of the social and political dimensions of the Civil War.

———. 1994. *The Presidency of Abraham Lincoln.* Lawrence: University Press of Kansas.

One of the volumes in the University Press of Kansas presidency series. Traces Lincoln's presidency from his election in 1860 to his assassination in 1865. The volume focuses on Lincoln presiding over the Civil War and initiating the plans for the postwar Reconstruction period.

Perman, Michael. 2003. *Emancipation and Reconstruction.* 2nd ed. Wheeling: Harlan Davidson.

Recent treatment of the period in which slavery ended and national government asserted extensive new authority during Reconstruction.

Ross, Michael A. 2003. *Justice of Shattered Dreams: Samuel Freeman Miller and the Supreme Court during the Civil War.* Baton Rouge: Louisiana State University Press.

Ross's volume is not a biography of Miller as such, but rather an attempt to reexamine the political as well as legal positions taken by Miller on such issues as capitalism and race. Ross argues that Miller's views were the product of "trans-Mississippi Republicanism, a faction of the party that lost out to the big business wing of the party in the late nineteenth century."

Urofsky, Melvin I., ed. 1994. *The Supreme Court Justices: A Biographical Dictionary.* New York: Garland.

A collection of essays about each of the 107 justices who have served on the U.S. Supreme Court. The essays contained in this volume were prepared by an extremely distinguished collection of authors and provide a brief but valuable analysis of the jurisprudence of each justice. See especially the essay by David J. Bodenhamer.

Urofsky, Melvin I., and Paul Finkelman. 2002. *A March of Liberty: A Constitutional History of the United States.* Volume I: *From the Founding to 1890.* New York: Oxford University Press.

A superb two-volume narrative on the history and development of the U.S. Constitution.

Wiecek, William. 1998. *The Lost World of Classical Legal Thought: Law and Ideology in America, 1886–1937.* New York: Oxford University Press.

Traces what Wiecek calls "legal classicism" from its apogee in the late nineteenth and the early twentieth century to its demise in the 1930s.

Index

Abolition, 12, 20, 107, 109, 115, 118, 128, 142–143, 151, 153, 164, 168, 172
  Booth and, 106
  Bradley and, 50
  Buchanan and, 108, 110
  Chase and, 22, 23, 25, 26
  Clifford and, 37
  growth of, 131
  Miller and, 43
  Wade and, 167
Abraham, Henry, 128, 132
Ackerman, Amos, 77–78
Adams, John, 125, 137, 145
Adams, John Quincy, 121, 165, 170
  Calhoun and, 110
  Clay and, 116
  Jackson and, 135
  Polk and, 150
Agricultural economy, 115
Alabama Supreme Court, Campbell and, 81, 111
Alaska, purchase of, 206
Alien and Sedition Laws (1798), 137
Allegheny District Court, Grier and, 35, 151
Allgeyer v. Louisiana (1897), 92, 211
American Party, 119, 129, 171
  described, 105
American System, 116, 150, 170
Amnesty Act (1872), 208
Anti-immigrant organizations, 105
Anti-Masonic Party, 128, 154, 157
Anti-Nebraska faction, 161
Antisecessionist movement, 119
Antislavery movement, 20, 154
  Wilmot Proviso and, 171–172
Appomattox Courthouse, 115, 118, 141, 143, 205
Army of Northern Virginia, surrender of, 118, 131
Articles of Confederation, 67, 125
Articles of War, 96

Baldwin, Henry, 35, 136, 151, 163, 164
Ballinger, William P., 61
Bank of the United States, 30, 166
  Jacksonian war against, 72
  Tyler and, 162, 163
Bankruptcy rules, 75
Barbour, Philip, 136
Barnburners, 130
Barstow, William, 112
Bell, John, 119
Biddle, Francis, 97, 98
Bill of Rights, 56
Bills of attainder, 59, 61
Bills of credit, 74
Bingham, John A., 139
Black Codes, 24, 113, 129, 138, 151
  described, 105–106
Black, Jeremiah, 109, 156
Blight, David, 87
Blockades, 37, 124, 142–143, 203
  constitutionality of, 8, 9
Bondholders, 10, 41
Booth, John Wilkes, 143, 155
  biographical sketch of, 106–107

Border states, 118, 144
Boston Bar Association, 134
Bradley, Joseph P., 75, 91, 93, 94
  career of, 50
  Chase and, 23
  legal tender and, 77, 78
  Miller and, 41
  nomination of, 132–133, 208
  portrait of, 51
Bradwell, Myra Colby, 84
  biographical sketch of, 107
Bradwell v. Illinois (1873), 23, 87, 209, 211
  described, 84–85
Breckinridge, John C., 21, 122, 138, 156
Brown, John, 106, 141
Brown, Joseph, 62
Browning, Orville Hickman, 64
  biographical sketch of, 108
Buchanan, James, 6, 19, 35, 122, 143, 151, 156
  biographical sketch of, 108–110
  Clifford and, 37
  election of, 153
  Morrill and, 147
  Nelson and, 33
  nominations by, 109
  Tyler and, 163
  Van Buren and, 166
Bucktails, 165
Burnside, Ambrose, 7
Burr, Aaron, 164
Bush, George W., 100
Butchers, slaughterhouse statute and, 80–81
Butchers' Union Co. v. Crescent City Co. (1884), 90, 211
Butler, Benjamin F., 139

Calhoun, John C.
  biographical sketch of, 110–111
  Clay and, 116
  Jackson and, 135–136
  nullification and, 29
  Van Buren and, 165
California Supreme Court, Field and, 46
Camden and Amboy Railroad, 50
Cameron, Simon, 156
Campbell, John Archibald, 80–81, 83, 148
  biographical sketch of, 111
  resignation of, 5, 6, 19, 143, 204
  on universal suffrage, 82
Carlisle, James M., 9
Carpenter, Matthew Hale, 64, 84, 107
  biographical sketch of, 111–112
Carter, Jimmy, 48
Cass, Lewis, 160
Catron, John, 19, 35, 206
  career of, 30, 32
  Chase and, 27, 30, 136
  death of, 73
  Nelson and, 33
  portrait of, 11, 31
  Wayne and, 29
Charles River Bridge Company v. Warren Bridge Company (1837), 159, 211
Chase Court
  key decisions of, 4, 10, 11, 87, 98, 100–101
  portrait of, 11, 16
  traits of, 5, 19, 85, 87
Chase, Salmon Portland
  career of, 20–27
  as chief justice, 3, 10, 16, 23, 55, 85, 136
  death of, xiv, 23, 41, 85, 87, 88, 133, 169
  health problems for, 23, 79, 83
  impeachment and, 63
  legacy of, 85
  Lincoln and, 7, 20, 22, 23, 67, 144
  nomination of, 205
  politics and, 20, 65
  portrait of, 11, 16, 21
Cherokee Tobacco Case (1871), 208, 211
Chicago Board of Trade, 91
Chicago, Burlington and Quincy Railroad, 108
Chicago fire, 208
Chicago, Milwaukee and St. Paul Railroad Co. v. Minnesota (1890), 91, 211
Citizenship, 79, 82, 88, 214
  Chinese immigrants and, 112
  federal/state, 113, 123
  freedmen and, 112, 161

Civil liberties, 14, 95, 99, 162, 214
constitutional protection for, 58
wartime and, 100
Civil rights, 13–14, 206, 214
black, 113, 129, 130, 151
denial of, 161
discrimination and, 113
federal, 129
laws, 93, 113–114
protection of, 130
violations of, 140
Civil Rights Act (1866), 151, 158, 161, 206
Browning and, 108
Campbell and, 81, 82
described, 112–113
Johnson and, 138
Reconstruction and, 112
Trumbull and, 162
veto of, 126
violation of, 27
Wade and, 168
Civil Rights Act (1870), 132
described, 113–114
Civil Rights Act (1871), described, 113–114
Civil Rights Act (1875), 94, 170, 209
described, 114–115
Civil Rights Cases (1883), 89, 93, 94, 114, 211
Civil Service Reform Commission, 208
Civil War, 57, 70, 120, 151
amendments, 127, 161
Booth and, 106
Bradwell and, 107
Chase and, 3, 22
Davis, J., and, 45
described, 98, 115, 118
Grant and, 132
Lincoln and, 115, 142–143
Seward and, 154–155
slavery and, 4
Stevens and, 157
Wade and, 167
Waite and, 169
Clay, Henry, 164, 171
American System and, 170
biographical sketch of, 115–117
Calhoun and, 110
Douglas and, 122
Fillmore and, 128
Jackson and, 135, 136
Lincoln and, 141
Polk and, 150
Taylor and, 160
Tyler and, 163
Van Buren and, 165
Clifford, Nathan, 27
career of, 37, 39
Catron and, 32
Chase and, 30
nomination of, 109
portrait of, 11, 16, 38
Clinton, DeWitt, 165
Clinton-Livingston faction, 164–165
Collector v. Day (1871), 208, 211
Bradley and, 71, 100
described, 71–73
Nelson and, 71
Commerce, 70, 146
Commerce Clause, 69, 214
Committee on Reconstruction, 126, 138, 151, 206
Committee on Territories, 121, 140
Committee on the Rebellious States, H. Davis and, 119
Compromise of 1850, 130, 131, 153, 171
Buchanan and, 109
Calhoun and, 111
Campbell and, 111
Catron and, 30
Clay and, 117
described, 117–118, 139
Douglas and, 117
Evarts and, 124
Fillmore and, 117
Nelson and, 33, 35
Pierce and, 148
Stevens and, 158
Tyler and, 163
Van Buren and, 166
Confederate Constitution, 118, 203
text of, 181–194
Confederate House of Representatives, 163

Confederate States of America
described, 118
public support for, 7, 143
surrender of, 118, 120, 131
Conkling, Roscoe, 52, 88, 133
Connecticut Supreme Court, 169
Constitutional Convention, 125, 168
Contract Clause, 159, 170
Contracts, 41, 75, 92, 146, 161, 218–219
Cooke, Jay, 25, 72
Cooley v. Board of Port Wardens (1851), 29, 32, 33, 211
Copperheads, 143
Corps of Engineers, 141
Court martials, 96
Court of Appeals Act (1891), 124
Court packing, 49, 50, 73, 98–99, 132
Crandall v. Nevada (1868), 207, 211
described, 68–70
Credit Mobilier scandal, 209
Creek Indians, 135
Crescent City Live Stock Landing and Slaughterhouse Company, 80, 90
Cummings, Father John, 59
Cummings v. Missouri (1867), 65, 66, 83, 206, 211
Chase and, 24–25, 72
described, 58–59
Field and, 46, 58, 59, 127
Miller and, 58, 72
symbolism of, 61–62
Curtis, Benjamin Robbins, 33, 109, 128, 139
Cushing, Caleb, 133

Dana, Richard Henry, 9
biographical sketch of, 118–119
Daniel, Peter V., 144, 166, 167
death of, 6, 19, 109, 143
Daniell, William, 29
Davis, Alexander, 146
Davis, David, 57, 58, 93, 94, 98, 99–100
career of, 43, 45
Lincoln and, 45, 56, 144
nomination of, 144, 204
politics and, 19
portrait of, 11, 16, 44
Stone and, 99
Davis, Henry Winter, 12, 167
biographical sketch of, 119–120
Davis, Jefferson, 115, 118, 203
biographical sketch of, 120–121
Evarts and, 124
inaugural address of, 178–181
Johnson and, 138
Lincoln and, 119, 120
Pierce and, 148
treason charges and, 119
Declaration of Independence, 136
Deep South, 5, 8, 118
Democratic Party, 64, 105, 131
Calhoun and, 110
described, 121
division within, 21, 153, 156
Jackson and, 135
Jefferson and, 121
Johnson and, 138
Milligan and, 146
Pierce and, 148
Polk and, 150
Tyler and, 163
Van Buren and, 166, 167
Democratic-Republican Party, 121, 125
Denio, Hiram, 52
Discrimination, 26, 114, 129
barring, 93, 94, 161
civil rights and, 113
public accommodation, 115
voting, 127, 132
District of Columbia, slave trade in, 117
Doctrinal divergence, 15
Douglas, Stephen A., 21, 111, 203
biographical sketch of, 121–122
Browning and, 108
Buchanan and, 109
Clay and, 117
Fessenden and, 126
Fillmore and, 128
Grant and, 131
Lincoln and, 142
Pierce and, 148
Draft law, 157, 158, 204

Dred Scott v. Sandford (1857), 5, 109, 123, 128, 147, 211
  Campbell and, 111
  Catron and, 30
  Chase and, 15
  Curtis and, 123
  described, 122–123
  Grier and, 35
  McLean and, 123
  Nelson and, 33
  reversal of, 129
  Taney and, 94, 123, 160
  Tyler and, 163
  Wayne and, 29
Dual sovereignty, 160
Due process, 14, 56, 91–92, 95–100, 215–216, 221, 222
Due Process Clause, 92, 100, 129, 170
Duvall, Gabriel, 159

Economic growth, xiii, 4, 5, 10
Ellsworth, Oliver, 145
Emancipation, 22, 106, 116, 119, 147, 162
Emancipation Proclamation (1862), xiv, 108, 143, 148, 204
  described, 123–124
  legal effect for, 161
  text of, 194–195
Enrollment Act (1863), 156
Equal protection, 14, 90, 100, 129, 130
Equal Protection Clause, 100
Era of Good Feeling, 121
Evarts Act. *See* Court of Appeals Act
Evarts, William Maxwell, 9, 139
  biographical sketch of, 124–125
Ex parte Garland (1867), 58–59, 65, 66, 83, 206, 211
  Carpenter and, 112
  Chase and, 24–25, 72
  described, 59–62
  Field and, 58, 60
  Miller and, 58, 60, 61, 72
Ex parte McCardle (1869), 207, 211
  Carpenter and, 112
  described, 62–65
  Field and, 63, 64–65, 127
  Grier and, 64–65
Ex parte Merryman (1861), 6, 211
Ex parte Milligan (1866), 61, 62, 63, 65, 66, 87, 143, 146, 205, 211
  Chase and, 72
  Davis, D., and, 45, 56, 57, 58, 98
  described, 55–58
  Field and, 58, 127
  impact of, 95, 97–98, 99
  military commissions and, 100
  Miller and, 58, 72
  Stone and, 99
  three-part test for, 97
Ex parte Quirin (1942), 99, 211
  Milligan and, 95, 97–98
Ex parte Vallandigham (1864), 7, 10, 45, 205, 211
Ex parte Yerger (1869), 65, 207, 211
Ex post facto laws, 59, 61
Executive branch, judicial branch and, 66
Executive clemency, 60

Fairman, Charles, 69, 74
Farni v. Tesson (1862), 204, 211
FBI, saboteurs and, 95, 96
Federal Enforcement Act (1870), 89, 112, 132, 162, 208
  described, 140
Federalism, 3, 67, 68–70, 82, 216
Federalist Party, 3, 110, 121, 159
  described, 125
Fessenden, William Pitt, 72
  biographical sketch of, 125–126
Field, David Dudley, Jr., 19, 46, 55, 61, 63
  biographical sketch of, 126–127
Field, Stephen J., 55, 61, 64, 77, 91, 92, 126
  career of, 46, 48
  Chase and, 23, 48
  Clifford and, 37
  death of, 127
  Lincoln and, 127
  nomination of, 25, 144, 204
  politics and, 19, 46
  portrait of, 11, 16, 47
  Wayne and, 30

Fifteenth Amendment (1870), 14, 72, 108
  described, 127
  enforcement of, 114, 208
  proposal of, 207
  ratification of, 88, 208
  suffrage and, 152
  Swayne and, 39
  text of, 201
  Trumbull and, 162
  voting discrimination and, 132
  Waite and, 89
Fillmore, Millard, 111, 117, 154, 171
  biographical sketch of, 127–129
First Cavalry, 141
First Division, 155
First Enforcement Act. *See* Civil Rights Act (1870)
First Inaugural Address (Lincoln), excerpts from, 173–178
First Reconstruction Act (1867), 63, 108, 126, 139, 157, 163, 206
  passage of, 66, 152
First Regiment of Mississippi Volunteers, 120
Fish, Hamilton, 133
Force Bill, 29, 150
Fort Sumter, 5, 6, 8, 20, 39, 110, 115, 118, 142, 203
Fourteenth Amendment (1868), 61, 65, 89, 113, 126, 151, 153
  Bradwell and, 107
  Campbell and, 81, 82, 111
  Carpenter and, 112
  Chase and, 79, 87, 100
  described, 87, 129–130, 206
  discrimination and, 94
  enforcement of, 14, 91, 208
  Field and, 46, 59, 84
  Holmes and, 93
  Johnson and, 79, 138
  liberty of contract and, 92
  Miller and, 43, 83, 84, 90, 91
  ratification of, 139, 207
  state police power and, 79–83
  Stevens and, 158
  text of, 200
  Trumbull and, 162
  Wade and, 168
  Waite and, 170
  women and, 87, 88
Fourth Infantry, 131
Franklin, Benjamin, 137
Free states, 142
  slave states and, 4, 147
Freedman's Bureau, 13, 14, 138
  Browning and, 108
  creation of, 205
  disbandment of, 130
  Johnson and, 130
  Trumbull and, 162
  Turner and, 26
  Wade and, 167–168
Freedman's Bureau Act (1866), 126, 130, 138, 158
Freedmen, 12, 43, 89, 106, 113, 169
  citizenship for, 112
  rights of, 68, 130
Free-Soil Party, 119, 148, 160, 166, 171
  described, 130–131
  Republican Party and, 153
Fremont, John Charles, 134, 153
French Revolution, 137
Fugitive Slave Act (1793), described, 131
Fugitive Slave Act (1850), 164
  Dana and, 119
  described, 131
  Evarts and, 124
  Pierce and, 148
  Stevens and, 158
  Wade and, 167
Fugitive slaves, 117, 131, 134, 158
Fuller, Melville W., 169

Gadsden Purchase, 139, 148
Gadsden Treaty, 148
Garfield, James, 55
Garland, A. H., 59, 60
Gelpcke v. Dubuque (1864), 205, 211
Gender equality, 107
Geneva Arbitration, 169
Georgia v. Stanton (1868), 206, 211
  described, 66

Gettysburg address, 204
Gettysburg Council, 157
Gibbons v. Ogden (1824), 146, 211
Gilded Age, 25, 87, 88
Gillette, William, 37, 39, 43
Gould, Jay, 127
Granger Cases. See *Munn v. Illinois*
Granger Laws, 91
Grant, Ulysses S., 65, 139, 141, 152, 153
  appointments by, 25, 48, 52, 73
  biographical sketch of, 131–133
  command for, 205
  election of, 48, 64, 132, 207, 209
  Fessenden and, 126
  Hoar and, 134
  Lee and, 10, 115
  Lincoln and, 143
  Nelson and, 77
  nominations by, 74, 75, 88, 132–133, 157, 169, 208, 209
  Sherman and, 155, 156
  Stanton and, 157
  Strong and, 49, 50
  Swayne and, 41
  Trumbull and, 162
Graves v. New York (1939), 100, 211
Greeley, Horace, 209
  letter to, 194
Greenbacks, 23, 37, 43, 48, 49, 83
  Chase and, 25, 72, 73, 74
Grier, Robert Cooper, 27, 64, 76
  career of, 35, 37
  Catron and, 32
  Nelson and, 33
  nomination of, 151
  portrait of, 11, 16, 36
  resignation of, 73, 132, 208
Grundy, Felix, 149

Habeas corpus, 55, 65, 146, 216–217
  seeking, 62, 63, 68, 97, 98, 99
  suspension of, xiv, 6, 7, 56, 119, 143, 156, 158
Habeas Corpus Act (1867), 64
Hale, John, 131, 148
Hamblin, Hannibal, 203
Hamilton, Alexander, 121, 125
Harlan, John, 93, 94
Harper's Ferry, 106, 141
Harper's Weekly on Chase, 85
Harrison, William Henry, 133, 158
  death of, 163, 171
  Van Buren and, 165, 166
Hayes, Rutherford B., 85, 93–94, 124
Hepburn v. Griswold (1870), 208, 211
  described, 73–77
  Miller and, 73, 74–75, 75–76
  reaffirmation of, 77–78
  Strong and, 48, 78
  See also Knox v. Lee; Parker v. Davis
Hill, Robert, 63
Hoar, Ebenezer Rockwood, 48, 75, 76, 85, 132
  biographical sketch of, 133–134
Holmes, Oliver Wendell, Jr., 92, 93
Homestead Act (1862), 5, 167, 204
  described, 134
Homesteading, 134, 153
Hornblower, William, 50
House of Representatives, 63, 68, 88, 132, 149, 162
Howe, Timothy P., 133
Hunt, Ward, 81, 89, 133, 209
  career of, 52
  portrait of, 53
Hyman, Harold, 24

Illinois Bar Association, 107
Illinois House of Representatives, 45
Illinois Supreme Court, 107, 161
In re Turner (1867), 24–25, 26, 211
Inaugural Address of the Confederacy (J. Davis), 178–181
Industrial growth, 4, 10, 15, 92
Insurance Co. v. Ritchie (1867), 206, 211
Interstate commerce, 70, 146
Involuntary servitude, 27, 161

Jackson, Andrew, 23, 151, 171
  biographical sketch of, 135–136
  Buchanan and, 108
  Calhoun and, 110

Jackson, Andrew, *cont.*
Catron and, 30
Clay and, 116
Douglas and, 121
nominations by, 27, 136
opposition to, 170
Polk and, 150
Taney and, 159
Tyler and, 162
Van Buren and, 165, 166
Wayne and, 29
Jacksonian Democrats, 24, 27, 30, 37, 39, 52, 121, 135, 138, 159
Japanese Americans, internment of, 95
Jay, John, 145
Jay Treaty (1794), 125
Jefferson, Thomas, 116, 121, 125
biographical sketch of, 136–137
Jeffersonian Democrats, 3
Jeffersonian Party, 170
Jeffersonian Republicans, 110, 116
Johnson, Andrew, 15, 48, 67, 73, 106, 150, 151, 155, 169, 205
biographical sketch of, 137–139
Browning and, 108
Campbell and, 81
civil rights and, 14
Dana and, 119
Davis, J., and, 119
Evarts and, 9, 124
Fessenden and, 126
Garland and, 60
Grant and, 132
impeachment of, 25, 64, 65, 66, 126, 132, 139, 152, 157, 158, 168, 207
Lincoln and, 12, 138, 153
Milligan and, 45, 55
Stanton and, 126, 157, 162, 206, 207
Trumbull and, 162
Wade and, 167
Johnson, Herschel V., 203
Johnson, William, 29, 137
Judicial activism, 6, 66, 217
Judicial branch, executive branch and, 66
Judiciary Act (1789), 65
Judiciary Act (1801), 137
Judiciary Act (1863), 41
Jurisprudence, 8, 218
Justice Department, 208

Kansas-Nebraska Act (1854), 109, 147, 154
Browning and, 108
described, 139–140
Douglas and, 122, 140
Evarts and, 124
Fessenden and, 126
Lincoln and, 142
Pierce and, 140, 148
Republican Party and, 140, 153
Trumbull and, 161
Tyler and, 163
Van Buren and, 166
Wade and, 167
Kens, Paul, 90
Kentucky Resolutions (1798), 137
Kentucky v. Dennison (1861), 203, 211
King, Edward, 163–164
Knights of the Golden Circle, 106
Know-Nothing Party, 119, 129, 171
described, 105
Knox v. Lee (1871), 76, 208, 211
Chase and, 72, 73
described, 77–79
Evarts and, 124
Strong and, 50
Ku Klux Klan, 132, 152
Ku Klux Klan Act. *See* Federal Enforcement Act

Laissez-faire, 93, 218
Land-grant program, 134, 147, 204
Laws of war, 96
Lee, Robert E., 131
biographical sketch of, 141
surrender of, 10, 115, 205
Leffingwell v. Warren (1862), 204, 212
Legal tender, 74, 75, 77, 78
Legal Tender Act, 25, 49, 50
Legal Tender Cases. See Hepburn v. Griswold; Knox v. Lee; Parker v. Davis

Liberty Party, 153
  described, 130–131
License Cases (1847), 212
Lincoln, Abraham
  appointments by, 6, 20, 27, 41, 43, 46
  assassination of, xiv, 8, 10, 11, 12, 13, 106, 131–132, 138, 153, 155, 205
  biographical sketch of, 141–145
  Chase and, 7, 20, 22, 23, 67, 144
  election of, xiii, 23, 109, 118, 153, 171, 203, 205
  inaugural addresses of, 173–178, 198–199
  letter from, 194
  nominations by, 19, 45, 143–144, 204
Literacy, free state/slave state, 4
Literacy tests, 15, 127
Livingston, Brockholst, 137
Loan Association v. Topeka (1875), 209, 212
Lochner v. New York (1905), 92, 212
Louisiana Military Seminary, Sherman and, 155
Louisiana Purchase territory, slavery in, 147
Loyalty oaths, 25, 59, 60, 61, 62, 143, 151, 168

Madison, James, 121
Manufacturing, free state/slave state, 4
Marbury v. Madison (1803), 145, 212
Marcy, William, 154
Maritime law, 9
Marriage, interracial, 106
Marshall Court, 3, 159
Marshall, John, xiv, 24, 43, 48, 67, 69, 71, 75, 116, 125, 137
  biographical sketch of, 145–146
  death of, 145, 159
  nationalism of, 160
  tenure of, 3
Martial law, 57, 97, 219
Massachusetts Supreme Court, 134
McCardle, William H., 62
McCulloch v. Maryland (1819), 69, 71, 145, 212
McKinley, John, 128, 166
McLean, John, 33, 136
  death of, 6, 19, 39, 143, 144, 203
Melville, Herman, 11
Memphis, rioting in, 14
Merryman, John, 6
Mexican War, 117, 133, 148, 156
  Grant and, 131
  Lee and, 141
  Lincoln and, 142
  Sherman and, 155
  Taylor and, 160
Military commissions, 7–8, 45, 55–58, 62, 95, 98, 100, 146
  saboteurs and, 96–97
  trial by, 64, 99
Military Division of Mississippi, 155
Military justice, 58, 96
Military Reconstruction Act (1867), 158, 162
Military tribunals, 57, 95, 99, 100, 127, 130
Miller, Samuel Freeman, 90, 133
  on black suffrage, 62
  career of, 41, 43
  Chase and, 22, 23, 75, 76, 77, 85
  nomination of, 10, 144, 204
  politics and, 19
  portrait of, 11, 16, 42
  Swayne and, 41
Milligan, Lambdin, 45, 55, 56, 57, 58
  biographical sketch of, 146
Minor v. Happersett (1875), 88, 209, 212
Minor, Virginia, 88
Mississippi v. Johnson (1867), 206, 212
  described, 66
Mississippi Volunteers, 120
Missouri Compromise (1820), 117, 140
  Clay and, 116
  Davis and, 120
  described, 146–147
  nullification of, 148
  Scott and, 122, 123
Missouri Supreme Court, 33, 122
Monroe, James, 110, 121
Morrill, Justin S., 147
Morrill Land Grant Act (1862), 5, 167, 204
  described, 147

Morrill Tariff Act (1861), 203
Morton, Oliver P., 133
Mudd, Samuel A., 139
Municipal bonds, 10
Munn, Ira, 91
Munn v. Illinois (1877), 94, 212
  Bradley and, 50, 91
  Browning and, 108
  Miller and, 91
  Waite and, 90–91, 170

National banking system, 5, 30, 72, 73, 121, 135, 136, 153, 159, 162, 163, 166
National Labor Union Reform Party, 19
National Republicans, 170
National Union Party, 12
Naturalization, 105, 219
"Necessary and proper" clause, 145
Nelson, Samuel, 27, 76, 77, 164
  career of, 32–35
  Catron and, 32
  Grier and, 35
  portrait of, 11, 16, 33
  retirement of, 52, 133, 209
New Deal, 93
New Hampshire General Court, 148
New Orleans
  rioting in, 14
  sanitation regulations in, 80
New York Constitutional Convention, 32
New York Court of Appeals, 52
New York Sixth Circuit Court, 32
New York Supreme Court, 133
Nixon, Richard M., 94
Northern Democrats, 35, 109, 171
Northwest Ordinance, 171
Nullification, 29, 136, 137, 150, 171
  Calhoun and, 110
  Catron and, 30
  Van Buren and, 166

Ohio Supreme Court, 156, 169
Old Republicans, 162
Omnibus Bill, 128, 160
Order of the Star-Spangled Banner, 105

Paludin, Philip, 3, 90
Paper money, 23, 37, 43, 48, 49, 83
  Chase and, 25, 72, 73, 74
Parker v. Davis (1871), 72, 73–79, 124, 208, 212. *See also Hepburn v. Griswold; Knox v. Lee*
Passenger Cases (1849), 212
Patronage appointments, 22, 23, 128, 132
Paul v. Virginia (1869), 70, 71, 207, 212
Peckham, Rufus, 92, 93
Pennsylvania House, 157
Pennsylvania Supreme Court, 48–49, 156
Philadelphia and Reading Railroad Co. v. Pennsylvania (1873), 209, 212
Pierce, Franklin, 109, 120, 128, 166
  biographical sketch of, 147–48
  Campbell and, 5, 81, 111
Politics, 5, 11, 19, 20, 27, 129
Polk, James Knox
  biographical sketch of, 149–151
  Buchanan and, 108–109
  Clay and, 116
  Clifford and, 37
  election of, 164
  Johnson and, 138
  nominations by, 35, 151
  Stanton and, 156
  Taylor and, 160
  Tyler and, 163
  Van Buren and, 166
Popular sovereignty, 117, 122
Populists, 162
Potter, Clarkson, 77
Privileges and Immunities Clause, 107
Prize Cases (1863), 8, 204, 212
  Carlisle and, 9
  Catron and, 30
  Dana and, 119
  Evarts and, 124
  Grier and, 9, 37
  Nelson and, 34–35
  Taney and, 9
Proclamation of Amnesty and Reconstruction (1863), 143, 151, 168
  text of, 196–198

Property rights, 10, 112, 123, 146, 159, 161, 170
Public opportunity, equal opportunity to, 209

Quakers, 164

Racism, 11, 12, 24, 50
Radical Republicans, 58, 138, 153
  Browning and, 108
  Evarts and, 124
  Grant and, 132
  Johnson and, 12, 13, 24, 25, 61, 139, 152
  Milligan/test oath holdings and, 63
  Reconstruction and, 63, 150, 151, 157, 158, 162, 168
  Stanton and, 206
  Trumbull and, 162
Railroads, 10
  regulating, 50, 169
  transcontinental, 5, 22, 69, 139, 140, 153, 207
  See also Underground Railroad
Read, John Meredith, 164
Reconstruction
  amendments, 79, 82, 89
  Campbell and, 81
  Carpenter and, 112
  Catron and, 32
  Chase and, 24, 26, 67, 68, 87, 88
  civil rights and, 112, 140
  Clifford and, 37
  congressional, 62, 63, 65, 66, 72, 79, 88, 95, 157, 168
  constitutional change during, 61
  Davis, H., and, 119
  Democrats and, 64
  described, 151–152
  end of, xiv, 72, 88, 93–94, 132
  Evarts and, 124
  Fessenden and, 126
  Grant and, 132
  Grier and, 37
  Hunt and, 52, 81
  Johnson and, 13, 14, 62, 66, 139, 150, 151, 152
  Lincoln and, 11–12, 23, 143, 150, 155
  Miller and, 43
  presidential, 13, 23, 168
  proposals for, 11–12
  Radical Republicans and, 63, 150, 151, 162, 168
  Stanton and, 157
  Stevens and, 157
  Trumbull and, 162
  Wade and, 167
  Waite and, 169
  Wayne and, 30
Regulation, 5
  commercial, 32
  economic, 70
  immigrant, 32
  insurance, 70
  private property, 146, 159
  railroad, 50, 169
  sanitation, 80
  state, 88, 91, 170
Repeal Act (1802), 137
Republican Party, 39, 105, 115, 171
  Browning and, 108
  Chase and, 21–22
  described, 153–154
  Douglas and, 122
  Evarts and, 124
  Fessenden and, 126
  Field and, 127
  formation of, 148, 154
  Hayes and, 94
  Hoar and, 134
  Hunt and, 52
  Jefferson and, 137
  Lincoln and, 142
  Stevens and, 158
  Trumbull and, 161–162
  Wade and, 167
Roberts, Owen J., Justice, 74
Roosevelt, Franklin D.
  court packing and, 73, 98–99
  military commissions and, 96–97, 98
Roosevelt v. Meyer (1863), 205, 212
Royall, Kenneth, 97
Ryan, Edward, 112

Saboteurs, habeas corpus and, 95, 96, 97, 98, 99
Sanitary conditions, 80, 92
Schools, segregation of, 106
Scott, Winfield, 148, 160, 171
Secession, 12, 19, 23, 25, 35, 109, 110, 123, 142, 151, 163
  Catron and, 32
  Chase and, 24
  Deep South and, 5
  issues arising from, 10
  Texas and, 67–68
Second Cavalry, 141
Second Continental Congress, 137
Second Enforcement Act. *See* Civil Rights Act (1871)
Second Inaugural Address (Lincoln), text of, 198–199
Second Military Department, 160
Second National Bank, 135, 136
Second Reconstruction Act (1867), 157, 206
Sectional crisis, 128, 129, 140, 148, 156
Securities, recovering, 67
Segregation, 106
Self-restraint, judicial, 33, 217
Seminole Indians, 135, 165
Senate Finance Committee, 126
Senate Judiciary Committee, 64, 162
Separation of powers, 145, 222
September 11, 2001, 58, 95, 100
Seward, William Henry, 22, 106
  biographical sketch of, 154–155
  Evarts and, 124
  Fillmore and, 128
  Lincoln and, 142, 154–155
  Stanton and, 156
Seymour, Horatio, 207
Sherman, John, 39
Sherman, William Tecumseh, 13, 205
  biographical sketch of, 155–156
Silvester, Francis, 164
Slaughterhouse Cases (1873), 55, 70, 84, 88, 89, 91, 129, 130, 209, 212
  Campbell and, 111
  Carpenter and, 112
  Chase and, 23, 85
  described, 79–83, 87
  Field and, 83
  Hunt and, 52, 81
  Miller and, 43, 82–83, 92
  Waite and, 90, 169–170
Slaughterhouse statute, 80–81, 82
Slave states, 118, 142
  free states and, 4, 147
Slave trade, 117, 137
Slavery, 4, 13, 94, 105, 108, 111, 120, 168
  Chase and, 21, 22, 23, 24, 25
  Clifford and, 37
  conflict over, 3, 117, 118, 122, 158
  end of, 5, 12, 26, 115, 142, 153, 155, 161, 204, 205, 206
  expanding, 115, 171
  Hunt and, 52
  Lincoln and, 142–143
  Nelson and, 33
  Northern Democrats and, 109
  opposition to, 22, 122, 153
  property rights and, 123
  Stevens and, 158
  Strong and, 48
  Swayne and, 39
  in territories, 109, 116, 146
  Wade and, 167
  Wayne and, 29
Smith, William, 166
Social development, free state/slave state, 4
South Carolina v. Katzenbach (1966), 127, 212
Southern District of New York, 124
Southern Unionists, 62
Spencer, Herbert, 93
Spencer, John C., 163
Stanbery, Henry, 139
Stanford, Leland, 46
Stanton, Edwin McMasters, 48
  biographical sketch of, 156–157
  death of, 75, 132, 157
  removal of, 126, 132, 139, 152, 157, 162, 206, 207
State authority, 88–94
State Department, 156
State police power, 79–83

States' rights, 82, 112, 118, 137, 146, 159, 170
- Calhoun and, 116
- Clay and, 171
- Davis and, 120
- Johnson and, 113
- Van Buren and, 165

Stephens, Alexander H., 118
Stevens, Thaddeus, 88, 139, 150, 151, 152
- biographical sketch of, 157–158
- Reconstruction and, 14

Stockbridge, Henry, 26, 27
Stone Court, 99, 100
Stone v. Mississippi (1880), 170, 212
Story, Joseph, 151
Strauder v. West Virginia (1880), 89–90
Strong, William, 75, 76
- career of, 48, 50
- legal tender and, 77, 78
- nomination of, 132–133, 208
- portrait of, 49

Stuart, John T., 141
Suffrage. *See* Voting rights
Sumner, Charles, 88, 93, 114, 167
Supplementary Enforcement Act (1871), 208
Supreme Court of Louisiana, 81
Swayne, Noah H., 58
- career of, 39, 41
- nomination of, 10, 144, 204
- portrait of, 11, 16, 40

Tammany Hall, 127
Taney Court, 3, 122, 128, 147, 160
- Catron and, 30
- Grier and, 35
- Wayne and, 29

Taney, Roger Brooke, 3, 24, 94, 123, 132, 145
- biographical sketch of, 158–160
- Chase and, 27
- death of, 23, 124, 144, 159, 205
- Grier and, 35
- Lincoln and, 6–7, 55
- Nelson and, 33
- nomination of, 136
- Wayne and, 29

Tappan, Benjamin, 156
Tariff Act (1870), 208
Tariff Act (1872), 209
Tariffs, 22, 116, 121, 153, 165
- increase in, 5, 209
- opposition to, 29

Taxation, 68, 69, 70, 71
Taylor, Zachary, 130, 154, 171
- biographical sketch of, 160
- Evarts and, 124
- Fillmore and, 128
- Grant and, 131
- Lincoln and, 142
- Polk and, 150–151
- Van Buren and, 166

Tennessee Supreme Court, 135
Tenth Circuit, 144
Tenure of Office Act (1867), 132, 152, 157
- passage of, 139, 206
- violation of, 207

Terrorism, xiii, 114
Test Oath Cases. See Cummings v. Missouri; Ex parte Garland
Texas Republic, annexation of, 150
Texas v. White (1869), 66, 207, 212
- Chase and, 24–25, 26, 72
- described, 67–68

Third Brigade, 155
Third Enforcement Act (1871), described, 140
Third Reconstruction Act (1868), 157, 207
Thirteenth Amendment (1865), 113, 138, 151, 153, 155, 206
- adoption of, 205
- Campbell and, 81
- described, 161
- involuntary servitude and, 27
- passage of, 26
- text of, 199
- Trumbull and, 162

Thompson, Smith, 33, 163
Tilden, Samuel J., 93, 112, 124, 162
Todd, Thomas, 137
Toth v. Quarles (1955), 100, 212
Transportation, 106

Treasury Department, Chase and, 22, 71, 72, 74
Trumbull, Lyman, 112, 113, 142, 151
biographical sketch of, 161–162
Freedmen's Bureau and, 13, 130
Trustees of Dartmouth College v. Woodward (1819), 159, 212
Turner, Elizabeth, 26, 27
Tween, William "Boss," 127
Twenty-first Illinois Volunteer Infantry, 131
Two Years before the Mast (Dana), 9, 119
Tyler, John, 33, 35, 110, 171
biographical sketch of, 162–164
nominations by, 163–164

Underground Railroad, 131
described, 164
Union Army, 4
blacks in, 124, 155
draft for, 204
Union Navy, blockade by, 8
Union Party, 14
United States v. Butler (1936), 74, 212
United States v. Cruikshank (1874), 89, 170, 212
United States v. Harris (1883), 140, 212
United States v. Reese (1875), 89, 212
Urbanized population, free state/slave state, 4
U.S. Army, 8, 29, 141
U.S. Military Railroads (USMRR), 4–5
U.S. Navy, 95
USMRR. *See* United States Military Railroads

Vallandigham, Clement, 7
Van Buren, Martin, 130, 135, 136, 151
biographical sketch of, 164–167
Calhoun and, 110
Catron and, 30
nominations by, 166–167
Polk and, 150
Taylor and, 160
Veazie Bank v. Fenno (1869), 207, 212
described, 70–71
Virginia Constitution, 145
Virginia House of Burgesses, 137
Virginia House of Delegates, 137, 145
Virginia v. Rives (1879), 90, 212
Voting rights, 14, 82, 89, 127, 132, 207
black, 15, 62, 72, 79, 139, 152, 168, 170
woman's, 88, 107, 112
Voting Rights Act (1965), 127

Wade, Benjamin F., 12, 39, 139
biographical sketch of, 167–168
Wade-Davis Act (1864), 12, 119, 151, 167
described, 168–169
Lincoln and, 143, 168, 169
Waite Court, 169, 170
Fifteenth Amendment and, 89
Third Enforcement Act and, 140
Waite, Morrison Remick, 88, 133, 209
biographical sketch of, 169–170
Walworth, Reuben H., 163, 164
War Democrats, 138
War Department, 4–5, 157
War Hawks, 110, 116
War of 1812, 27, 30, 116, 135
War of Independence, 135, 145
Warren Court, 127
Washington, George, 125, 137, 145
Wayne, Henry, 29
Wayne, James, 35, 73, 206
career of, 27, 29–30
Catron and, 30, 32
judicial avoidance by, 8
military commission and, 7–8
nomination of, 136
politics and, 29
portrait of, 11, 28
Ways and Means Committee, 158
Webster, Daniel, 67, 78, 116, 128, 165, 171
Weed, Thurlow, 154
Welles, Gideon, 64
Whig Party, 130, 133, 154
Browning and, 108
Clay and, 116
Davis, H., and, 119
described, 170–171

Douglas and, 122
Fessenden and, 126
Fillmore and, 128, 129
Johnson and, 138
Lincoln and, 142
Tyler and, 163
Van Buren and, 165, 166, 167
Whyte, George, 116
Williams, George H., 133
Wilmot, David, 110–111, 150, 171
Wilmot Proviso, 109, 130, 142, 150, 163
described, 171–172
Wirt, William, 20
Women's Christian Temperance Union, 209
Woodbury, Levi, 128, 151
Woodward, George W., 151

Yellowstone Park, 208

About the Author

Jonathan Lurie is professor of U.S. legal history at Rutgers University. He is the author of *History of the United States Court of Appeals for the Armed Forces* and *Military Justice in America.*

www.ingramcontent.com/pod-product-compliance
Ingram Content Group UK Ltd.
Pitfield, Milton Keynes, MK11 3LW, UK
UKHW050418051026
15470UKWH00022B/1652